Agency Operations and Sales Management

Principles of Agency Management

Segment A

Christopher J. Amrhein, AAI
Vice President of Industry Affairs
Independent Insurance Agents of America

Daniel P. Hussey, Jr., CPCU, AAI, ARM
Director, Western Region
American Institute for CPCU/Insurance Institute of America

Coordinating Editor
Christine O. Quay, AAI
Associate Director
American Institute for CPCU/Insurance Institute of America

Second Edition

American Institute for Chartered Property Casualty Underwriters/
Insurance Institute of America
720 Providence Road, Malvern, Pennsylvania 19355-0716

Second Edition • Third Printing • February 2004

Library of Congress Control Number: 2001098687
ISBN 0894621637

Printed in Canada.

Foreword

The American Institute for Chartered Property Casualty Underwriters and the Insurance Institute of America are independent, nonprofit organizations serving the educational needs of the risk management, property-casualty, and financial services businesses. The Institutes develop a wide range of curricula, study materials, and examinations in response to the educational needs of various elements of these businesses. The American Institute confers the Chartered Property Casualty Underwriter (CPCU®) professional designation on people who meet its examination, ethics, and experience requirements. The Insurance Institute of America offers associate designations and certificate programs in the following areas:

- Accounting and Finance
- Agent Studies
- Business Writing
- Claims
- Global Risk Management and Insurance
- Information Technology
- Insurance Fundamentals
- Management
- Marine Insurance
- Performance Improvement
- Personal Insurance
- Premium Auditing
- Regulation and Compliance
- Reinsurance
- Risk Management
- Surety Bonds and Crime Insurance
- Surplus Lines
- Underwriting

The American Institute was founded in 1942 through a cooperative effort between property-casualty insurance company executives and insurance professors. Faculty members at The Wharton School of the University of Pennsylvania in Philadelphia led this effort. The CPCU designation arose from the same type of business and academic partnership at Wharton as the Chartered Life Underwriter (CLU) designation did in 1927.

The Insurance Institute of America was founded in 1909 by five educational organizations across the United States. It is the oldest continuously functioning national organization offering educational programs for the property-casualty insurance business. It merged with the American Institute in 1953.

The Insurance Research Council (IRC), founded in 1977, is a division of the Institutes. It is a not-for-profit research organization that examines public policy issues that affect property-casualty insurers and their customers. IRC research reports are distributed widely to insurance-related organizations, public policy authorities, and the media.

The broad knowledge base in property-casualty insurance and financial services created by the Institutes over the years is contained mainly in our textbooks. Although we use electronic technology to enhance our educational materials, communicate with our students, and deliver our examinations, our textbooks are at the heart of our educational activities. They contain the information that you as a student must read, understand, integrate into your existing knowledge, and apply to the tasks you perform as part of your job.

Despite the vast range of subjects and purposes of the more than eighty individual textbook volumes we publish, they all have much in common. First, each book is specifically designed to increase knowledge and develop skills that can improve job performance and help students achieve the educational objectives of the course for which it is assigned. Second, all of the manuscripts for our texts are reviewed widely before publication, by both insurance business practitioners and members of the risk management and insurance academic community. In addition, the revisions of our texts often incorporate improvements that students and course leaders have suggested. We welcome constructive comments that help us to improve the quality of our study materials. Please direct any comments you may have on this text to my personal attention.

We hope what you learn from your study of this text will expand your knowledge, increase your confidence in your skills, and support your career growth. If so, then you and the Institutes will truly be *succeeding together*.

Terrie E. Troxel, Ph.D., CPCU, CLU
President and CEO
American Institute for CPCU
Insurance Institute of America

Preface

The Accredited Adviser in Insurance (AAI) program is designed to meet the educational needs of insurance producers, customer service representatives, and other agency and brokerage personnel. In that regard, the courses in the AAI program focus on three primary areas: (1) the technical aspects of the insurance business, including coverage and pricing; (2) the marketing of insurance products, including producer relationships with both clients and underwriters; and (3) the operation and management of insurance agencies and brokerages.

AAI 83, *Agency Operations and Sales Management*, is the third of the three AAI courses. It contains three segments that group topics of a similar nature. This text, *Principles of Agency Management*, is the first segment of AAI 83. It begins this course by discussing insurance agency formation and the environment in which producers work. The second assignment introduces the traditional principles of management and includes a description of some recent management trends. The third and fourth assignments apply the basic management principles to insurance agency management and personal production planning, respectively.

This text is not intended to be "proscriptive." That is, it does not attempt to tell any agency principal the perfect way to run an agency. Rather, it describes sound applications of management principles to the business of running an agency. It also describes how all agency personnel fit into the operation of an agency and how their efforts contribute to the success of the agency.

Although this text is identified as the second edition, it is based on the former *Agency Operations and Sales Management* texts. Those two volumes were first published in 1982 and were in the third edition. Many people contributed to those texts as authors and reviewers during the three editions. The American Institute for CPCU and the Insurance Institute of America recognize their efforts, especially two of the principal authors of the early editions, Peter R. Kensicki, D.B.A., CPCU, CLU, FLMI, and Carol A. Hammes, CPCU.

The principal author of this edition of the text is Christopher J. Amrhein, AAI, Vice President, Education, Florida Association of Insurance Agents. Chris has contributed to the texts in all three AAI courses, having been involved with the program since its inception. Chris is also a member of the AAI Advisory Committee, which reviews the content of the courses and composes the national examinations.

The coordinating author of this and the balance of the AAI texts is the director of the AAI program, Daniel P. Hussey, Jr., CPCU, AAI, ARM. Several reviewers from both outside and inside the AICPCU/IIA also contributed to this edition of the text to ensure that the material was correct and complete. The primary outside reviewer was Jo Conway Roberts, Vice President, ACORD.

The authors accept full responsibility for all errors and omissions. Readers detecting errors or wishing to add to the content of future editions are encouraged to send their contributions and criticisms to the Institutes.

Daniel P. Hussey, Jr.

Contents

Agency Formation and Environment

Assignment 1

Assignment Objectives

After completing this assignment, you should be able to:

1. Explain the legal aspects of agency.
   In support of the assignment objective listed above, you should be able to do the following:
   a. Describe the duties agents owe to their principals.
   b. Identify the remedies a principal has when its agent fails in his or her duties.
   c. Describe the duties principals owe to their agents.
   d. Identify the remedies an agent has when its principal breaches the agency contract.
2. Given a case regarding the authority of an insurance agency, explain the relationships among the agency, the client, and the principal (insurer).
   In support of the assignment objective listed above, you should be able to do the following:
   a. Illustrate the different distribution systems used in property-liability insurance sales.
   b. Differentiate between an agent and a broker and describe how their relationships differ when dealing with insurers and insureds.
   c. Illustrate the different types of authority an agent might have.
3. Explain the advantages and disadvantages of the fee system in insurance sales.
4. Describe the major sections of an insurance agency contract.
5. Explain the factors that are included in a typical profit sharing (contingent commission) agreement.
6. Given an insurance agency case, explain the organizational forms available to the insurance agency.
   In support of the assignment objective listed above, you should be able to do the following:
   a. Describe the legal forms of insurance agencies.
   b. Describe the optional operating affiliations available to insurance agencies.
   c. Explain the advantages and disadvantages of agency clusters.
   d. Describe the decision process used in forming an agency cluster.
   e. Explain the process used in evaluating operating affiliations.
7. Define or describe the Key Words and Phrases for this assignment.

Assignment Outline

I. Legal Aspects of Agency

II. The Agency-Principal Relationship
   A. Duties of the Agent
   B. Remedies of the Principal
   C. Duties of the Principal
   D. Remedies of the Agent

III. Insurance Producers and the Law of Agency
   A. Distribution Systems
   B. Duties of Insurance Agents
   C. Agent Versus Broker
   D. Authority of Insurance Agents
   E. Ratification
   F. Agent as Independent Contractor
   G. Undisclosed Principal
   H. Nonexistent Principal
   I. Licensing

IV. Insurance Agency Contracts
   A. Major Sections of an Agency Contract

V. Organizational Forms of Insurance Agencies
   A. Legal Form
   B. Operating Affiliation
   C. Evaluating Operating Affiliations

VI. Summary

Assignment 1

Agency Formation and Environment

Orient yourself to this assignment by reading the following introduction.

As the distribution of insurance has become technical and specialized, it has become more and more important that the successful producer have an effective support system in order to compete favorably in the marketplace.

There are many definitions of "producer," but the term as used in the AAI texts is defined as follows:

> A **producer** sells insurance and related services. The producer may be an **agent**—the authorized representative of an insurance company—or a **broker**—the authorized representative of an insured. For the sake of simplicity, the producer's employer or office will be called "the agency" throughout the AAI program. In this sense, the independent agent in Pierre, South Dakota, the sales representative of Liberty Mutual in Chicago, the State Farm agent in Belpre, Ohio, and the broker in New York all work out of "an agency."

The successful producer must have a base from which to operate. An agency is a key element leading to success for most producers. The function of the agency is to support the sales effort by freeing the producer to sell, being assured that his or her clients will be entrusted to a competent service organization.

There is no one ideal environment for a producer. What works well for an agency in a metropolitan area may not work at all for an agency in a small farm community. The internal structure of a large firm will differ significantly from an agency with a staff of three. Agencies affiliated with regional, national, or international organizations will not be operated in the same manner as firms that have independent and local ownership. All agencies, however, share certain fundamental legal and business characteristics.

This assignment begins by exploring the legal aspects of agency in general, followed by emphasis on the distribution of insurance, including a discussion of insurance agency contracts. The third major topic is the alternative operating forms available to, and possible operating affiliations for, insurance agencies.

Read the definition of the *Key Words and Phrases* that follow. Being familiar with these important words will help you better understand the first part of this assignment. *Key Words and Phrases* appear in bold in the text when they are defined.

Producer Sells insurance and related services

Agent An authorized representative of an insurance company

Broker An authorized representative of the insured

Agency A fiduciary relationship in which the principal authorizes the agent to act on its behalf in business dealings with third parties

Covenant not to compete An agreement by an agent not to compete with the principal or not to become employed by a competitor

Nonpiracy agreement An agreement wherein the agent agrees not to contact any existing clients of the principal for a given length of time but is free to pursue new prospects

Direct writing system The agent is an employee of the insurer and places business exclusively with that insurer

American Agency System Independent agents who may represent many insurers and are allowed to place business with any of them

Exclusive agency system Agents who are independent in the operation of their offices and are not employees of the company but are obligated to place business with one insurer

Dual agency A person representing two parties to conduct a transaction between them

Express authority Legal agreement, either oral or written, between the agent and the principal

Implied authority Unwritten set of rules that broadens the agent's authority, by law or custom, to carry out express authority

Apparent authority Authority that is not specified but is based on a third party's reasonable belief that the agent is acting within its authority

Authority by estoppel A theory that if the principal creates the appearance of authority in an agent, and a third party relies on that appearance, the principal cannot deny the agent's authority

Ratification A form of post-contract authority where the principal accepts a transaction that exceeds an agent's express or implied authority

Independent contractor A person who enters into a contract to accomplish a particular task without guidance from the person hiring that independent contractor

Study the first part of this assignment, which includes the following sections:

I. Legal Aspects of Agency
II. The Agency-Principal Relationship
III. Insurance Producers and the Law of Agency

Legal Aspects of Agency

Agency is a fiduciary relationship in which one entity (the principal) authorizes another (the agent) to act on its behalf in business dealings with third parties. Both the principal and the agent must agree to the relationship. The rights and responsibilities among parties when one represents another in dealings with third parties are the subject of the law of agency. In this assignment, agency, and agent are often discussed in the general sense of these terms. These terms are applied to insurance agencies and insurance agents as well as other types of agency relationships.

The relationship is a fiduciary one because of the high degree of trust and confidence involved. In this and in other fiduciary relationships, the law imposes a higher standard of conduct than in the usual course of business. The agent owes a duty to act primarily for the benefit of the principal and to deal fairly with the principal in every way.

The Agency-Principal Relationship

In an agency relationship, the parties have certain powers and authority. At the same time, the parties have duties and remedies if those duties are not performed.

Duties of the Agent

Agency normally results from a contract between the parties, and the agency contract imposes specified duties of performance. In addition to these contractual duties, the law implies other duties as a result of the fiduciary nature of the relationship. The special fiduciary duties imposed on the agent by the unique nature of the relationship include (1) loyalty, (2) obedience, (3) reasonable care, (4) accounting, and (5) giving information.

Violation of any of the duties subjects the agent to discharge and to liability for damage that may result to the principal, because failure to carry out these implied duties is a breach of the agency relationship, even though those duties are not mentioned in the contract. The law imposes a higher standard of conduct on the agent than would be expected in usual business dealings, and an agent must not represent the principal only to their mutual advantage. The agent owes a duty to act primarily for the benefit of the principal.

I. Legal Aspects of Agency
II. The Agency-Principal Relationship
A. Duties of the Agent
B. Remedies of the Principal

Duty of Loyalty

One of the agent's most important duties is undivided loyalty to the interests of the principal. Generally, the agent must not undertake any business venture that competes with or interferes in any manner with the business of the principal. An agent may not secretly represent the agent's own interests or the interests of a third person in a transaction for the principal. Any transaction that violates this rule may be voided by the principal, even if the agent was entirely fair to the principal. The rule is absolute and unqualified in order to remove all question of an agent's motivation or incentive when dealing on his or her own behalf.

The duty of loyalty also prohibits the agent from using or revealing trade secrets gained during the course of the agency. An agent, for instance, who learns of a secret process of the principal may not use such information for the agent's own purposes either during or after the termination of the agency. The principal may sue to enjoin the use of such information and may obtain from the agent any profits the agent makes from selling the information to others.

Mere knowledge and skill obtained through experience are not trade secrets, however. Agents may use the fruits of their experience in later employment or in working for themselves.

The duty of loyalty extends beyond the period of the agency itself, and many difficult problems can arise in applying this rule. For example, although the duty of loyalty may not prevent an agent from contacting previous customers of the principal, the agency agreement itself may contain restrictions on the agent's right to compete with the principal upon termination of the agency. (See Exhibit 1-1.) In order that such a limitation not be held unenforceable as an unreasonable restraint of trade, the limitation must be necessary to the protection of the principal's interests and must be reasonable. Considering the type of business involved and other circumstances surrounding the agreement, an agreement by an agent not to compete with the principal or not to become employed by a competitor will be upheld if the agreement restricts the agent for a reasonable period and within a reasonable distance from the former principal's business. Such provisions are often called a **covenant not to compete**, and if such an agreement exists, one may not compete even if one only relies on memory to recall customers.

A variation of the covenant not to compete is an agreement wherein the agent agrees not to contact any existing clients of the principal for a given length of time. In return, the principal agrees that the agent is free to pursue any other prospects for his or her services, thus allowing the agent to continue earning a living while the principal's customer base is protected. Such an arrangement is known as a **nonpiracy agreement**, and is far more likely to be upheld by the courts as a reasonable provision for both principal and agent.

Agent Tip

It is neither uncommon nor unreasonable for a principal (or agency) to require either a covenant not to compete or a nonpiracy agreement. From an agent's perspective, the nonpiracy agreement is by far the better choice. It allows you to continue doing what you do best, while preserving the agency's right not to have you "steal" its current customers. Be certain, before signing any contract, to determine whether such a clause is included, which type of clause it is, and whether you can live with its consequences. If it is not acceptable, ask to have it changed or don't sign the agreement.

Exhibit 1-1
Trade Secrets Agreement

In consideration of my employment by ____________ Insurance Brokers (hereinafter called ____________), I agree that I will regard and preserve as confidential all trade secrets (as defined below) pertaining to the business of _______ that have been or may be obtained by me by reason of my employment. I agree that I will not, without written authority during my employment or thereafter for a period of eighteen months immediately following the termination of my employment, except as required in the line of my employment with __________, divulge any trade secrets or confidential information connected with the business of __________. I further agree that I will not either during my employment or thereafter for a period of eighteen months immediately following the termination of my employment, either directly or indirectly, make known to any person, firm, or corporation the names or addresses of any of the clients of _____, or any other confidential information pertaining to them, or call on, solicit, or take away, or attempt to call on, solicit, or take away any of the clients of ________, on whom I may call or with whom I may become acquainted during my employment with _______, either for myself or for any other person, firm, or corporation.

I agree that all records of the accounts of clients, client lists, and any other records, books, and documents relating in any manner whatsoever to the clients of ________, whether prepared by me or otherwise coming into my possession, shall be the exclusive property of _______. I agree to immediately return to __________ on termination of employment, all such books, records, or documents.

For purpose of this Agreement, "Trade Secrets" shall include, but not be limited to, information encompassed in all marketing and sales plans, financial information, information related to the needs of particular clients and their methods of doing business, information relating to ________'s method of doing business with particular clients, clients' names and addresses, and all concepts or ideas in or reasonably related to the business of ________ that have not previously been publicly released by a duly authorized representative of _______.

Dated:__________, 19______

____

Employee

Duty of Obedience

An agent owes a duty to obey the lawful instructions of the principal. If the agent disobeys a reasonable order, the principal may bring an action for damages that result and may also terminate the relationship. Generally, the agent may not challenge the instructions unless they call for illegal or immoral acts. The fact that the instructions seem impractical or are distasteful to the agent does not affect the agent's duty to obey.

Duty of Reasonable Care

An agent is required to exercise the degree of care and skill that a reasonably prudent person would exercise under the same or similar circumstances. An agent with special skills or training is held to the higher standard of care of a reasonable person possessing those skills, that is, an insurance broker is required to exercise the care of a reasonably prudent insurance broker. The duty of exercising reasonable care does not require the agent to ensure the success of the undertaking. To be liable, the agent must fail to exercise the degree of care required under the circumstances.

An agent's failure to act, when action is reasonably required, also constitutes a breach of duty. The agency contract implies that the agent will carry out the duties of the agency with reasonable care in order to avoid injury to the principal.

Marketing Tip

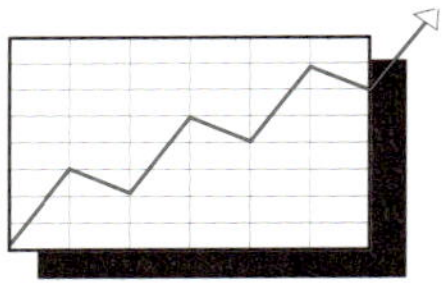

Use the duty of reasonable care to your advantage. If it's reasonable to assume that your clients are looking for the best coverage, offer it to them! You may be pleasantly surprised how often they accept your offer. Even if they refuse the offer this time, you have advised them of a need for which they might purchase coverage at the next renewal.

E&O Alert!

The reverse is also true—not offering the best coverage can become a lawsuit. The duty of reasonable care is easily violated by a producer who assumes too much about what an insured either wants or is willing to pay for. In far too many E&O cases, the producer defends, "Well, even if I had offered him the coverage, he wouldn't have bought it." What a mistake—this producer not only gave up the commission from a possible sale and incurred an E&O claim, the producer called the client a cheapskate. Give the insured every opportunity to accept the broadest coverage; then document all refusals.

Care of Gratuitous Agent

It makes no difference whether the agent is paid or not paid for the services. All agents owe their principals the duty to exercise reasonable care under the circumstances. Liability is generally imposed on gratuitous agents under the theory of tort rather than contract. Gratuitous agents cannot be compelled to perform the duties of the agency, but once they commence performance, they are held to the standard of reasonable care under the circumstances.

Limiting Agent's Liability

The agent and principal may enter into an agreement that the agent is not to be liable to the principal for ordinary negligence. Such agreements, called exculpatory agreements, are generally binding between parties since it is recognized that an agent may limit as well as expand his or her liability to the principal. An agent, however, may not be insulated from liability for gross negligence or from exercising reasonable care when performing a public duty.

Duty of Accounting

An agent owes a duty to account to the principal for all property and money of the principal that comes into possession of the agent. As part of this duty, the agent must keep the property and money of the principal separate from that of the agent. If the agent commingles the property, it is assumed that it all belongs to the principal unless the agent clearly proves otherwise. Money held by the agent should be deposited in a bank in a separate account in the name of the principal.

In accounting to the principal, the agent is entitled to set off any amounts, such as commissions, that the principal may owe the agent in the conduct of the agency. The agent may not, however, set off amounts due the agent from outside, nonagency transactions between the principal and agent.

The agent's accounting may be informal and need not involve keeping books. The time of accounting may be specified by the parties or upon a reasonable demand by the principal. During the course of the agency and at the termination of the agency, the agent must make full accounting of all property and money of the principal. The principal has a right to make reasonable inspection of the agent's books of account, including the original entries.

The agency relationship implies that any benefits arising from the agency belong to the principal and not to the agent. The agent is entitled only to established compensation from the work as an agent.

Management Tip

Some states require that insurance producers maintain premium funds in trust for the insurer and that the producer cannot even invest the funds without specific authorization from each insurer whose funds the producer holds. This topic is discussed in detail in another segment of this course. Be sure to verify if your state has such a requirement.

Duty To Give Information

An agent owes a duty to keep the principal informed of all facts relating to the agency relationship. The principal is entitled to all information that materially affects his or her interests. Since the knowledge the agent obtained during the course of performing the principal's business is imputed to the principal, the law imposes on the agent the duty of giving the information to the principal. Failure to perform this duty makes the agent liable to the principal for loss resulting to the principal.

Remedies of the Principal

The principal has four possible remedies for the default or wrongdoing of an agent. The selection of the appropriate legal remedy has important implications. When an agent makes improper use of the principal's property, the principal has the option to (1) bring an action for breach of the agency contract, (2) sue in tort for the harm done, (3) sue for the value of the benefit received by the agent, or (4) sue to require the agent to transfer to the principal the property improperly held. The selection of the appropriate remedy depends on the circumstances of the breach.

Duties of the Principal

Just as the agent has various duties to the principal, so does the principal have duties to the agent. The principal has the duty to perform according to the contract with the agent. The principal is also obligated to continue the relationship in accordance with the terms of the agreement, to provide an opportunity to work, to compensate the agent, to reimburse the agent for expenses, and to indemnify the agent or sub-agent.

Period of Employment

A contract of employment may normally be terminated at the will of either party unless the agreement specifies a fixed period. An agreement to pay a salary by the month or year does not necessarily indicate that employment is assured for the stated period. The promise of an agent to serve, or a principal to employ, for a specified period makes the parties liable for breach of their agreement within that period. When the employment contract provides for a specified period of employment and the principal goes out of business, it is generally held, as an implied term of the contract, that employment shall terminate because of changed conditions and not merely to avoid contractual duties.

An agent who has been discharged by the principal during a specified period of employment may maintain an action for compensation for the remainder of the period. In absence of special legislation affecting the rights of labor, the agent may not successfully maintain an action for specific performance requiring the principal to continue the employment.

The principal always retains the power, if not the contractual right, to terminate the relationship.

Opportunity To Work

A duty is inferred from the agency contract that the principal will afford the agent the opportunity to work. The principal is required to make reasonable efforts to enable the agent to continue performing as required by the terms of the contract of employment.

If the principal gives the agent the exclusive right to represent the principal in a particular area, the principal may not grant to another a right to sell in that area. Granting an exclusive right to sell also precludes the principal from selling in competition with the agent.

Duty of Compensation

The principal has a duty to pay the agent the agreed compensation for the services performed by the agent. If one appoints an agent who normally would be paid for services, compensation is required for the reasonable value of the service even if payment is not mentioned. An agent may, of course, agree to work on a contingent salary basis or for no income at all. An agent who breaches the duties of the agency relationship is not entitled to compensation.

In absence of a contrary agreement, a sales agent is entitled to recover when the sale is made, even though the sale is not actually carried through or performed. Thus, when a real estate agent obtains a firm offer from a responsible buyer, the owner-principal cannot deprive the agent of a commission by refusing to deal with the prospective purchaser. The commission is also earned when the owner contracts with the buyer, even if the buyer does not go through with the agreement. The owner is generally held to assume the risk of performance upon executing the contract with the buyer who has been presented by the agent. Contract language between the parties may provide otherwise, and in such cases the contract provisions are binding.

Duty of Reimbursement

The principal is under a duty to reimburse or repay the agent for any disbursements and expenses necessarily incurred for the proper discharge of agency duties. The agent may not, however, recover disbursements made for illegal purposes, or for expenses incurred through the agent's own negligence or fault. The principal is also required to reimburse the agent for any advances made on behalf of the principal by the agent. If, for example, the principal requires the agent to incur travel and advertising expenses, the principal must reimburse these expenses. If the agent's negligent conduct results in unnecessary expense, the agent bears that expense rather than the principal.

Duty of Indemnity

The principal owes a duty to indemnify the agent for any losses or damages suffered without the agent's fault, but arising on account of the agency. If the agent, at the direction of the principal, commits a wrong against a third party, and if the agent did not know the act was wrongful, the agent is entitled to be indemnified for the amount the agent is required to pay.

Any expenses that the agent incurs in defending actions by third persons brought because of the agent's authorized conduct, the agent again being innocent of intentional wrongdoing, the principal must indemnify. In most instances, however, the agent is not entitled to indemnification if the agent's own intentional conduct was responsible for the expense incurred. An agent who knowingly commits an illegal act ordinarily has no right to indemnity from the principal even though the principal has directed that the act be committed. The agent is barred from indemnity by the illegality of the transaction.

Remedies of the Agent

If a principal breaches the agency contract, the agent normally has the option to (1) sue the principal for the reasonable value of the agent's services up to the date of the breach or discharge from service; (2) treat the contract as continuing to exist and sue for damages sustained, which include what the agent would have earned had the contract been completed according to the agreement; or (3) sue at the expiration of the contract period for damages that flowed from breach of the contract, if the agent tries to mitigate damages by seeking other employment or by performing in the best way possible after the breach.

Insurance Producers and the Law of Agency

To this point this assignment has reviewed the agent and principal relationship as it applies to all business agreements. Although there are many unique aspects to the relationship between insurers and their agents, that relationship is still firmly based upon the concepts and legal doctrines discussed in the preceding section. This section will devote itself to the specific concepts and doctrines affecting *insurance* agents.

In the distribution of insurance, those on the sales force are generally referred to as agents or brokers. All independent insurance agents operate under the law of agency. Although there is a functional difference among an agent, a broker, a general agent, and so forth, the law generally fails to draw a significant distinction in their legal responsibilities. The determining factor is not the name under which the producer operates, whether "agent" or "broker" or some other term, but the type of activity in which the producer is engaged.

Distribution Systems

Initially, sales representatives of American insurers were employees of insurance companies located in large cities on the East Coast. As the country expanded west, agents were appointed who traveled over large territories and had binding authority (for property and liability insurance if not for life insurance). The agents made daily reports to the insurers listing the details of each sale, and thus the phrase "daily" or "daily report" has come to mean an abstract of an insurance policy used for file purposes by both producers and insurers. Policy declarations pages are sometimes referred to as "dailies."

As the nation continued to push westward, insurers authorized some of their agents to appoint sub-agents and act as intermediaries between the sub-agents and the insurer. These "general agents" often became large organizations representing many different insurers, and compensation to the general agent frequently included not only commissions but also operating expenses. The general agents were independent business owners who, by contract, fulfilled many of the functions of the insurer, including underwriting, loss control services, claims adjusting, accounting, and so on.

In the property and liability field, insurance company branch offices have replaced many of the general agencies. General agents continue to work in the life insurance field, but they usually do not have underwriting or claims authority since their primary function today is sales management.

There are three major insurance distribution systems. In the **direct writing system**, agents are employees of the insurer (such as Liberty Mutual) who place business exclusively with that insurer. Producers who are a part of the **American Agency System** ("independent" agents) have the option of representing many insurers, and may place business with any or several of them, depending on the unique needs of each insured. In the **exclusive agency system**, agents (such as those employed by State Farm) are obligated to place business with one insurer, but remain independent in the operation of their offices and are not employees of the company. If an exclusive agent's insurer does not accept a certain type of business, the agent's contract may or may not allow the exclusive agent to submit that business to another insurer or residual market such as the FAIR plan.

A current trend among the American Agency System companies is the assignment of underwriting, loss control, policy writing, and claims adjusting functions to their agents. This trend, facilitated by modern communications and computer technology, enables those insurance companies that grant broad authority to their agents to reduce the size and number of their branch offices. This trend, if it continues, may again result in the linking of the agency force directly to insurance company home offices, but by electronics rather than by mail, and the result will be a new kind of general agency system.

Duties of Insurance Agents

Agents of insurance companies owe the same duties to their principals as do agents in other businesses. The duty of loyalty owed by the insurance agent raises some special considerations. Normally, a person who is employed by two others to conduct a transaction between them (all facts being known to both parties) is the agent of both and owes a duty to each to deal with them fairly. This is known as **dual agency**. The essential question is whether the insurance agent owes primary allegiance to the general employer (the insurer) or to the insured.

E&O Alert!

Dual agency is an unavoidable reality for insurance agents, so carefully study the following discussion. If the agent is seen as unduly favoring either the insurer or the insured in a given situation, the slighted party may resort to an E&O claim to recover its loss.

An insurance broker, who represents the insured in obtaining insurance, may owe duties to both the insured and the insurer depending upon the particular act. For example, the broker may be the agent of the insured in securing a policy and, as is generally required by specific statute, may also be the agent of the insurer in receiving premiums. The problems of dual agency and of allegiance to two principals in insurance transactions come from the fact that a person may be an agent for one principal for part of a transaction, and an agent for the other for the remainder of the transaction.

In the usual insurance company-agent relationship, courts tend to infer that the fiduciary duties of the agent are owed to the insurer. Statutes in many states stipulate that insurance agents are agents of the insurance company and not of the insured so that information given to the agent, or payment made to the agent, is binding on the insurance company. Attempts by insurers to include contractual provisions that stipulate that the agent is the agent of the insured have not been recognized by the courts. Whether a producer can collect fees in addition to commissions depends on state law, but when the agent receives additional compensation, all parties to the transaction should be aware of the charges.

A producer in a dual agency role might take a bargaining position between the insurer and the insurance buyer, but this is a difficult position to take and to maintain objectively. The courts recognize the dual agency status of agents and brokers as an exception to the general rule of serving only one principal. The producer generally represents the insurance company when binding insurance, keeping records, collecting premiums, and issuing and canceling policies, and the producer generally represents the client when suggesting and selecting coverages or insurers.

E&O Alert!

The American Agency System puts the producer in a dual agency capacity. The independent agent has traditionally advertised service to the insurance buyer and yet is contracted to the other party to the transaction—the insurer. At various points in the transaction the agent or broker will shift from representing one party to representing the other party. If you are an independent agent, be careful not to violate your duties to either.

Agent Versus Broker

Whether an insurance producer is an agent or a broker depends on whose interest he or she represents. When the producer represents the buyer of insurance, the producer is a broker. When the producer represents the seller of insurance (an insurance company), the producer is an agent. Under the law of agency, the client is always the principal of the broker, and the insurer is the principal of the agent, as Exhibit 1-2 shows.

Exhibit 1-2

Agent-Principal Relationship in Insurance Production

	Principal		Agent		Third Party
Brokerage	Client	→	Broker	→	Insurer
Agency	Insurer	→	Agent	→	Client

Most courts and state insurance regulators have taken the position that general agency law could unjustly penalize the public for dealing with brokers and at the same time allow insurance companies to escape responsibility for broker acts for which the insurance companies should be responsible. Thus, as a matter of consumer protection, the broker is sometimes considered an agent for the insurer. The nature of the circumstances rather than the strict legal relationship of the parties determines whether the producer is an agent of the insurance company or an agent of the policyholder. For example, most states make the broker by statute the legal agent of the insurance company for the purpose of premium collection. Such laws permit the general public to rely on the certainty that payment to their insurance broker is payment to the insurer. As this situation illustrates, the broker can be the insured's agent for some aspects of an insurance transaction and the agent of the insurance company for other aspects of the same transaction. (See the previous discussion of "dual agency.")

Insurers grant authority to their agents by an agency contract written and executed by both principal and agent. Brokers rarely obtain written agreements with insurance buyers in the same way that public accountants secure an engagement letter, but it is good practice for a broker to have a written agreement covering any fees that a client may be charged. Because the broker represents the buyer of insurance, it is rare to find a written agreement granting binding authority between a broker and an insurer. A broker who places business regularly with an insurer may have a written agreement governing such matters as the terms of premium payment, but such brokerage agreements go to great lengths to make clear that the broker is not an agent of the insurer.

Brokers are generally paid a commission, which is part of the insurance premium. In this regard, they are no different from agents who transact business in the same manner. Many brokers (especially when dealing with large commercial accounts) have moved away from the traditional

II. The Agency-Principal Relationship
III. Insurance Producers and the Law of Agency
B. Duties of Insurance Agents
C. Agent Versus Broker
D. Authority of Insurance Agents
E. Ratification

commission arrangements toward a fee basis where the client pays for the professional services rendered by the broker in addition to paying the insurance premium to the insurer. When a broker charges a fee, the insurance is usually "written net" by the insurer, that is, the premium is reduced to eliminate the producer commission. The broker is then free to negotiate a fee based on the work to be performed, irrespective of the size of the insurance premium. This approach also prevents violating any laws that prohibit a producer from taking both a commission and a fee.

The fee system provides certain advantages for the broker. For example, the potential for conflict of interest is minimized since the insurer no longer pays a commission. In addition, the fee can reflect the amount of compensation the broker requires for service, overhead, and profit. In a competitive market where premiums (and therefore commissions) are shrinking, the broker's fee may remain constant or even increase.

The fee system also has disadvantages for the broker. Fees are visible to the insurance buyer, while the commission is a part of the premium. When the insured knows the fees charged, that insured can evaluate the cost of producer service separately from the cost of insurance protection. Such visibility highlights the amount of the fee and allows the client to negotiate it separately.

Marketing Tip

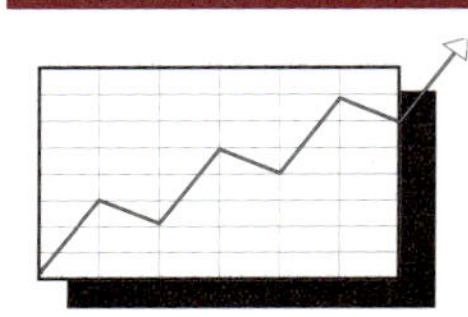

As commission levels that carriers pay to agents change (usually going down), many agents have begun looking to the fee system as a possible alternative. If after considering the pluses and minuses a fee system still looks attractive, be careful to review applicable state laws and regulations before implementing fees. Even if the insured is fully aware of the fee and agrees to pay, you may be conducting an illegal practice. Find out under what circumstances fees are allowed (if at all) and what necessary disclosure arrangements are applicable in your marketing territory.

Authority of Insurance Agents

Authority is the legal power of the agent arising from the agency relationship. An agent's power to bind the principal is determined from the agent's "authority" derived expressly, by implication, or from the facts of the situation. These types of authority are called, respectively, express authority, implied authority, and apparent authority.

Express Authority

An agent's **express authority** is anything legal that is agreed to by the agent and the principal. The law recognizes two degrees of agency. A general agent has authority to perform all acts that are "usual and customary" in such a capacity. A special agent is usually restricted to just those acts "essential" to the situation. (The terms "general agent" and "special agent" used here should not be confused with the day-to-day use of these terms by producers.) Most property and liability insurance producers are general agents in the legal sense with authority, within expressed limits, to make or to modify contracts of insurance, and to perform all of the other activities necessary in the efficient performance of an insurance agency.

A more detailed discussion of insurance agency contracts follows later in this assignment, but every producer should be aware of the limits of the express authority each represented insurance company grants. Express authority can be given through oral or written instructions from the principal to the agent. In the business of insurance, instructions from insurer to agent are normally written, and they are a part of the negotiations that establish the agency relationship or modify it from time to time. The agency contract offered by an insurance company and signed by the agency's owners contains express authority for the agency to represent the insurer. Agreements by two different insurance companies illustrate various aspects of insurance agency contracts.

The express grant of authority in an insurance agency agreement will include a statement like this:

> IT IS HEREBY AGREED between the Company and the Agent as follows: (1) The Company hereby grants authority to the Agent to receive and accept proposals for insurance and to issue contracts of insurance on policy forms provided by and at premium rates promulgated or adopted by the Company covering risks as authorized in the addenda attached hereto within the state of
>
> Name of State
>
> subject, however, to restrictions placed upon the Agent by applicable state laws and to the terms and conditions hereinafter set forth and to such instructions as may be given to the Agent by the Company from time to time.

Or the wording might be more detailed:

> COMPANY HEREBY GRANTS AUTHORITY to Agent to receive and accept proposals for contracts of insurance which Company lawfully has authority to make covering risks located in the state first above mentioned (on a schedule earlier in the contract) and any other state in which Agent is authorized to engage in an insurance business, subject to all restrictions placed upon Agent by law and subject further to the following terms and conditions:
>
> 1. EXTENT OF AGENT'S AUTHORITY
>
> (a) Authority granted hereunder shall apply only with respect to such and so many of the lines of business as are specifically designated in the Schedule of Appointment, which may be amended or supplemented from time to time. Agent agrees to follow all underwriting rules and regulations of Company as respects such lines of business.
>
> (b) Agent shall have authority to accept and bind proposals for contracts of insurance to which this agreement applies only as specifically authorized and provided in Schedules forming part of the Agreement, which Company may amend or supplement from time to time by

II. The Agency-Principal Relationship
III. Insurance Producers and the Law of Agency
C. Agent Versus Broker
D. Authority of Insurance Agents
E. Ratification

> written notice of not less than thirty (30) days from Company to Agent. Agent agrees to forward copies of all evidences of insurance issued by Agent, or otherwise to report to Company all insurance accepted and bound, no later than the close of the tenth business day following the effective date or the date of acceptance of such insurance, whichever first occurs.

Express authority according to these agreements generally gives instructions regarding binding and issuing policies, collection and remittance of premiums, and commissions. Of course, the general statements in the agency contract are expanded by references to the law, to attached "addenda" or "schedules," and to company underwriting rules—all of which will explicitly limit agency authority.

Implied Authority

No agency contract can encompass every possible contingency. Therefore, the agreement is broadened by law and custom to include other acts deemed necessary to carry out the agent's express authority. In other words, the agent has the **implied authority** to carry out the express authority. Notice there can be no implied authority without express authority. For example, an insurance agent has the implied authority to advertise that the producer represents a certain insurance company, even if the agency contract does not spell this out. The right to advertise representation is implied because advertising is necessary to carry out the agent's commitment to solicit insurance on behalf of the insurer.

An agent should be able to believe that any actions in accord with accepted custom are within the scope of the authority granted. Usually, this authority would be similar to that of other agents in a similar position. Implied authority is simple in principle but can cause problems in practice because it is nebulous. When a producer is in doubt as to the extent of implied authority, he or she should ask the principal for clarification.

Implied authority also may arise from a principal's conduct that could be construed as intending to confer such authority. If an insurance agent has for years been able to bind property submissions without limit on value, that agent has, by implication, the right to continue to do so until the insurance company expresses otherwise.

E&O Alert!

When, through any of its employees or solicitors, an insurance agency exceeds its express or implied authority with an insurance company, the agency may be liable to both the client and the insurance company for financial loss caused as a result of the exceeded authority. Care should be taken that all personnel in the agency are well aware of their individual authority as well as the authority of the agency itself. Any limitations on an agent's authority of an unusual nature must be communicated to third parties, and the insurance producer operating under special limitations on authority must be very careful not to exceed those limitations.

Apparent Authority

Apparent authority is not authority given to the agent by the principal but is based on the third party's reasonable belief, based on appearances created by the principal, that the agent has authority. It is often called **authority by estoppel** on the theory that if a principal creates the appearance of authority in an agent, and a third party reasonably relies on that appearance, the principal should be estopped (prevented) from denying that authority.

Apparent authority is derived from the circumstances of the situation. In a society as interrelated and complex as ours, the existence of agency is a common occurrence, but few members of the general public know the exact extent of the expressed and implied authority relationships that exist between agents and their principals. For instance, how many policyholders have seen the agency contract between their agent and insurance company?

Thus, whether apparent authority is present is determined by how the third party perceives the situation. If the third party perceives that the supposed agent has authority, the courts will hold the principal to obligations made by the supposed agent so long as the agent operated in accordance with the accepted customs and traditions of the business.

For example, suppose an unlicensed clerical employee of an insurance agency bound coverage while the licensed producers were away from the office. Since it would be reasonable for a member of the public to assume that the clerical person had the necessary authority to bind the coverage, the insurance company would be held liable for the coverage even though an agent did not prepare the binder.

E&O Alert!

In this situation, the insurance company may have a right of action against the agency for any damages it sustained in paying the claims. Apparent authority, however, assures that the public is still protected.

The concept of apparent authority may sound unfair to the principal, and in some cases it may be, but apparent authority allows an innocent third party to recover from the principal when the principal has made it appear either intentionally or unintentionally that the agent has authority to act.

Third parties, however, cannot depend so completely upon appearances created by the agent that they are absolved of all responsibility to act as reasonable and prudent consumers. The public has a responsibility to protect itself and must always be on guard to note special or unusual situations. When an agent acts in a way that appears to be adverse to the best interests of the principal, the third party has a duty to determine the extent of the agent's authority by a direct inquiry to the principal.

Ratification

In addition to entering into an agency contract, an agency and an insurer can create agency by **ratification**, which is, in essence, a form of post-contract authority.

When an agent exceeds the express or implied powers granted by the principal, the agent in effect has made a contract for himself or herself rather than for the principal, since the agent has breached or exceeded the authority granted by the principal. However, if, after the transaction has been completed, the principal with knowledge of the unauthorized act ratifies (approves) the agent's conduct, it is as if such authority had been granted in the first place. The ratification could come about by a written confirmation or simply by not rejecting the transaction.

These are the requirements for ratification:

1. The agent must purport to act for the principal at the time of the original transaction.
2. The principal must ratify the entire transaction.
3. The principal must ratify before the third party elects to withdraw.
4. The principal must have full knowledge of all of the facts.
5. The contract must be legal.

If all of these elements are present, the principal ratifying the act of the agent is bound by the contract, and the inception of the agreement dates from the time of the original contract. If the principal does not ratify the agent's act, the agent alone is liable on the specific contract.

For example, an agent's contract with the insurer expressly limits property insurance binding authority to $1,000,000 per building. An existing client calls, asking for coverage on his newly purchased $2,000,000 building. The agent binds the coverage, then calls the insurer asking that the insurer honor the binder. The underwriter refers the agent's request to the insurer's home office, which agrees to honor the binder three days later. The binder is now ratified, and coverage exists from the moment the agent originally bound the risk.

Although the licensing requirements of the state may affect the legal relationships between the insurance company and the purported agent, as far as the third party is concerned the ratified insurance contract is binding on the insurer.

Agent as Independent Contractor

An **independent contractor** is a person who enters into a contract to accomplish a particular task without guidance from the person hiring that independent contractor. If the person engaging the contractor begins to exert control over the contractor in the performance of the task assigned, the status of independent contractor may be lost, and the parties become employer and employee.

The advantage to the principal in dealing with an independent contractor is the absence of liability for the actions of the independent contractor. For example, the principal is not responsible for accidents caused by those independent contractors with their own automobiles. Using independent contractors instead of employees is one way to transfer some of the liability exposures (particularly tort and criminal liability) that can arise from the actions of employees.

Insurance agency contracts generally afford independent contractor status to the agency. An example of wording establishing independent contractor status comes from an agency agreement, which states the following in a section entitled "Agent's Relation to Company":

> This Agreement is not a contract of employment, and nothing herein contained shall be construed to create the relationship of employer and employee between Company and Agent. Agent is an independent contractor and shall be free to exercise judgment and discretion with regard to the conduct of business as Agent for Company.

These same provisions may apply to independent or exclusive agents. For instance, State Farm refers to its agents as "independent contractor agents" and has established that relationship with producers in just the same manner as insurers who permit their agents to represent more than one insurance company.

Undisclosed Principal

An undisclosed principal asks the agent to act as if the *agent* were the principal. A commonly used example is a prospective land purchaser who is afraid prices will jump if the owners know the prospective purchaser is in the market. Thus, the land purchaser instructs the agent to act as if the agent were the prospective purchaser, hiding the agency relationship from the sellers. When a third party deals with an agent for an undisclosed principal and later learns of the existence of the principal, the third party has the choice of suing the agent or the principal for performance on the contract should the principal attempt to back out of the contract. In other words, the agent does not drop out of the picture, as the agent normally would if the principal had been disclosed. The third party is in a superior position after discovering the principal than if that third party had dealt with an agent of a disclosed principal. This rule protects the public.

A similar relationship, known as a partially disclosed principal, might also exist. A partially disclosed principal has the agent acknowledge the existence of a principal, but the agent does not disclose the identity of that principal. The legal protection for the third party is virtually the same as with an undisclosed principal.

Although insurance producers will seldom have a principal ask to be undisclosed, producers must be aware of the pitfalls of failing to fully disclose the principal for whom they act. Consider, for instance, the producer who meets a client on the street who mentions the purchase of a new truck. The producer says, "The truck will be insured as soon as I get back to the office. I'll send you a bill for the premium with the policy when it is issued." In this case the producer probably had no insurer in mind at the time of the conversation.

Assume that an accident involving the truck happens before the producer returns to the agency. If the producer is a broker, the vehicle could not have been insured without the producer's contacting an insurer and obtaining a binder for the coverage. Because the broker is an agent of the insurance buyer, the only possible claim against the broker by the client would be for negligence in seeking an insurer for the truck. In view of the facts of this situation, it is unlikely such a claim could be sustained because so little time elapsed.

If the producer is an agent, however, the producer and the agency would bear the truck's loss. A court would probably hold that the producer had represented a partially disclosed principal or had breached the warranty of authority to the client that the producer had an insurance company with which to place the exposure.

Finally, if the producer had binding authority and had selected an insurer, the insurance company would have been bound by the conversation (even in the absence of a written binder) and obligated to pay the loss. If the producer had no binding authority, only a ratification by the insurance company after the loss would bind the insurer to pay.

E&O Alert!

This hypothetical example emphasizes the importance of an independent agent naming an insurer to the client when coverage has been promised. Further, producers must issue a written binder of insurance to both the insurer and the client as quickly as possible so that the terms of the insurance and the identity of the insurer are certain.

Nonexistent Principal

The term nonexistent principal is used when an agent gives the third party the impression that the agent is dealing for a principal when, in fact, there is no principal. For example, assume the producer is presented with an exposure that the producer knows will have to be placed through Lloyd's of London because of the unusual or difficult nature of the exposure. Suppose the producer says to the client, "I'll insure you through Lloyd's." Because Lloyd's is not an insurer, but rather a physical location where underwriters meet to accept or reject submissions, Lloyd's is not a disclosed principal. In this case, the producer is operating for a nonexistent principal and will bear any loss from the time the client reasonably believes the coverage is in force until the underwriters at Lloyd's actually accept the submission.

Licensing

A unique aspect of the law affecting insurance producers and their authority is licensing by the states. Each state issues a license to those producers domiciled and doing business in that state. Producers transacting insurance in more than one state need to obtain a nonresident license in the states where their clients are situated. Without proper licensing, state insurance laws prohibit an insurer from giving any authority to an agent, and this prohibition is also reinforced by wording in the agency contract terminating it automatically if the agent's license is suspended or terminated.

Whether an insurance producer is called an agent or a broker, the laws of each state provide for testing and licensing before the producer can represent an insurer or an insured. Some states have a number of different licenses, such as those for insurance consultants or for employees of agents or brokers (who are licensed as "solicitors"); some states license only agents. Engaging in the insurance business without first complying with the licensing requirements makes the noncomplying parties subject to possible prosecution and fine. A lack of licensing will not prevent or hinder a policyholder's suit against an agent or an insurer for error or omission. It may, however, restrict the agent's ability to recover from the insurance company and vice versa.

Licensing may also affect how commissions are split in a particular instance. In California, agents of the same insurance company may share commissions on a policy. They cannot, however, share commissions with agents who are not licensed to represent the same insurer. Brokers, on the other hand, are permitted to split commissions among themselves as they see fit without regard to an agency appointment by the insurance company concerned.

Each state has its own legal qualifications and testing standards for insurance producers. The tests are usually administered by the state insurance department, which issues the appropriate license to the producer upon satisfaction of its requirements. Requirements for "surplus" or "excess" lines brokers who write insurance through nonadmitted insurance companies may be even more rigorous. In addition, this type of license often requires the producer's regular financial disclosure to the state since such producers act in many ways like insurers. Many states require that the producer post a license bond promising faithful performance.

State regulations also specify the circumstances under which a producer's license can be revoked. Termination by an insurance company of the right of an agent to write business for that company does not result in cancellation of the agent's right to be licensed with other companies.

Engaging in the insurance business as an agent thus involves the twofold process of being licensed by the state and being granted the privilege of representing a particular insurer. A broker need only be licensed by the state.

Check your understanding of the *Key Words and Phrases* found in the first part of this assignment.

Producer (p. 1)

Agent (p. 1)

Broker (p. 1)

Agency (p. 3)

Covenant not to compete (p. 4)

Nonpiracy agreement (p. 4)

Direct writing system (p. 11) – Agents are employees
– company owns expirations

American Agency System (p. 11) – independent contractors
– represent many carriers
– agent owns expirations (agency)

Exclusive agency system (p. 11) – one insurer (& FAIR PLAN)
– can be company or agent owned expirations

Dual agency (p. 12)

Express authority (p. 14) – written

Implied authority (p. 16) – implied by express AUTHORITY

Apparent authority (p. 17) – what appears to someone as AUTHORITY
– perceived

Authority by estoppel (p. 17)

Ratification (p. 18)

Independent contractor (p. 18)

Review the concepts presented in the first part of this assignment by answering the following questions. **Note: Acceptable answers to all questions appear at the end of this segment.**

1. What is the primary function of an agency? (p. 3)

2. What are the duties an agent owes to his or her principal? (p. 3)

   Loyalty, obedience, reasonable care, accounting, and ~~giving~~ relay information "LORAR"

3. What remedies does a principal have when its agent fails in his or her duties? (p. 8)

   1) action for breach of agency contract
   2) sue in tort for the harm done
   3) sue for the value of the benefit received by the agent
   4) sue to require

4. What duties do principals owe to their agents? (p. 8) "WIREC"

   W - opportunity to work
   I - Indemnity
   R - reimbursement (i.e. travel expenses)
   E - period of employment
   C - salary compensation

5. When might an insurance broker be legally considered an agent for the insurance company as well as the insured? (p. 12)

   dual agency

6. How does an insurance agent sometimes become a dual agent? (p. 12)

   Service to buyer
   Contracted to insurer

7. Why might a producer prefer being compensated by commission rather than by a fee? (pp. 13-14)

Fees are visible
Commission built into premium

8. Describe the types of authority an agent might have. (pp. 14-17)

Express - written
Implied - i.e. advertising - follows express authority
Apparent - perceived by outside party

9. What problem might an agent have when facing a loss with an undisclosed principal? (p. 19)

Insurance company
i.e. Chubb

Apply the concepts presented in the first part of this assignment by answering the following questions.

1. Some persons believe that once an agent makes the sale for the insurer, the agent drops out of the picture and has no further obligations in the matter legally because he or she is not a party to the insurance contract. Explain whether this belief is true.

2. An agent has authority to represent the principal in an insurance transaction. Explain how each of the three major types of authority relates to the following:

   (a) a written contract

   (b) customary business procedures

(c) an insurer's plaque on the agency's wall

(d) an oral binder for an umbrella policy

3. Because of the contractual relationship between the principal and agent, both parties have a number of duties and obligations that they must fulfill under that relationship.
   (a) Explain the five duties the agent owes to the principal.
   (b) Explain the five duties the principal owes to the agent.
   (c) What remedies does the principal have if the agent fails to fulfill the duties owed?

Read the definitions of the *Key Words and Phrases* that follow. Being familiar with these important words will help you better understand the second part of this assignment.

Run-off provision A contract provision allowing current clients to be renewed for a specified period of time following the termination of an agency's contract

Account current A type of billing system in which the agency bills and collects premiums from insureds and pays the insurer based on the insurer's billing records

Direct bill A billing procedure in which the insurer bills the client directly

Arbitration clause A clause that provides a formal method for the agency and insurer to resolve disagreements arising under the contract

Profit sharing (contingent commission) agreement A supplemental contract arrangement provided by the insurer offering incentive compensation for producers who exceed benchmarks for profitability and volume of business

Trade loss ratio A measure of profitability using the ratio of incurred losses to earned premiums

Sole proprietorship A business owned by a single individual

Partnership A voluntary association of two or more persons who are co-owners of a business operating for profit

Corporation A business enterprise that is a legal entity in and of itself and is owned by its stockholders

Limited liability company (LLC) A form of business structure created under state laws with specific tax and liability provisions

Agency cluster A group of agents sharing services and insurers

Study the second part of this assignment, which includes the following sections:

IV. Insurance Agency Contracts
V. Organizational Forms of Insurance Agencies

Insurance Agency Contracts

This section of this assignment will consider the common features of typical agency contracts that property and liability insurance companies offer to their independent contractor agents. Although contracts vary from one insurer to another, certain topics are part of virtually every contract. Attempts have been made to standardize insurance agency contracts. The Independent Insurance Agents and Brokers of America, Inc. (IIABA), for example, has studied agency contracts and recommended certain criteria in *The Independent Agent's Guide to Agency-Company Agreements*, which forms the basis of the following discussion.

The fact is, however, that an insurer and an agency individually enter each contract, and the relative bargaining power of the two parties determines how much the contract the insurer originally offers is modified to favor the agency. The wise producer will seek as much authority as possible on the most favorable terms. Often an insurer will have a number of alternative standard contracts, and an assertive agent can obtain a better contract than the agent who merely accepts what the insurance company's marketing representative offers.

Agency agreements vary considerably and often alter the general duties of the principal and agent, and many producers overlook the importance of their own duties in connection with their agency contracts. Because of the convenience offered by an agency appointment with an insurance company (like the ability to bind certain coverages and eligibility for profit sharing agreements), even most brokers have agreements with the insurers they use most frequently. Producers must understand the agency contract, since the agency owner is liable for the conduct of producers. Acts committed by a producer that are contrary to the agency contract could jeopardize that contract.

Major Sections of an Agency Contract

Major provisions of agency contracts include the term of agreement/termination, rehabilitation, ownership of expirations, payment procedures, indemnification, amendments to contract, arbitration, and sale of the agency.

Term of Agreement/Termination

Many contracts allow the insurer to terminate the contract for any reason as long as the specified notice is given. The agent, however, may be unable to attempt long-term planning with any assurance the insurer will still continue the relationship.

A better provision would be to have the contract written for a specific term, with automatic rollover/renewal unless the agent violates the agreement. Such violations should be specifically spelled out in the contract (loss of license, for example), and only if the violation is committed by the agent can the insurer cancel the contract.

Terminations should not be based upon volume or mix of business placed with the insurer, unless the insurer has clearly informed the agent of such requirements in writing, and enough in advance of termination to allow the agency a reasonable chance of meeting the requirements. The contract should preclude any such termination if the failure to meet the requirements was due to the insurer's underwriting practices. It is clearly unfair for an insurer to establish high-volume requirements, then impose such strict underwriting guidelines that the agency has no chance to meet those requirements.

Similarly, agency loss ratios should only be a basis for termination if the agency's tendency to write consistently bad business is documented over a period of years. Shock losses (catastrophes such as earthquakes and tornadoes) and uninsured motorist losses (clearly outside the underwriting control of the agency) should be excluded from the loss ratio calculations. If, following these considerations, the agency's loss ratio still appears to the insurer to be unacceptable, the agency should be notified and given a reasonable chance to improve before being terminated.

When cancellation is to occur, 180 days' written notice should be given, and the notice should include the specific reason(s) for the termination. A reasonable exception that would allow a shorter length of notice is the agency's failure to pay premiums due the insurer. The insurer should provide the agency time (10 days following notification of the past due amounts, for example) to pay. Routine bookkeeping errors and legitimate disputes over amounts owed should not activate this exception.

When the contract is terminated, what happens to the agency's clients currently insured by that insurer? Since a key issue for independent agents is ownership/control of expirations (discussed in a following section), the insurer must nonrenew all the policies currently written for the agency's clients. But such a mass nonrenewal may cause confusion and hardship on the individual insureds. To allow for a smooth transition for the insured from the terminating insurer to the new insurer chosen by the agency, a **run-off provision** is necessary. This contract provision allows current clients to be renewed for a specified period of time following the agency's termination. For example, all insureds coming up for renewal within the twelve months following the contract termination should be renewed for at least one additional year, assuming current underwriting conditions are met. The rate of commission and other policy terms would the same as those in effect on the date of the agency termination. The agency would continue to have the responsibility to service such business.

Run-off provisions are being increasingly complicated by the growing number of state or other governmental restrictions on policy terminations. What happens, for instance, if a regulation requires the insured's policy to be renewed beyond the time period the agency and insurer agreed to in the contract? The agency contract has been terminated, but the insurer must legally keep the policy in force. The agency, of course, wants to retain control/ownership of the expiration. Since the cause of the complication lies outside the control of either the insurer or agency, perhaps the best compromise is a provision continuing a limited agency contract only for such policies, granting the agency control of the policy whether it is ultimately replaced or continued in force with the current insurer. Without such a provision, the insurer may intend to move the policy to another of its agents for servicing, in effect assuming ownership of the expiration.

Rehabilitation

Assuming the termination of the contract is always the least favorable resolution to an agency's failing to fulfill an insurer's requirements, a rehabilitation clause provides a length of time during which the agency can work to avoid termination. The insurer agrees to make a good-faith effort to agree with the agency on exactly what the agency must do to retain the contract. Although the length of time for the rehabilitation is negotiable, an agency should request a minimum of one year.

Ownership of Expirations

Although the customer is the only one who truly controls or "owns" his or her policy expirations, in any contract between an insurer and agency a key provision is which party has the right to control the relationship with a client. Especially in today's evolving marketplace, where many insurers are dealing directly with the clients (whether to "assist" the agency or "eliminate" the agency from the transaction is an often argued question), both the insurer and the agency must clearly understand who has the final word on client communications and solicitations.

In the case of agents who represent one company exclusively, the insurer often owns the expirations, not the agent. But for independent agencies, ownership of policy expirations determines whether an agency is truly independent. Although commissions on the sale of products are the major ongoing income source, the long-term value of the agency—the price at which it can be purchased or sold, or its value when passed on to heirs—is based upon control and ownership of the book of business. Any restrictions or limitations on such control lessen the agency's value.

Agency ownership of its book of business is well established in common law, but the specific wording in many company contracts often varies. Some insurers require joint ownership of expirations. Others may claim ownership from the agency if the contract is terminated for certain reasons. Others require the agency to give the insurer a security interest in the expirations. These provisions are included in contracts to assure payment of all premiums due the insurer. Ideally, the contract should avoid limitations or provisions and recognize the independent agency's clear and complete ownership of expirations under all circumstances.

Payment Procedures

The provisions of a contract between the agency and insurer must clearly delineate procedures for collecting and remitting the amounts of money arising from the sale of insurance products. Who will bill the client? If the agency, how and when will the insurer be paid its share? If the insurer bills the client, how and when will the agency receive its commissions? The resolutions to these questions must be included in the contract.

When the agency handles the billing and premium collection for a particular policy, that policy is typically referred to as being on an **account current** basis. In this system, the insurer submits a billing for its share of the premiums to the agency, typically on a monthly cycle. The agency, after verifying the accuracy of the insurer's billing, pays it. While this billing method is typically used on large commercial accounts, some agencies prefer account current on as much of their business as possible because it gives them control of the funds, and possibly a significant investment income on the premiums invested between the time collected and the date paid to the insurer.

Direct bill is the procedure in which the insurer bills the client directly. The agency's commissions are then remitted to the agency by the insurer, again typically on a monthly cycle. Nearly all personal lines business is now direct billed, with a growing percentage of small and medium commercial business moving to this method.

Direct billing was extremely controversial when introduced because it seemed to many agencies that the insurer was trying to control the agency-client relationship. Once the client began receiving bills directly from the insurer, with the insurer's name prominently displayed, and the client began paying premiums directly to the insurer, some argued that the client would no longer consider himself or herself the customer of the agency but rather the customer of the insurer. Since the ownership of expirations is important to independent agencies, this situation could clearly become a threat. Also, since billings often update the customer regarding renewals and policy changes, the agency faced the possibility of being cut out of the loop of customer communications.

The agency contract should address payment issues by clearly addressing several questions. Which types of business will be put on direct bill and which on account current? For account current, when will the premiums be due for new business, renewals, and changes or endorsements? Will the agency collect the first premium payment on a direct billed policy? How prominently will the agency name be displayed on direct bill communications with an insured? Will copies of all direct bill communications of any type be furnished to the agency before being sent to the client? Will the insurer accept all responsibility for potential errors and omissions arising from direct bill procedures? If the contract is terminated, will the insurer supply the agency with a complete list of all direct billed policyholders, their expiration dates, and necessary policy details?

Indemnification

When an error and omissions claim arises, the contract should clearly delineate when the insurer will indemnify, defend, or hold harmless the agency if the claim arises solely or partially through the insurer's error.

An agency should avoid any clause that bases carrier indemnification of the agency upon a contributory standard. Such a clause might state, for example, the insurer will only indemnify the agency for claims "caused solely and directly by error of omission of Company." With this wording, if the agency is even 1 percent at fault, the insurer has no obligation to indemnify for *any* of the claim.

A comparative negligence guideline that holds the agency responsible for its percentage of responsibility for the claim and the insurer responsible for its percentage is the fairest method. Wording for this clause might agree to indemnification by the insurer for any "Company act or omission, except to the extent the agent has caused such error." Under this guideline, if the agency is found 1 percent at fault, the insurer will still indemnify and defend for the other 99 percent of the claim.

Defense of E&O claims is just as important as indemnification for them. An agent should verify that the insurer will defend as well as indemnify, or if not, that the agent's E&O coverage is adequate for this purpose.

E&O Alert!

Under no circumstances should an agency agree to indemnify an insurer. The agency has fewer available resources compared to the potential deep pockets of the insurer. A relatively minor claim for an insurer could wipe out the financial resources of an agency.

Some contract indemnification clauses impose certain requirements on the agency's E&O insurance coverage. Such requirements should be as specific and reasonable as possible, and then only agreed to if compliance is available to the agency.

Amendments to Contract

Since the agency's ability to establish long-term plans is based upon the stability of its contracts, the ease and frequency of amending the terms are vital. Although an agency and insurer might agree to amend a contract at any time, many contracts can be amended by the insurer—with an average of ninety days' notice—regardless of the agency's consent. Far too often such unilateral changes made on short notice have a financial effect on the agency, such as commission schedules.

If the contract allows the insurer to make changes unilaterally, a recommended provision for amendments would give the agency more notice of changes. One-hundred-and-eighty days is a minimum. To assist the agency in its financial planning, any changes to commission schedules should remain in effect for at least twelve months. Ideally, all amendments should be made only with the agreement of the agency and the insurer.

Miscellaneous Provisions

Other provisions the agency should analyze in the contract include arbitration clauses and procedures upon sale of the agency.

The **arbitration clause** provides a formal method for the agency and insurer to resolve disagreements arising under the contract. Good faith efforts should first be made to settle the issues, but if they fail, an arbitration agreement is an excellent alternative to litigation or the termination of the contract. Generally, the rules of the American Arbitration Association are followed, wherein each party appoints a representative. These two arbitrators then agree on a third person, or, if failing to do so, the Association chooses the third arbitrator. The decision of the arbitrators is then binding and final on both the agency and insurer. Both parties bear equally costs for the proceeding, unless one party is found to have acted in bad faith.

When an agency is sold, the buyer may be basing a percentage of the agency's value upon the insurer's extending its contract to the new owner. The contract may specify a reasonable notice to be given to the insurer of any impending sale, and if the insurer does not plan to appoint the new owner as an agent, it will at least continue the contract for some period of time to allow the new owner to move the business to another insurer.

Commissions

Commissions are normally detailed in a schedule, which may either be a part of the contract or a separate agreement. If provided in a separate agreement, the provisions for changing the schedule follow the same guidelines as previously discussed for the contracts. A minimum twelve-month interval before a given commission level can be changed again will give some stability to the agency's financial planning.

Commission rates vary by line of business. For example, the rate may be fairly low (such as 2 percent) for large workers compensation accounts and be at their highest (often 30 percent) for bonds. The rates for "preferred" types of policies may be lower than standard or specialty products to keep their premiums competitive.

Management Tip

Many agents seem unaware that commission schedules may be negotiable with certain insurers. Since commissions form the backbone of agency income, a complete understanding of the commission schedules and their variation possibilities is crucial. Also, you should determine what your bottom line is for commission percentages. If commission percentages approach that minimum, you should look toward fees as an alternative income source.

Commission rates can also vary by agency. An agency that can deliver the business an insurer prefers in markets, spread of business, volume of business, loss ratios, or other criteria may be in an excellent position to negotiate a higher commission schedule. The agency should be certain to discuss with the insurer exactly what criteria will lead to a better commission schedule. Conversely, the agency should also learn what criteria or actions will lead the insurer to lower the commission rates.

Profit Sharing Arrangements

Insurance companies often provide incentive compensation for producers who exceed established benchmarks for profitability and volume of business. These supplemental arrangements are known by various names, such as **profit sharing agreements** and **contingency commission agreements**. These supplemental contracts are not uniform. Profit sharing commissions can contribute significantly to agency revenues, and for agencies that provide insurers with a steady stream of profitable business, these bonuses can provide up to 10 percent or more of total agency revenues.

Generally, the factors that determine whether an agency receives a profit sharing payment at the end of a year can include (1) profitability of business written by the agency based upon the **trade loss ratio** (the ratio of incurred losses to earned premiums) of the book of business, (2) meeting minimum volume commitments, (3) meeting growth incentive levels based on a percentage growth in premiums, and (4) the average profitability of the book of business over a period of years.

Producers interested in a detailed analysis of profit sharing agreements should refer to *A Report of the Profit Sharing Agreements Task Force, Independent Insurance Agents of America,* which provides a guide for agents in negotiating such contracts with insurers. Profit sharing computations can be complex, and since they are generally prepared by the insurance company, the agency should verify the figures. A partial checklist for such agreements is found in Exhibit 1-3.

Some of the factors to be taken into account by a producer negotiating a profit sharing agreement include the qualifying volume requirement, the lines of business included and excluded, how insurance company income is computed, how losses are defined, whether a stop loss provision applies to exclude claims over a certain dollar amount, how the profit is to be calculated, and when the profit sharing will be paid to the agency. Other considerations include whether the amount is subject to arbitration and what happens if the agency is terminated.

Changing market conditions make it difficult to determine exactly what is the best profit sharing agreement for an agency at any given time. Agreements based upon premium volume, for example, deliver exceptional bonuses in a hard market with rising prices, but a soft market of dwindling premiums could result in no bonus being paid (due to decreasing premium and an increasing loss ratio) despite the producer's working much harder to keep the business on the books. If an agency's bad loss ratio is at least partly the result of insufficient pricing and underwriting by the insurer, should the agency's bonus suffer? When a market (such as workers compensation) delivers high premiums but has claim costs that

Exhibit 1-3
Partial Checklist for Incentive Agreements (See Appendix for an entire copy.)

CHECKLIST FOR INCENTIVE AGREEMENTS

This checklist includes only general information and comments, and is not intended to provide specific advice about individual legal, business or other questions. It was prepared solely for use as a guide, is not a substitute for Agents' independent evaluation of any provision in a contract, and is not a recommendation that the contract be signed or rejected. If specific legal or other export advice is required or desired, the services of an appropriate, competent professional, such as an attorney, should be sought.

I. AGREEMENT

A. The Agreement should have a specific effective date. Retroactive effective dates should be avoided.
B. The Agent and the Company should be required to sign the Agreement. This should insure that the Agent and the Company are working from the same version of the Agreement.
C. The Agreement should indicate clearly if it is a new agreement or an amendment to an existing agreement.

II. CALCULATIONS

A. All formulas used to calculate the amount of incentive compensation should be clearly stated and easy to apply.
B. The definitions should be clearly stated for all terms/components in the formulas used to calculate the amount of incentive compensation.

III. QUALIFICATION IN ORDER TO RECEIVE INCENTIVE COMPENSATION

A. The minimum premium volume requirement and growth rate in premium volume, if any, should be specified.
B. Clarify if there is a separate incentive agreement for personal and commercial lines. If so, determine if there are separate minimum premium volume requirements for each line or one combined minimum premium volume requirement.
C. Clarify if only specific lines of business are eligible for incentive compensation under the Agreement.
D. Determine if the Agreement specifies a maximum loss ratio.
E. Determine if the Agreement contains a minimum policy count or policy growth rate requirement.
F. Note if and to what extent retention of business is a condition to receive incentive compensation under the Agreement.
G. Determine if the Agreement requires a specific success ratio.
H. Clarify if incentive compensation is affected by the timeliness of premium payments.
I. Determine if the Agreement requires any interface participation.

IV. TYPICAL EXCLUSIONS

A. Determine which, if any, policies are excluded from the Agreement. Policies often excluded from incentive compensation agreements following:
   i) specific policies, by mutual agreement;
   ii) policies written in specific classes of business;
   iii) policies in pools or associations;
   iv) boiler and machinery policies; and
   v) loss sensitive policies.

often are beyond the agency's or insurer's control, should the line be included in or excluded from the calculations of profitability?

Because of these and many other questions, insurers and agents should constantly review profit sharing agreements in an ongoing effort to provide the optimal mix of reward and incentive intended.

Organizational Forms of Insurance Agencies

The term "organizational form" comprises (1) a legal form and (2) an operating affiliation. The legal form refers to whether the agency is a sole proprietorship, partnership, or corporation. Operating affiliation refers to whether the agency is operated as an independent agency, an exclusive agency, or a member of some other agency grouping.

Legal Form

The legal forms of business organization consist of sole proprietorships, partnerships, or corporations.

Sole Proprietorships

The **sole proprietorship** is a business owned by a single individual. The key advantage to sole proprietorships is the minimum of legal formality necessary to establish a new business. The only requirements that must be met in order to operate an insurance agency as a sole proprietorship are licensing by the state insurance regulatory authority and, in most jurisdictions, a filing in compliance with fictitious trade name regulations if the sole proprietor's name is not the name under which the agency is to be operated.

For instance, Kathy Adams, operating Adams Insurance Agency as a sole proprietor, would have to register the name Adams Insurance Agency. Legally, the sole proprietorship would be referred to as Kathy Adams d/b/a Adams Insurance Agency (d/b/a is an abbreviation for "doing business as").

Kathy can then set her own hours, be her own boss, and know that her hard work is going directly into building her own business. She is literally a solo enterprise, with all the potential and freedom that entails.

But being on your own in business has its inherent disadvantages as well. For example, when an insurance agency, or any type of business, is operated as a sole proprietorship, the legal entity literally lives and dies with the owner, and if the owner dies or becomes seriously disabled, the enterprise is terminated by action of law. A sole proprietor like Kathy Adams can make provisions in advance for the sale of the business if she dies, becomes disabled, or wishes to retire. Legally, however, the firm of Kathy Adams d/b/a Adams Insurance Agency ceases with the death of Kathy Adams.

IV. Insurance Agency Contracts
V. **Organizational Forms of Insurance Agencies**
A. **Legal Form**
B. Operating Affiliation

Other disadvantages of the sole proprietorship as a form of business include unlimited personal liability for debts and judgments arising from the operation of the firm, difficulty in raising capital, and the uncertainty of future employment for the employees and producers who are associated with, but not owners of, the firm.

Thousands of insurance agencies operate successfully as sole proprietorships in the United States. Many firms begin as sole proprietorships and later change legal form to a partnership or corporation for the reasons discussed in the following sections.

Partnerships

A **partnership** is a voluntary association of two or more persons who are co-owners of a business operating for a profit. For instance, if Kathy Adams decided that operating an insurance agency alone was hindering her ability to make a profit, she might decide to join forces with Bob Jones to form Adams & Jones Insurance Agency. As with sole proprietorships, partnerships are easy to begin. The only requirements for an insurance agency are the necessary insurance licenses and the registration of the fictitious name, which in this case would be Kathy Adams and Bob Jones d/b/a Adams & Jones Insurance Agency. The partners may not even realize that they have created a partnership as a legal business form, but they are legally operating as a partnership. A well-thought-out partnership will have a written agreement between the partners so that all partners will know their rights and obligations in operating the firm and so that there will be an orderly transition in the event of the death, disability, or retirement of one or more of the partners. Some very large entities such as law firms or public accounting firms remain as partnerships in spite of their size. In the case of insurance agencies, once firms reach a size where the partnership becomes difficult to manage, incorporation generally follows.

The partnership has some of the disadvantages of the sole proprietorship, such as limited duration depending on the health and life of the partners, and unlimited personal liability of each partner—even for the acts of one partner. By law, the partnership also terminates upon the death or, possibly, the disability of any of the partners. A formal contract of partnership usually makes provision for a new partnership of the remaining partners to be created automatically on the death, disability, or retirement of a partner. Raising capital and spreading management responsibilities are easier for the partnership than the sole proprietorship, but the security of the employees does not increase to any great extent when compared to the sole proprietorship. Significant numbers of insurance agencies operate successfully as partnerships with gradual changes in ownership as new partners join or as partners depart through retirement or death.

A partnership can be either a general partnership or a limited partnership. In a general partnership, all of the owners are general partners with all of the rights and obligations of a partner who operates the enterprise. A limited partnership includes at least one general partner and at least one limited partner. Of course, there can be many partners in either category. The advantage of a limited partner is that the maximum personal liability of each limited partner is the value of the capital invested by that partner. As an illustration, assume Kathy Adams and Bob Jones decide that they require additional capital in their firm to continue to expand. They approach Jack Brown, one of their major clients, and he agrees to invest funds in the agency but wants to act only as a limited (that is, only a financial, "silent," or "money") partner because he is not going to be active in the running of the business and does not want to share Kathy's and Bob's unlimited personal liability for the partnership activities. The firm continues to do business as Adams & Jones; however, it must amend its fictitious name filing (and possibly insurance licenses) to reflect the new ownership. The limited partnership form of business principally enables the firm to raise capital from outside investors who are assured of limited personal liability so long as they are not active in the business.

Corporations

The final legal form of organization to be considered is the corporate form of business enterprise. The government of a state gives life to a **corporation** by issuing a charter to the incorporators. The corporation, once chartered, becomes a legal entity in and of itself. It has a life beyond that of the owners and is unaffected by the death or disability of an owner. The ownership of a corporation is through shares of stock that can be given away, sold, or willed. The corporation offers limited liability to all of the owners similar to that afforded to limited partners, so that the maximum that an owner of a corporation stands to lose is the amount of his or her investment. To continue the example of Adams & Jones Insurance Agency, suppose that the three owners decide to take advantage of the corporate form of business ownership. They would have to petition their state government for a charter, and once granted, the state would create Adams & Jones Insurance Agency, Incorporated. Kathy Smith, Bob Jones, and Jack Brown would become stockholders in the corporation. The amount of stock each holds would be determined by the size of their investments in the initial firm and the strength of their respective bargaining positions when they incorporated. They could each then transfer their own stock as they saw fit. Most closely held corporations (those owned by only a few stockholders), such as Adams & Jones Insurance Agency, Inc., have a written buy and sell agreement giving surviving stockholders the right and obligation to acquire the stock of a departing stockholder.

Many insurance agencies in the United States are incorporated because of the distinct advantages of limited personal liability and unlimited life, and also because the corporate legal form may facilitate capital acquisition. Further, a corporation may have tax advantages over the other forms of business organization. Disadvantages of the corporation as a legal form are the additional work and costs required to document the activities of the corporation, including the keeping of a corporate minute book, the filing of a corporate tax return, and so on.

IV. Insurance Agency Contracts
V. Organizational Forms of Insurance Agencies
A. Legal Form
B. Operating Affiliation
C. Evaluating Operating Affiliations

S Corporations

S corporations—named after a section of the tax code—are corporations that have elected to be taxed as partnerships under federal tax laws. Whether a corporation should elect to be taxed as a corporation or as a partnership is a question the tax adviser for that corporation should answer. In the example cited above, Adams & Jones Insurance Agency, Inc., could elect to be an S corporation for income tax purposes.

Limited Liability Companies

A relatively new form of business structure is the **limited liability company (LLC)**. It has three major features: (1) for federal and most state taxes, the LLC is treated as a partnership (with more tax flexibility than that of an S corporation); (2) the personal assets of the members are shielded, as in a regular corporation, from the LLC's liabilities and obligations; and (3) it has substantial flexibility in management arrangements and sharing of economic benefits among the members.

LLCs are created under state laws and must have a minimum of two members. If a sole proprietor wished to take advantage of becoming an LLC, a spouse could be brought into the company to meet the member requirements. Their tax advantages, flexibility in sharing economic benefits, liability protection for members' personal assets, and various other features (best left to the business owner's tax advisors and attorneys to decipher) have helped the LLC become a popular replacement for general partnerships, limited partnerships, and S corporations as the business entity of choice for closely held business enterprises. This form of corporation is currently most popular with service-type businesses such as engineering, real estate, and investment firms.

Choice of Legal Form

The choice of legal form for an insurance agency is a complex one that requires the advice of legal and tax experts. While this is an important business decision for the owners of an agency, it has relatively little to do with the day-to-day operations of the agency and is probably of little concern to the insurers represented by the agency or to the clients of the agency. The existence of the agency does not automatically disclose the business form, and some states do not even require that corporations identify themselves as such by requiring the use of the words "Incorporated" and "Inc." in the name of the firm. The fictitious name filing made with the county where the firm is located might identify the nature of the ownership of the firm. The legal form taken by an insurance agency, or by any other kind of enterprise, depends on such issues as personal liability of the owners, continuity of the business, the owners' desire to control the business, and taxation.

Operating Affiliation

Operating affiliations help the agency reach its goals. The nature and purposes of various entities with which an agency can affiliate are diverse, so the discussion in this text can only concern certain typical opportunities available to an agency for affiliation. Trade associations such as the Independent Insurance Agents and Brokers of America and the National Association of Professional Insurance Agents and professional associations like the CPCU Society are not considered in this context. Although trade organizations and professional organizations are wonderful resources for the agency, their primary purposes include general objectives like political advocacy or enhancing the profession through education. They are not founded primarily to assist a particular agency in reaching its production and financial goals. The operating affiliations considered here are those entities that contribute to the competitive stance of an agency by providing services to the agency or making competitive products available to it.

Agency Clusters

The idea of agents banding together—clustering—to share services and insurers is not new. Recent interest in clustering has, however, been fostered by agencies' need for automated systems and an awareness of the special treatment offered to larger agencies by insurance companies. The **agency cluster**, first described in-depth in 1965 by Morrison and Bakst as the "Worcester Plan" in *Agency Purchases & Mergers*, has been likened to the professional association arrangement in the medical profession. Cluster members share support services and often physical space, but each member of the cluster retains ownership of his or her individual book of business.

A cluster differs from a merger in that (1) a separate entity, the cluster, is created—usually a partnership or corporation—in which shares of stock are owned by cluster agencies, and (2) ownership of policy expirations remains separately with the participating agencies.

The form and function of the cluster can vary greatly depending upon the needs of the members. Clusters range from a collection of agents cooperating to attack a specific market segment to an arrangement that, from all appearances, resembles a full-fledged merger. This appearance of one entity extends to the insurers that the cluster represents, because all business produced by the cluster is treated as coming from one agency.

Advantages of Clusters

Cluster members report the following advantages of the clustering arrangement:

- "Significant" producers often receive special treatment from insurance companies. By combining premium volume, members often receive such treatment from their companies.
- Cluster members have greater clout for negotiating agency-company contracts. Some cluster members report a 2 to 3 percent increase in average commissions.
- For members who have fallen behind in automation because of limited resources, the cluster arrangement can provide an impetus to upgrade to a more productive system by providing the funds.
- Insurance companies deal with one entity, instead of several, and realize economies and efficiencies in communication and work flow.

- A cluster can bring specialists together to form a new entity that can better serve client needs and provide expertise in a variety of coverage areas.
- For the entrepreneur who cherishes his or her independence, the cluster provides an alternative to merging or selling the agency.
- Many agents report that they enjoy delegating personnel administration and other management tasks to an operations manager and returning to selling.
- The cluster arrangement can provide economies in physical space, staffing, and insurer relations.
- Advertising expenditures can be pooled effectively.
- A cluster can provide the "engagement" period before the "marriage" for agents who have reservations about whether a merger is appropriate for them.

Disadvantages of Clusters

Clusters may present these disadvantages:

- Independent businessowners may have difficulty agreeing on agency management issues. An individual who has successfully built an agency may not wish to share decisions that affect that business.
- Members of the cluster must share financial information with other members. Loss of privacy in financial matters may make many businessowners uncomfortable.
- Members lose direct, personal control of agency cash flow.
- Most clusters report the necessity of hiring an operations manager, and some agents may have difficulty letting go of the administration of the agency.

Forming a cluster requires patience and perseverance, attendance at many meetings, and a tolerance for potential members who lose interest in the project. For agency owners who are used to taking decisive action, the process often moves too slowly.

The Decision Process in Forming a Cluster

First, it is helpful in the planning process to develop a questionnaire profiling potential cluster members. Drafted by the group, the questionnaire should focus on the information agents want to know about each other, such as business mix, premium income, numbers of accounts, commission income, percentage of direct-billed business, automation capabilities, staffing, plans for perpetuation, areas of specialization and expertise, agency goals, loss ratios, areas of interest to the agency principals, and level of commitment toward beginning a cluster. This process of self-analysis can be a revealing and useful exercise in itself.

The second step is for interested agents to inventory the insurance companies that potential members represent and the products that those insurers offer. All members must analyze the insurers they represent objectively because all members of the cluster will represent the insurers they decide to retain. This process allows the members to keep the insurers that will do the best job for the cluster and terminate those that will not.

A third major decision is whether participating members should occupy the same building or whether the cluster should be established as a separate entity apart from member offices. Consolidating offices is not essential. The decision on whether to occupy one building should be made based on the goals and objectives of the group. For example, if the primary interest of the group is to consolidate space, supplies, and overhead, a physical move will achieve that goal. On the other hand, if the intent of clustering is to present an image of an agency with a variety of servicing locations, a physical move is neither necessary nor desirable.

Fourth, start-up committees are often appointed. Various committees might address these issues:

- *Resources*. This committee would review the profile questionnaires and determine the sincerity and level of commitment of potential cluster members. The committee would also analyze the potential members' automation systems, staff, capital, and other resources.
- *Finance*. This group would analyze financial statements, search for start-up capital, and project cash flow and costs for the new cluster.
- *Management*. This committee would develop an organizational chart and investigate alternatives for the legal structure of the cluster.
- *Automation*. This committee would assess the members' strengths, weaknesses, existing systems, and future needs.
- *Personnel*. This committee should evaluate the needs of the emerging cluster and analyze the talents and training of existing employees.

A fifth major decision is how the board of directors of the cluster will be structured. Many cluster arrangements have a "one agency-one vote" rule, regardless of the member agencies' size. Other clusters rotate the leadership position among members so that each member has the chairman position at some time. The members must also decide how new members can join the cluster.

Insurance Company Affiliations

Insurance companies form groups of affiliated agencies for the purposes of marketing specialized products. Entities like Famex, established by Fireman's Fund, fit into this category and have been established to sell commercial group insurance programs. The producer normally pays a fee to the insurer for the right to represent exclusive programs in a particular geographical area. The benefit to the producer in affiliating with an insurance company marketing organization is that the producer gains access to an exclusive product of the insurer not available to the "regular" agents. Usually, these organizations are set up for mass marketing programs to industry trade groups, and the insurers create the sales opportunity by directly soliciting the group or by underwriting it for one of their agents (often called an originating agent) who agrees to permit the network to make the direct sales.

IV. Insurance Agency Contracts
V. Organizational Forms of Insurance Agencies
A. Legal Form
B. Operating Affiliation
C. Evaluating Operating Affiliations

When a producer affiliates with such an organization, the insurer often gives territorial exclusivity, which prevents other agents from access to sales opportunities in a defined territory. The insurer provides leads to the agency, which is responsible for the sales and service aspects of the transaction. This affiliation can be a productive source of sales opportunities if the programs are good ones. However, independent producers sometimes resent the degree of sales management the insurer exercises. They understand the purpose for it, but the practical day-to-day requirements cause difficulties for producers who are used to controlling their own activities. Many agents affiliate defensively to prevent their competitors from acquiring the affiliation. The insurers, however, are looking for agencies that will sell the programs; not firms that will just sign up for the programs to prevent their competitors from having them.

Specialty Marketing Groups

Another type of organization, called specialty marketing groups, is also mass marketing oriented, and they have created a network much like the networks sponsored by insurance companies. The differences are that these groups are independently owned and the programs are underwritten by more than one insurer. ARM (Associated Risk Managers) and MMI (Marketing Management, Incorporated) are examples of this kind of organization. As the company-sponsored affiliations, the primary purpose of these entities is to create mass marketing sales for the affiliated producer by soliciting groups at a national or regional level and by providing leads to the affiliated agencies that make the sales. These organizations earn their revenue by taking an overriding commission from the insurer to cover profit and the costs of the marketing programs they operate. These affiliations may be available to a producer who, not representing an insurer with a network, otherwise would be unable to take advantage of national mass marketing. The programs of these organizations, like those of insurance company affiliations, are only as good as the producer makes them. If the programs are not competitive in a particular area or if the sponsoring organization or the underwriting insurance company is weak in the producer's territory, the affiliation with this sort of specialty group will be of little benefit to an agency. If the programs are salable, however, such an affiliation can greatly benefit the affiliated producer.

General Purpose Groups

General purpose groups are broader in scope than the affiliations that primarily market commercial group insurance products. The purpose of organizations like InsGroup Corp. or Group 500 is to provide the affiliated agencies with a diverse package of resources including educational opportunities, preferential treatment for affiliated agencies from certain insurers, a forum in which to exchange information with other agencies, and management assistance. These organizations feature meetings of affiliated agencies where marketing and management information is exchanged. An annual fee paid by each affiliated agency supports the group's activities, and many of the meetings and seminars offered may be additional costs to the affiliated agency. These groups are trying to attract top agencies so that the exchange of information is beneficial to those participating. An affiliated producer can learn much by meeting with producers from other areas of the country with similar problems and perceptions.

Common Identity Groups

Common identity groups are established to give the participating firms the image and resources of national or international strength. An organization like Assurex International offers affiliated agencies facilities in major insurance centers throughout the United States and elsewhere. The primary emphasis of such an organization is account servicing, and the participants are likely to be larger agencies who require reliable affiliates for local service on interstate or international accounts. Such organizations may also participate in a common advertising program or otherwise identify themselves as participants. Current members of such groups tend to be selective in allowing new affiliates so that they can be certain that the quality of the participating firms remains high. The costs of operating the network are paid by the participating firms in an annual service fee.

Evaluating Operating Affiliations

Producers have many opportunities to affiliate with various kinds of support organizations. Producers must determine whether any of these organizations can benefit their agency, and they must consider a number of factors. A producer considering an affiliation of any kind should talk not only to those who are offering the affiliation but also to some participants. It is also useful to find references who are not satisfied with the affiliation or those who rejected it so that negative factors could be considered as well as positive factors. In deciding on an affiliation, a producer should evaluate the topics that follow.

Services Provided

Any organization seeking affiliated insurance agencies will offer a variety of services to the prospects. Some of these services will be attractive to the producer considering affiliation, and others may be seen as not useful or even harmful. The producer looking for a way to service national accounts from a single location will be attracted to an affiliation that will provide contacts across the United States. A producer who wants products to sell may be attracted by commercial group insurance programs, and a producer who feels the need for management assistance might find some form of cluster desirable. With some programs, unfortunately, there is more hype than substance, and the producer needs to investigate each service carefully to see exactly how it is going to be delivered to the agency. More emphasis should be placed on those services that are actually being provided than on those that are promised for some time in the future.

Personnel

Evaluating the available services is important, but evaluating who will be responsible for them is crucial. Services might look outstanding on paper or in current practice, but the individuals behind the services will ultimately determine the success of any affiliation. A producer considering affiliation must verify references given by those in the services organization to be certain not only that the people are reliable but also that they are experienced insurance professionals.

Exclusivity

Many of the possible organizations with which an agency can affiliate are in one way or another exclusive. Often this exclusivity makes the organization attractive to a producer. It is important to determine how many other agencies in the immediate marketing area can join. It is also important to determine the legal nature of the exclusivity and just how tight the contract is written in describing the rights of an affiliated agency to a particular territory. Another factor is the reputation of those firms already participating in the program. Prestige and image from the affiliation can be derived only if others participating are up to the standards described by the sponsoring organization.

Fees

A major factor in determining whether to affiliate will be the cost of the affiliation. Some of the groups available to the producer cost little or nothing; others can be expensive. The question is whether the services offered are worth the price being charged. Often similar services may be available from other sources, so the producer considering an affiliation must try to unbundle the services offered and price them separately. All costs should be known to the agency in advance so that there will be no surprises once it has made the affiliation. Sometimes the prices quoted can be negotiated, so the producer should investigate this as well, especially in the case of new organizations.

Contract

The agency considering an affiliation should look carefully at the contract to be signed between the agency and the sponsoring organization if the association is going to be a formal one. The documents should be examined to determine the responsibilities of the agency and to see what benefits are guaranteed by the contract to the agency. Certainly, an attorney should review any agreement that the producer is considering.

Financial Stability

The larger the commitment the sponsoring organization undertakes, the more important are the financial resources to assure delivery of the services. It is not sufficient to determine that the resources are present; the producer also needs to be certain that the resources are committed to the project. Even large financial organizations change their corporate priorities, and the producer considering affiliation should assure himself or herself as much as possible that the commitment is firm. The best way to determine this is to talk to the top personnel and to get an impression of their commitment to the program under consideration.

Check your understanding of the *Key Words and Phrases* found in the second part of this assignment.

Run-off provision (p. 28)

Account current (p. 30) Agency bills insured

Direct bill (p. 30) Insurer bills insured

Arbitration clause (p. 32)

Profit sharing (contingent commission) agreement (p. 33)

Trade loss ratio (p. 33)

Sole proprietorship (p. 35)

Partnership (p. 36)

Corporation (p. 37)

Limited liability company (LLC) (p. 38)

Agency cluster (p. 39)

Review the concepts presented in the second part of this assignment by answering the following questions.

10. What are the major sections of a typical agency contract? (p. 27)

- Term / termination
- rehabilitation
- ownerships of expirations
- Indemnification
- payment procedures
- amendments
- arbitration, commissions

11. Why is the arbitration clause an important part of an agency contract? (p. 32)

- how disputes will be handled.

12. What factors might be included in an agency's profit sharing agreement? (p. 33)

loss ratio
growth
average profitability

13. Describe the different legal forms an agency might choose. (pp. 35-37)

ends with death of { Sole propietorship - licensed & file fictious name
partnership - licensed & Fictious name }
corporation - limited personal liability; cumbersome paperwork
- entity unto it self; tax advantages

14. What are two advantages and two disadvantages of the corporate form of ownership of an agency? (pp. 37-38)

15. What are the advantages and disadvantages of agency clusters? (pp. 39-40)

economies of scale | - loss of control
- privacy of financial info.

16. What factors should a producer evaluate when considering an affiliation with some type of support group? (pp. 41-42)

S corp. - tax as partnership
LLC - limited liabity; tax flexibility

Apply the concepts presented in the second part of this assignment by answering the following questions.

4. The producer must be exceedingly careful about the language found in the agency contract. Explain eight important portions of a typical agency contract and describe how each area should be dealt with under the contract.

5. The concept of direct billing came with the advanced use of computers in insurance company accounting departments. This billing system was intended to be an important source of paperwork relief for the agency. It has not been an entirely favorable process for the producer, however. Explain the advantages and disadvantages of the direct billing concept from the perspective of the producer.

Disadvantages - No float of $
- lose contact w/client
- not uniform billing system with insurers

Advantages - get rid of bad debt
- less paperwork

6. Agency profit sharing agreements or contingent commission agreements are usually based, in part, on the trade loss ratio of the agency's book of business. Many producers feel this is not an equitable system, particularly during a time of falling insurance rates. Illustrate the problems associated with using the trade loss ratio in profit sharing formulas.

$\frac{\text{incurred losses}}{\text{earned premium}}$ = loss ratio - Producers have no control over these factors.

7. Many agencies have found that affiliations with other agencies or organizations have been profitable in certain areas. Identify four different types of affiliations and explain how they might help your agency.

Summary

The discussion of agency formation began with an analysis of the legal aspects of agency, including types of distribution systems, the distinction between an agent and a broker, types of authority granted to insurance agents, contract ratification, and licensing. The agency-principal relationship imposes certain duties on both agent and principal and prescribes remedies to both parties in the event of conflict. Agents have the duties of loyalty, obedience, reasonable care, accounting, and giving of information. Principals have the duties of employment, an opportunity to work, compensation, reimbursement, and indemnity. Both agents and principals have remedies should the other party fail in its duties or break the contract between the parties.

Insurance agency contracts vary from company to company and from agency to agency, but most contain major sections pertaining to term of agreement/termination, rehabilitation, ownership of expirations, payment procedures, indemnification, amendments to contract, arbitration, and sale of the agency. Many times a separate contingent or profit sharing contract is also completed.

The organizational form of an insurance agency involves two elements—legal form and operating affiliation. The legal form may be sole proprietorship, partnership, or corporation. Operating affiliations include clusters, insurance company affiliations, special marketing groups, general purposes groups, and common identity groups. Any of these affiliations should be evaluated on the bases of services provided, personnel, exclusivity, contract, and financial stability.

Appendix

CHECKLIST FOR INCENTIVE AGREEMENTS

This checklist includes only general information and comments, and is not intended to provide specific advice about individual legal, business or other questions. It was prepared solely for use as a guide, is not a substitute for Agents' independent evaluation of any provision in a contract, and is not a recommendation that the contract be signed or rejected. If specific legal or other export advice is required or desired, the services of an appropriate, competent professional, such as an attorney, should be sought.

I. AGREEMENT

A. The Agreement should have a specific effective date. Retroactive effective dates should be avoided.
B. The Agent and the Company should be required to sign the Agreement. This should insure that the Agent and the Company are working from the same version of the Agreement.
C. The Agreement should indicate clearly if it is a new agreement or an amendment to an existing agreement.

II. CALCULATIONS

A. All formulas used to calculate the amount of incentive compensation should be clearly stated and easy to apply.
B. The definitions should be clearly stated for all terms/components in the formulas used to calculate the amount of incentive compensation.

III. QUALIFICATION IN ORDER TO RECEIVE INCENTIVE COMPENSATION

A. The minimum premium volume requirement and growth rate in premium volume, if any, should be specified.
B. Clarify if there is a separate incentive agreement for personal and commercial lines. If so, determine if there are separate minimum premium volume requirements for each line or one combined minimum premium volume requirement.
C. Clarify if only specific lines of business are eligible for incentive compensation under the Agreement.
D. Determine if the Agreement specifies a maximum loss ratio.
E. Determine if the Agreement contains a minimum policy count or policy growth rate requirement.
F. Note if and to what extent retention of business is a condition to receive incentive compensation under the Agreement.
G. Determine if the Agreement requires a specific success ratio.
H. Clarify if incentive compensation is affected by the timeliness of premium payments.
I. Determine if the Agreement requires any interface participation.

IV. TYPICAL EXCLUSIONS

A. Determine which, if any, policies are excluded from the Agreement. Policies often excluded from incentive compensation agreements following:
   i) specific policies, by mutual agreement;
   ii) policies written in specific classes of business;
   iii) policies in pools or associations;
   iv) boiler and machinery policies; and
   v) loss sensitive policies.

V. DEFINITION OF INCOME
The types of include the
A. Clarify what constitutes "income" under the Agreement. Specifically, determine the following:
   i) if written premium is used for qualification for incentive compensation;
   ii) if earned premium is used to determine profitability;
   iii) if any other factors are used to determine qualification and/or profitability.

VI. OUTGO

A. Clarify if the Agreement includes IBNR in determining outgo and if so, at what percentage? Also, verify that the Agreement credits the Agent for the prior year's IBNR before it assesses an IBNR percentage for the current year.
B. Verify that the Agreement defines and clearly states any stop loss provision and any buy down option.
C. Determine how loss adjustment expenses are calculated. Specifically, note how the Agreement defines allocated vs. unlocated loss adjustment expenses. Costs in the Company operating expense column should not be charged as unlocated adjustment expenses.
D. Determine if salvage, subrogation, and reinsurance adjustments are made under the outgo clause.
E. Determine if the outgo includes any other losses or loss expenses, such as acquisition costs, Company profit, commissions, operating expenses, policyholder dividends reinsurance costs, residual market costs, stop loss charges, taxes arid fees, and other miscellaneous costs. It is important that these terms be clearly defined.

VII. YEARS INCLUDED IN CALCULATIONS

A. Determine if the Agreement bases incentive compensation on a single year's or multiple years' premiums and losses.
B. Note the method of calculating incentive compensation and what factors are used in the calculation (e.g. loss carryovers, averaged losses, premiums).
C. If the Agreement changes from a single to a multiple year calculation, determine if the Agreement is retroactive or begins with next year's numbers.

VIII. PAYMENT

A. Determine on what date the Company closes its books for the incentive compensation under the Agreement.
B. Clarify when the Company must make the incentive compensation Agent and if the Agent is entitled to interest on late payment.
C. Determine if there is a "lock-in" provision, and if so, the cost of such a provision.
D. Determine if the Agreement creates a "cap" on the amount of the Company's payout to the Agent.
E. Determine if the Company's payment to the Agent can be reduced or voided by the Agent's action or inaction (e.g. late payment of premium or termination of the Agent's appointment prior to the end of the term of the Agreement).
F. Determine if the Agent allows the Company to offset any money owed to the Company by the Agent under other contracts.

IX. AMENDMENTS

A. Verify that the Agreement includes a requirement that the Agent receive advance written notice of all amendments to the Agreement.
B. Determine if the notice must include the proposed changes to the Agreement.
C. It is recommended that the Agreement require that the Agent receive at least one hundred eighty (180) days prior written notice of all changes proposed to take place in next calendar year.

X. TERMINATION

A. Verify that the Agreement includes a requirement of advance written notice to the Agent prior to termination of the Agreement.
B. It is recommended that the Agreement require that the Agent receive at least one hundred eighty (180) days prior written notice of termination of the Agreement.

C. Determine if the Agent is paid a pro-rated portion of incentive compensation in the year that the Agreement is terminated. It is recommended that the Agreement not contain a provision which allows the Company to avoid payment to an Agent who otherwise qualifies for payment merely because the Agent's appointment has been terminated.

XI. ARBITRATION

A. Determine if the Agreement allows for or requires the use of binding arbitration, and if it specifies the location of the arbitration, the allocation of arbitration costs and attorney's fees, and the state law that will be applied.

Organizational Management

Assignment 2

Assignment Objectives

After completing this assignment, you should be able to:

1. Describe the four major activities in the management function and illustrate the steps in each function.
2. Describe the information included in organizational plans, functional plans, strategic plans, and action plans.
3. Explain the nature and importance of:
   a. short-term budgets
   b. long-term budgets
4. Explain why budgets, policies, and procedures are necessary.
5. Differentiate among the different forms of organizational structure and explain the advantages and disadvantages of each type of structure.
6. Illustrate the information included in job descriptions and job qualifications.
7. Explain how a person's needs influence or motivate action.
8. Describe monetary and nonmonetary incentives.
9. Describe the sources of error and bias that can adversely affect the value of an employee evaluation.
10. Illustrate three management methods that focus on quality.
11. Define or describe each of the Key Words and Phrases for this assignment.

Assignment Outline

I. A Note About Management Approaches
   A. Management Defined
II. Planning
   A. Characteristics of a Plan
   B. Planning Areas in an Organization
   C. Types of Plans
   D. Steps in the Planning Process
   E. Monitoring the Plan
   F. Budgeting as a Planning Tool
III. Organizing
   A. Organization Defined
   B. Organizational Structure
   C. Job Descriptions
   D. Job Qualifications
   E. Hiring
IV. Leading
   A. Delegating
   B. Motivating
   C. Managing Differences
V. Controlling
   A. Developing Reporting Systems
   B. Developing Standards
   C. Measuring Results
   D. Correcting Deviations
   E. Rewarding
   F. Evaluating Employees
VI. Other Management Methods
   A. Total Quality Management
   B. Return on Quality (ROQ) and Continuous Quality Improvement (CQI)
VII. Summary

Assignment 2

Organizational Management

Orient yourself to this assignment by reading the following introduction.

This assignment gives an overview of management concepts and principles. The next assignment will apply those concepts and principles specifically to insurance agencies, with particular emphasis on sales management. Then the fourth assignment of this segment will focus on producers' personal production planning and how it fits into the overall framework of the agency.

Read the definitions of the *Key Words and Phrases* that follow. Being familiar with these important words will help you better understand the first part of this assignment. *Key Words and Phrases* appear in bold in the text when they are defined.

Management — Achieving organizational goals or a set of activities to achieve an organization's goals. These activities are planning, organizing, leading, and controlling

Planning — The process of setting an organization's goals and devising ways to achieve them

Organizational plans — Plans that address survival, independence, and public image

Functional plans — Plans that address profit, growth, product line, and personnel

Strategic business plan — Long-range planning to include ideas of what the organization hopes to achieve; a general plan that is three-to-five years long

Action plan — A detailed plan with concrete steps applied to the immediate future of the organization

Mission statement — A statement written to address the needs of potential customers, both internal and external

Strategy A specific plan for achieving an organization's goals

Goals The final target for the planning period

Objectives The intermediate steps required to achieve goals

Forecasting Attempting to project into the future

Budget An allocation of a scarce resource

Policies Generalized guidelines on how activities should be carried out

Procedure An established routine for normal and recurring activities

Management by exception A concept stating that management should monitor the goals and objectives falling outside the set parameters rather than spending time on items falling within the parameters

Organizing Allocating the total workload among the available personnel, establishing the relative authority and responsibility of each, supplying the proper work environment, and hiring staff to achieve the organization's goals

Activities analysis A process that helps managers find out what work has to be performed, what functions belong together, and how each activity should be emphasized in the organizational structure

Decision analysis A process that determines what kind of decisions are needed, where in the structure they should be made, and to what extent each manager should be involved

Relations analysis A process to determine who should work with whom and the respective contributions of each manager and employee

Line organization A structure of authority that flows vertically, in a direct line, from the top of the structure to the bottom

Functional organization A structure in which the principal retains line authority but can staff each function with an expert in the respective area

Line and staff organization A structure that includes both line organization (which develops general skills) and functional organization (which develops experts in specific fields)

Study the first part of this assignment, which includes the following sections:

I. A Note About Management Approaches
II. Planning
III. Organizing

A Note About Management Approaches

There are nearly as many approaches to management as there are managers. Any bookstore will gladly inundate you with dozens of the latest management texts, all claiming to offer the true path to success. Try to read them all and you will not only emerge bewildered by the literally hundreds of concepts and suggestions, but you will also see that many of the texts directly contradict each other. This confusion is exacerbated by management experts' tendency to emphasize the newness of their ideas by liberally inventing new terms and buzzwords—downsizing, rightsizing, reengineering, TQM, ROQ, and CQI are but a few.

This is not to say their ideas have no merit, just that a manager looking for solutions may have difficulty finding his or her way through the forest of concepts and jargon. For this text, the approach will be to give an overview of the basic framework that all management approaches must address. Many of these approaches are also described in detail in other assignments in this course.

One can choose from many management philosophies and theories. Each has its detractors and fervent advocates. Which, then, is the one true path? Or, more accurately, which is the path for you? Because the answers can vary, this text will focus on two approaches.

This assignment will review the basic management system that has prevailed in American business for several decades. This will serve first to establish a common foundation to help the student understand what the current management consultants and authors are maintaining must be changed. Second, the student needs to be aware that this traditional system is still in widespread use in many agencies. The better the student understands the structure and motivations of employers, the better equipped you will be either to succeed within the system or help it change.

The next assignment will apply this basic system to show how agencies use it. It will also review several of management theories bringing widespread changes to the way many agencies function and succeed.

Management Tip

At times, a student may feel studying management theory in general is unimportant. Why not focus immediately and specifically on agency management? Because agencies do not exist in a vacuum. You, your associates, and your clients are all in constant contact with other businesses and their ways of dealing with employees and customers. To study management in general first gives the student an awareness of how these same issues and ideas apply to all businesses. Insurance has its unique facets, but far too many agency owners and producers have ignored excellent new ideas simply because they were developed in noninsurance businesses.

> A successful manager must be flexible and be alert to concepts and techniques others use, whether in insurance or not, that may also improve his or her own agency operation.

Management Defined

Most management texts define **management** as achieving organizational goals or a set of activities intended to achieve an organization's goals. These activities are the following:

- Planning—determining the desired results and formulating ways to achieve them
- Organizing—managing activities and resources logically
- Leading—influencing employees to work together to achieve the organization's goals
- Controlling—monitoring activities and making revisions, if necessary, to achieve the planned results

Management Tip

All management systems, no matter the approach, involve people. Thus, a manager must adapt the chosen management system to his or her own personality. Sports teams may be organized under the same rules and all have the same goal of winning, but each coach defines the task in a different way, and the team, for good or ill, reflects the personality of the coach. So will it be for your team's management/coaching. Learn the basics, but then use your individual style to make the management system your own.

Planning

Planning is setting an organization's goals and devising ways to achieve them. Planning helps owners and managers decide what to do, how, when, and where to do it, and who to do it. Effective planning includes identifying the organization's needed resources and the relationship of the organization to its environment. Planning further recognizes choices the organization can exercise in using its resources.

Careful planning may seem most important to larger firms, but the results of improper or no planning can devastate smaller firms because they have less room for error. A great deal of activity alone—whether in sales or service—is never enough to ensure the success of the firm. However, planning the types of activities to be carried out can improve an agency's chances to succeed. Proper planning also reduces costs and increases profits.

Planning provides a means for the organization to progress from where it is to where it desires to be, and planning enables the organization to move toward a specific goal or goals.

Characteristics of a Plan

Plans sometimes become outdated and must be revised, but the planning process is indispensable and need not be difficult or complex to be effective. Planning does not require predicting the future with certainty or preventing all mistakes. Its aim is to minimize the degree to which an organization is surprised and assist in the revision of goals and objectives from planning period to planning period. The side benefits of the planning process, such as gaining a better understanding of the organization and how it functions, are worth many times the cost of the plan itself.

The planning process is essentially a function of management. However, agencies that involve the entire organization, eliciting the intelligent and enthusiastic participation of all managerial personnel as well as input from every member of the staff, often develop plans that are broader and more effective than plans of agencies that rely only on top management. A plan that involves many people must be simple, practical, severable, and flexible.

The best plan will not work unless the average employee can use it without intensive training and despite the day-to-day pressures of the job. Changes in an organization are never easy, so planning must offer objectives, results, and activities everyone can easily understand and readily support. When plans are developed with input from all employees, those employees will better understand and accept the plan.

A well-designed plan will indicate the implementation procedure. The manager is responsible for implementing the plan, within the determined time frame, and involving all the designated people.

If the manager does not promptly implement the plan, he or she will not meet time schedules. It is also the manager's responsibility to institute alternatives if the original plan lags or circumstances prevent scheduled participation of any designated parties. Promptly altering the plan will keep implementation on track and on schedule.

It is easy at times to get caught up in the process and believe the sole purpose of planning is to produce the plan. Many individuals have soured on the planning process when they have labored hard and long to develop a theoretically excellent plan that turned out to have no practical purpose. Planning must be practical. Employees need a practical process, adequate information, training, and technical assistance if planning is to benefit the most.

The final business plan is the summation of different desired results, and these parts must be separable and identifiable so that managers can see how they apply to their specific area. No manager should be required to use more of the plan than he or she can coordinate and consolidate in his or her own area of responsibility.

I. A Note About Management Approaches
II. **Planning**
A. **Characteristics of a Plan**
B. **Planning Areas in an Organization**
C. Types of Plans

For instance, assume an agency has a goal to sell 100 new homeowners policies. Because of the planned volume, the agency's administrative manager desires a new automation system. The sales manager agrees, and another goal, the installation of a new automation system with training for both sales and service personnel, is established. The plan should reflect the separate responsibilities of the administrative and sales managers in selecting the hardware and software, and personnel training.

An organization does not operate in a fixed, unchanging environment; therefore, the planning process must recognize and allow flexibility. The plan should be modified when a change is necessary. Unless it is flexible, the planning process cannot respond to the dynamic requirements of a fast-changing world. No plan can predict with 100 percent accuracy, and the longer the planning period, the less accurate the plan is likely to be. Consequently, mid-course revisions to the plan, often resulting from circumstances beyond the agency's control, can and must be made. Revisions should be made because of changes in the underlying assumptions of the plan, not just because the organization is unwilling to sustain the effort necessary to reach the desired goals.

Planning Areas in an Organization

An organization has two major areas of planning: organizational plans and functional plans.

Organizational Plans

Organizational plans address survival, independence, and public image.

When a manager recognizes survival as the prevailing goal, the firm should act to preserve assets and focus on customer retention, thus preventing revenues and profits from deteriorating.

Some people start a business to achieve independence. They want to have freedom from interference or control by others. They desire autonomy in exercising their initiative and ambition. This goal is acceptable to some and prized by others. But as the business grows, a built-in dilemma emerges: if inefficient, the business is likely to fail; if efficient and capable, the business succeeds and grows, causing the principals to lose some of the autonomy and control they sought in the first place.

"Image" is a word commonly used the way clients and potential clients perceive the organization. Image is what people believe to be true. Some businesses are concerned only with the economic rewards generated by their activities. Others are concerned only with how they appear in the eye of the public. Most fall between these two concerns, seeking the dual goals of prestige and profit. Fortunately, prestige in marketing can also enhance the organization's ability to make a profit. Thus, achieving both profit and prestige is desirable and attainable.

Developing a good public image, regardless of its position within an overall goal structure, can be accomplished by advertising, community service, good public relations, and many other techniques, which other assignments in this course treat in detail.

Agency owners should be concerned because the continued influx of customers depends on a favorable image. Since the picture of the organization that consumers have may or may not match actual conditions (unfortunately, clients sometimes believe things that are not true), the agency must identify and correct any image distortion. If consumers perceive an organization to be high-priced, low-service, and unconcerned, the business will suffer financially. Management may think the business can provide the right product at the right price, with the right terms, and the right advice, but the most important factor is the client's perception of the agency.

Functional Plans

Functional plans address profit, growth, product line, and personnel.

Virtually all agency owners seek a rate of profit commensurate with their efforts and investment. Unfortunately, most do not recognize the size of their investment. One way to measure profit is to take the organization's total assets and determine the relationship to net income (before bonuses to owners). A formula sometimes known as the return on assets ratio divides net income by total assets:

$$\text{Return on assets} = \frac{\text{Net income}}{\text{Total assets}}$$

The return on total assets should exceed the return on an equivalent investment if the owner decided to convert all agency assets to cash and invest the proceeds in a low-risk, interest-bearing security. Then the question can be asked, "Is the difference in the earnings worth the effort?" With interest rates high, the answer might be "No, the effort is not worth the return." This answer must also view long-term interest rates; each owner must decide on an acceptable rate of return.

Survival in business depends on making a profit. Given the ability to make a profit, or at least to avoid a loss, the next measure of business success is growth. Growth has economic significance because it should cause the net worth and income of the people involved in the enterprise to grow. In addition, growth has psychological and social significance. Many consider growth, even without a profit, a measure of success.

Some agency owners simply desire to be the largest organization in their locality. They frequently ignore maximizing short-term profit, believing that revenue will eventually take care of profit. An agency must be profitable to grow, but growth does not ensure any level of profit.

Other owners wish to grow large in order to challenge larger firms. To them this growth means the ability to hire additional people, to provide more services, and to compete more effectively for larger customers. This attitude frequently starts with a willingness to de-emphasize profit or accept a lower current profit in order to build for the future.

Another goal of owners seeking substantial growth is to become a more attractive merger or acquisition candidate. The purchase price of the agency would be based on the amount of commission the agency generates. Therefore, the better the growth, the more the agency would sell for.

I. A Note About Management Approaches
II. **Planning**
A. Characteristics of a Plan
B. Planning Areas in an Organization
C. Types of Plans
D. Steps in the Planning Process
E. Monitoring the Plan

Any organization with a product to sell must constantly review the needs of its market and customers. A great product that no one wants will lead to failure of the organization that produces it. Business lore is full of examples of technological achievements that went largely unrecognized, while others, marketing "low quality" or "less than cutting edge" products, made millions as consumers beat a path to their door. Focusing on customer wants and needs is a basic tenet of the "quality movement" (discussed at the end of this assignment).

The last issue that functional plans address is personnel. Part of every manager's job is assisting employees in achieving their personal employment goals. For most individuals, success is not the attainment of one static goal; on the contrary, success requires continuous effort and the constant development of new goals. Consequently, employees whose goal is to be successful in their jobs will be continually striving to improve job satisfaction and personal image as well as to increase their earnings. The manager's responsibility to assist employees, then, becomes a continuous process.

Some employees, however, may be willing to accept mediocre results as long as what they must do to achieve those results is relatively comfortable and pleasant. In order to make these people more concerned with overall organizational results, the manager should strive to make them feel a real part of the organization. Personal identification with work can generate an instinct for excellent performance and concern for the quality and results obtained.

Types of Plans

The level of detail and the structure of a plan depend both on the type of plan and on the length of the time period it encompasses. A **strategic business plan**, one that addresses what the organization hopes to become or achieve, is typically long-range, looking ahead three to five years. It is more general and less detailed than an **action plan** of concrete steps, which applies to the immediate future, generally up to one year. Both types of planning are necessary and must be coordinated to meet the challenges posed by technological change and business world competition.

Strategic Planning

The strategic plan (performed at the top management level) addresses long-range goals and helps direct the operation toward broad goals some three to five years in the future. To develop such a plan, management must have a clear idea of the nature of the organization today and the historical factors that created it. Management then needs to decide which of the agency's characteristics it wants to retain, either as is or in some revised form, and what new characteristics it would like to see at the end of the designated period. The final written strategic plan will delineate the organization's mission and the broad strategies needed to help achieve this mission.

Action Planning

Action plans, aimed at immediate goals and objectives, may be outlined by top management but must involve input from all personnel who will be responsible for carrying them out. Action planning is done within the framework of the strategic plan. Once the longer-term strategies are set, the shorter-term goals and objectives can be addressed. Action plans require careful and specific formulation and are often developed with individual employees as part of their performance evaluations.

The steps in the process of developing action plans are similar to those followed in putting together a strategic business plan; the differences are the plan's time frame and specificity.

Steps in the Planning Process

A plan is a guide to action. For an organization to be successful, a definite plan is required with a specified time period in which to do the job. A properly developed plan permits the organization to think (plan) first, act second, and then enjoy the fruits of labor. The planning process includes seven steps:

1. Setting a mission statement
2. Developing strategies
3. Setting goals
4. Setting objectives
5. Developing budgets
6. Setting policies
7. Establishing procedures

Although all seven of these steps can be part of the overall strategic business plan, the last five are specific enough to be part of the shorter-term action plan. They are part of the organizing functions of management. Frequently, an organization will set mission statements, strategies, and goals for a three- to five-year time span and then narrow goal setting by establishing objectives, budgets, policies, and procedures on a one-year schedule. To be effective, all steps in the planning process must be in writing.

Mission Statement

The first step in the strategic planning process is to develop a **mission** (or vision) **statement**. This statement should be written to address the needs of current and potential customers.

The mission statement should have these characteristics:

1. It should be broadly stated.
2. It should express the desire to meet the needs of clients or potential clients.

3. It should be generic (no specific products should be mentioned).
4. It should be directional.

Broadly Stated

The mission generally states the agency's business purpose. It refers neither to actual markets nor to anything specific.

In "Needs" Terms

The mission statement should mention which client needs the organization must address. "The insurance needs," for example, is extremely broad, encompassing life, health, and property-liability insurance. If an agency wants to address only property and liability insurance, the mission statement can be narrowed. The preferable alternative is to state the mission broadly, then narrow it through the strategy statements (discussed below). Since strategies are by design more flexible and subject to change, strategies are more appropriate to narrow than missions.

Generic

The specific products to be sold are not mentioned in mission statements. Similarly, the agency may want to refer to "insurance needs" rather than "property-liability insurance needs," or, even more broadly, to "risk management needs" rather than "insurance needs."

Nothing is inherently wrong in being more limited. If an agency's management knows definitely that it wishes to serve the needs of California school districts, then that limitation may be in the mission statement. However, leaving the mission statement broad (generic) allows for personal growth in knowledge and expanding interests in the future.

Directional

The final requirement of a mission statement is that it identify a direction for the agency while remaining broad enough to allow the producers to grow. The mission statement is then directional but not confining.

Sample Mission Statement

During a series of Agency Top Management Seminars held by the American Institute, seminar leaders asked the following questions: Why are you in the insurance business? What do you want from your business? To whom do you wish to sell? From the answers given, participants developed many mission statements:

- "To provide risk management services to my community." A broad statement.
- "To find those people or organizations I can serve within the restrictions of my agency contract." A narrower statement made by an agent of a direct writer.
- "To serve the financial needs of the greater Buffalo community." A statement broad in service and narrow in geographic area.

The three examples show that a mission statement, although meeting the four requirements, is still a statement that addresses the needs of clients.

By its nature, the mission statement does not address the needs of employees, members of the organization, or the person drafting the statement.

Strategy

A **strategy** is a specific plan for achieving an organization's mission. Strategies are important to commit to paper because they give everyone involved with the plan a specific sense of how to achieve the organization's mission. Furthermore, strategies are the foundations of specific short-range planning and should be relatively consistent for each planning period and among all members of the organization. In fact, strategies should be long range so that they include a number of planning periods.

Goals and Objectives

Goals are the final target for the planning period. In strategic planning, the planning period may be as long as five years.

Objectives are milestones or intermediate steps toward goals. Objectives always support a goal, and typically each goal has multiple objectives. Other than those two differences, everything that applies to goals also applies to objectives.

Sample Goals and Objectives

To meet a strategic goal of $1 million in commission income within the next five years, an insurance agency might devise the following objectives:

1. Design a sales campaign and a compensation plan that sufficiently rewards producers to motivate them to produce enough business to qualify, that is, bonuses, prizes, and so on. The office and sales managers will design the campaign within thirty days.
2. The office and sales managers will design a telephone campaign directed to current clients within 120 days. Clerical personnel should run the campaign; prizes, bonuses, and incentives may be included.
3. Have all producers participate in a mail sales campaign to (1) their current customers for policy upgrades and (2) prospects they have yet to contact; both should be done within seven months.

These are illustrations of possible objectives supporting one strategic goal for an agency. Each separate goal will dictate a different objective or set of objectives.

Characteristics of Goals and Objectives

Each effective goal or objective has four characteristics: (1) it is time bounded, (2) desired results are stated, (3) it is easily understood and measurable, and (4) the statement does not specify how it is to be accomplished.

Having an end result in mind when setting goals and objectives is important. A maximum time period in which to reach the desired result is also necessary. Deadlines are vital.

A goal or objective must show people what is expected of them. A production goal "to increase production" does little to reveal what is expected other than to produce more. On the other hand, a goal stating that the retail value of products manufactured must reach $1 million per week clearly shows the desired results.

The understanding characteristic means that precise words are used to convey meaning. Measurability means that at the end of the planning period, the goal or objective can be said either to have or not have been accomplished. The production goal above is stated in specific terms and is measurable in dollars. The goal could have been stated in percentage terms or any other appropriate unit of measure.

A strategic goal tells the organization where it wants to be. In determining how to reach the goal, those responsible for the day-to-day activities must be included. The top management level must tell employees where the organization wants to be, but the employees should help determine how to get there.

Forecasting for Strategic Goals and Objectives

In a large organization, **forecasting**, or attempting to project into the future, may be handled by staff whose full-time job is planning. But whether or not an organization has such staff or resources available for sophisticated forecasting, when strategic goals and objectives are set, the organization should use some or all of the forecasting techniques. Forecasting requires an understanding of the organization's current position and future considerations, a listing of all assumptions used to project the future, and the flexibility to go where the organization wants to go.

To reach any future point, it is necessary to determine the present location and the resources available to assist in reaching the firm's goals or objectives. Forecast information should be provided in the exact terms of the ultimate goals or objectives of the business. For instance, if the forecast is to be expressed in terms of sales revenue, investment income, and other income, the data provided about the current position of the organization should be in those same terms.

Forecasts of the future will also affect the quality of the goal setting. For example, if an insurance agency wants to include a production goal, typical questions that can be asked to determine the final goal include those relative to the current production level and forecasts about the future. Some questions of this type are shown in Exhibit 2-1.

A longer-run goal relative to agency perpetuation or continuation requires considerably more information over a broader area than the short-run production goal. Sample areas to determine forecasts necessary for this goal-setting are shown in Exhibit 2-2.

Although the sample questions appear to require a great deal of information, most is readily available within an agency. A logical and orderly approach to the accumulation of the necessary data will demonstrate that the information is manageable and will be vital in planning effectively.

Exhibit 2-1
Illustrative Questions To Establish a Production Forecast

1. What insurance lines will be sold?
2. What are the quality and price of the products?
3. What is the past production record with our insurer(s)?
4. Do the products best fit the needs of our clients?
5. What is our past production record with the type of client needed?
6. Do the producers have the expertise to produce the kind of business needed?
7. Do the producers have the time to produce the volume of business needed?
8. Will this plan affect other objectives of the firm?
9. Will the plan affect our relationship with our insurer(s)?
10. Could the time be spent more effectively on another objective?

Exhibit 2-2
Illustrative Data Needed for Agency Perpetuation

1. Financial conditions of the agency
2. Location of the agency
3. Physical property of the agency
4. Personnel of the agency
5. Present insurer relationships
6. Prospective insurer relationships
7. Effectiveness of competitive forces in the area
8. Competitive position of price, product, and service
9. Information about present customers
10. Information about prospective customers
11. Outside (political, economic, social, or technological) factors that could affect any of the above

Although predicting the future is risky, the possibility that the forecasts and the plan might be in error is not a good reason to forgo planning. Forecasts must be made using the best information available, and the plan must be based on these forecasts.

Forecasts, based on information developed from Exhibit 2-2, must be made in areas external to the firm as well as internal. Typically, the internal forecasts are easier to make, but the external forecasts are just as important. These forecasts are required in such areas as the demographic characteristics of the customers, the nature of the competition, economic conditions, government practices, market availability, and many others. Even a cursory examination of those areas indicates changing situations, since the agency is not operating in a static environment.

After the planners make the decisions, they should be recorded for future reference. Planners should expect deviations. Flexibility is needed to

I. A Note About Management Approaches
II. Planning
C. Types of Plans
D. Steps in the Planning Process
E. Monitoring the Plan

adapt forecasts, underlying assumptions, and the plan to changing conditions. The plan should be designed in such a manner that deviations from the forecasts can be promptly identified, the effects on the plans analyzed quickly, and appropriate corrective action taken with as little delay as possible.

Based on the data accumulated by the questions in Exhibit 2-1 (and the information supplied for Exhibit 2-2), assume an agency made the following two unrelated planning forecasts:

Production Forecast—Commercial Umbrella Market

- Internal procedures will enable the producers to make the necessary calls to reach sales goals.
- Time will permit the necessary follow-up sales work.
- Present customers have not previously purchased this type of coverage from us.
- Present customers will find the products attractive enough to buy from us.
- The sale/call ratio will be at least 1 to 5.
- The average sale will produce $350 in commission.

Perpetuation Forecast

- Further inroads by financial institutions into the insurance business will be significant.
- Coverage availability and pricing will remain stable for the next five years.
- Interest rates will rise no more than a total of 3 percent over the next five years.
- The present educational level of the community will continue for the next three to five years.
- Light and medium industries will continue to locate and expand in our area for the next five years.
- The agency's key staff will continue with the agency for the next five years, or replacements will be readily available.
- The agency will be able to employ a competent underwriting and office manager within a year to free producers to produce.

With a series of similar forecasts for other areas of sales, the agency has the information and best judgment to establish a projected or forecasted level of production. Based on the set of forecasts relative to perpetuation, the principals or owners can predict how disposition of ownership should be handled. An appropriate procedure to change the forecasts should be established if any of the underlying data prove inaccurate or if the assumptions prove false.

Budgets

A **budget** is an allocation of a scarce resource. Budgets are usually allocated in units of money but can also be expressed in other resources, such as time. It is top management's prerogative and responsibility to allocate the financial resources of the firm to various components of the action plan. Usually the person assigned the task requests funds, and top management allocates funds based on the priority and importance of the action plan. (Developing a cash budget will be explained later.)

Budgeting time is as important as budgeting financial resources. Both the strategic plan and the action plan contain a time constraint, and the person in charge of the plan must allocate his or her staff and personal time among all of the duties within the organization. (Time management will be covered in a later assignment.)

Setting Policy

Policies are generalized guidelines on how activities should be carried out. They may be stated narrowly or broadly, depending on the type of policy involved. For instance, a policy concerning producer time in an agency may be: "Each producer shall determine the appropriate amount of time to be spent in the office for administrative and other nonselling activities. Management encourages producers to delegate as much of such duties as possible." At the other extreme is a narrowly stated policy on overdue accounts: "Any account overdue by thirty days will be canceled by the forty-fifth day and notice of cancellation forwarded to the insured by registered mail. Any deviation from this policy must be approved by management."

In the first instance, the policy is broad, letting the producer decide the appropriate amount of time to spend in the office. In the second, the policy is narrow and is directed toward the person handling accounts payable.

Establishing Procedures

A **procedure** is an established routine for normal and recurring activities. Procedures are an important part of the planning process because they can help the agency to budget and control both time and money. Procedures, unlike most other planning activities for an agency, are usually established below the top level of the organization.

Procedures are most useful to employees new to the agency or new to a position within the agency. Procedures clearly describe what needs to be done, in what order, and within a time frame (if appropriate). Procedures are meant to ensure consistency of action and serve as a training device so that the new employee will know how to accomplish all assigned tasks.

E&O Alert!

Procedures also help to prevent E&O claims because they can eliminate many of the mistakes that might occur should no clear procedures exist. Agency planning should design procedures with this benefit in mind.

Monitoring the Plan

A crucial part of any overall plan is controlling or monitoring the plan to allow for any necessary corrections. As a result, a mechanism must be built into the planning procedure to examine and report to the manager the position of the organization in relation to the intended course and schedule. Expected results should be stated in clear, precise, and measurable terms.

The organization's records may not be detailed enough to give a good measure of certain portions of the strategic goals and objectives. When a deficiency of this nature is discovered, minor changes in the records will frequently improve their quality and enhance planning potential. For example, if a plan calls for increasing sales of a specific policy, records must be able to show the production volume for that type of policy. If such records are not available or if sales of that policy are combined with other policies, changes in procedures are necessary to generate the appropriate monitoring tool.

A time frame should be a part of every plan, and someone should keep track of the plan and how it compares within the stated objective. Regular reports of progress should be mandatory for all personnel. These progress reports do not have to be elaborate; in fact, the simpler the better. The plans will instill discipline and will focus on achievement, both of which are crucial to the timely and successful completion of the stated goals.

Monitoring should be regular and timely, and it should be tightly organized and formalized. The concept of **management by exception** is appropriate in the monitoring process. Management should spend little time and effort on those items that are within the parameters of the objective. However, results that are below the goal or objective should get prompt attention.

Improved performance should result if the evaluation is done in a spirit of objectivity. When a deficiency is identified and the cause is pinpointed, corrective action must be taken. In some instances only small corrections are necessary; in others, the plan may need to be modified significantly. Courage to make the necessary modifications will enable the organization to achieve the intended objective.

Budgeting as a Planning Tool

The best financial planning tool is a budget. Budget development forces management to think about revenues and expenses in detail and to plan financial results.

Without some type of workable budget, an organization will not know if it is incurring excess expenses or making a profit until the end of the year, when it is too late to make a meaningful adjustment. Good management dictates budgeting.

An organization may improve the use of its resources through budgets. A budget must be written, and realistic figures must be used if the organization is to accomplish its goals. In addition, when personnel help set the goals, not only are they aware of the goals, but they are also likely to work to achieve them if a budget communicates them. The person establishing the budget must be familiar with the organization, and key people should be used to help prepare the budget for their own areas.

An appropriate budgetary period is long enough to make effective planning possible. For example, the longest term for the cash budget would likely be one year and could be broken down into different quarterly, monthly, or even weekly segments. A capital budget, which would include the purchase of computer equipment or real estate, should be longer because of the nature of the expenditures. Five years would be appropriate for this budget. The length of time should be matched to the item being budgeted.

Types of Financial Budgets

From the projected figures, long-term (two to five years) or short-term (up to one year) budgets can be developed with the understanding that they will probably need to be revised. Budgeting should be more detailed in the short term than in the long term. The first year's budget should include monthly projections; the second year could be done quarterly; and the following years could be annual. As the first year nears its end, the second year's budget should be transferred from quarterly to monthly, and so on. The short-term budgets are the sales budget, the expense budget, and the cash budget. Long-term budgets include a sales and expense budget and a capital budget.

Sales Budget

Important for growth is forecasting sales for the next five years. However, for monitoring and control, the short-term sales budget should be monthly or even weekly.

The projected level of sales established can be broken into action plan sales goals. For example, how many calls and sales are necessary each week to meet the annual sales budget? By checking the level of sales against the budget, the organization can determine whether it is ahead of or behind the planned production schedule.

Expense Budget

Every major expense category should be itemized in the expense budget. The budget should project when the expense is incurred and when it is paid. For example, if a firm anticipates purchasing a large quantity of office supplies in June, the budget should indicate that the expense will be incurred in June. But if the expense will not be paid until August 1, then the budget should also reflect the cash payment when made on August 1. Expense budgets, if prepared properly, can be highly accurate and can pinpoint the amount of funds and the time at which funds are needed, making this part of the budget important for the total short-term budgeting procedure.

I. A Note About Management Approaches
II. Planning
E. Monitoring the Plan
F. Budgeting as a Planning Tool
III. Organizing
A. Organization Defined
B. Organizational Structure

Cash Budget

The short-term sales and expense budgets are combined into the cash budget. The cash budget can reveal when excess cash is available for short-term investment or when a loan is needed to cover a period during which expenses paid exceed cash available. The cash budget will greatly assist the organization in having enough cash or liquid assets on hand to meet its financial requirements in any situation.

The cash budget is based on the simple concept that the cash available minus the cash needed equals the cash balance. The cash available is determined by starting with the balance in last month's bank account. Add to this cash receipts from previous month's bills to be collected. In addition, include any liquidated investments, expected contingent commissions, or any item that would produce cash.

The cash needs are determined by adding up payments to suppliers, office expenses, sales expenses, salaries, investment costs, and equipment purchases.

The difference between the monthly cash available and the monthly cash needs will give an anticipated cash balance throughout the year that can be used for profitable activities. An example of this profitable activity could be short-term investments. Cash payments may exceed available cash, and in that case, the agency must plan for a short-term loan from a bank. The cash budget would be used to show the bank when the loan could be repaid.

An organization should try to earn income on excess cash at minimum risk. The key to this technique is investing excess cash in low-risk assets that can be quickly converted into cash so that the money will be available to pay accounts and bills as they come due. The most common method is using money market funds.

Long-Term Budgeting

Long-term budgeting is important for the organization's growth and profit. Unlike short-term budgeting, the long-term budget should be more general and have greater room for modification. As in strategic planning, the business cannot predict exactly what the market, the economy, or even its own organization will be like in five or ten years. The annual budget is based on the first year of a long-range plan, so the annual and long-range budgets should complement each other. The long-term financial budget would include a summarized sales and expense budget and a capital budget.

For longer-range budgets, sales and expense projections are combined in less detail for periods beyond one year. The short-range sales and expense budget may be used with appropriate increases based on projections.

In its long-term budgeting, the organization must consider its capital expenditures. Capital budgeting is the process of planning expenditures on assets whose returns are expected to extend beyond one year. New computer hardware is an example of a capital expenditure.

Another area of capital budgeting is long-term investment of excess cash. Some organizations do not have excess cash required for such investments. However, some businesses can invest large amounts of cash in anticipation of a capital item purchase such as a new office building. Such a business should evaluate the risk on long-term investments as well as the returns on those investments.

Revisions

One of the most important aspects of the budgeting process is the final document's flexibility. When the budget is established, alternative plans should also be drawn up in case of sudden and unanticipated inflation rates, a change in market conditions, or any number of economic factors.

Any discrepancies in the budget should be investigated immediately, and corrective steps must be taken. When the budget must be altered, deciding on alternative actions projected earlier is easier than deciding without prior consideration.

Every organization should use budgeting techniques to help fulfill its goals. The budget is not a path to the future, but merely a guide on that path. A budget is a tool, not an end in itself.

Organizing

The organization of activities determines how the work will be divided into manageable units. These activities include the following:

- Establishing the organizational structure or determining who will do what
- Defining relationships and who has authority and responsibility for activities
- Creating a job description for each position in the organizational structure
- Establishing job qualifications for the person who will fill each position
- Hiring the right number of people with the skills necessary to achieve the firm's goals

Organization Defined

The word "organization" has two specific definitions. One meaning refers to an organization as an entity in itself, and the second meaning refers to organization as a process. Regardless of the definition, organizing, or organization, is a fundamental function of management and becomes necessary when two or more people work together.

Organizations have three things in common: (1) each has a distinct mission, (2) each is composed of people, and (3) each has a degree of formality in the structure of the organization that affects its members' behavior. Thus, as an entity, an organization is a group of people bound together in a formal relationship to achieve organizational goals.

The second definition of organization involves arranging the parts of the organization or the process of structuring the organization. Three things are organized: (1) the work, (2) the people, and (3) the systems. The objective of organization is to provide a framework within which talented people can contribute to the common objective of their workplace and themselves. Thus, organizing is also the process of distributing the work among the staff, determining who is going to do the work, and deciding what will be the relative authority and responsibility among the organizational units formed by the work and the members of the firm.

Stated formally, as used in this text, **organizing** is allocating the total workload among the available personnel, establishing the relative authority and responsibility of each, supplying the proper work environment, and hiring replacement or additional staff to achieve the organization's goals. An organizational structure is determined, relationships are delineated, positions are described, qualifications for positions are established, and people are hired as needed to fill those positions.

Organizing must support the plan of the business. Whatever its goals are, the organization must be measured against those goals to determine its effectiveness. Unity of purpose and efficiency must be the underlying principles of the organization.

Organizational Structure

A firm's organizational structure indicates who has the authority and responsibility for activities. Consequently, this structure needs to be planned, identified, and periodically reviewed because a faulty structure will hinder achievement of the firm's goals.

One of the most common organizational problems is the failure to clarify organizational relationships. People need to know who is responsible for what, and the flow of authority and responsibility needs to be clearly delineated.

Likewise, enough authority must be delegated to allow people to carry out their designated responsibilities. The manager who holds employees responsible for activities over which they have no control creates an unworkable structure and often contributes to morale problems. Top managers need to retain some authority, but they must be willing to delegate as much as is necessary for people to handle their designated jobs effectively.

According to management consultant Peter Drucker, three analyses can determine the kind of structure a firm needs:

- Activities analysis
- Decision analysis
- Relations analysis

Activities analysis helps managers find out what work has to be performed, what functions belong together, and how each activity should be emphasized in the organizational structure. **Decision analysis** determines what kind of decisions are needed, where in the structure they should be made, and to what extent each manager should be involved. **Relations analysis** involves the determination of who should work with whom and the respective contributions of each manager and employee.[1]

There are three basic forms of organizational structure based on delegated authority and responsibilities: line, functional, and line and staff.

Line Organization

Authority in a **line organization** structure flows vertically, in a direct line, from the top of the structure to the bottom. Responsibility flows in the opposite direction. This is likely to be the type of structure adopted by a small insurance agency. The principal (agency owner) issues orders directly to the office personnel. A simple line organization is shown in Exhibit 2-3.

Exhibit 2-3
Simple Line Organization

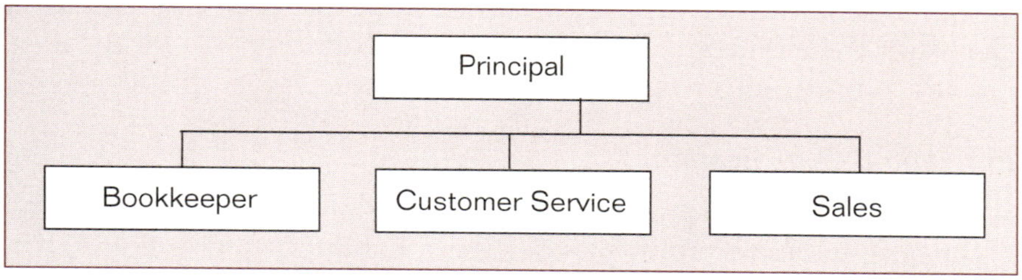

As the firm grows, the owner finds it necessary to spend more time on outside activities. As a result, authority for internal operations is delegated to a supervisor who becomes responsible to the owner for internal operations.

The delegation of the inside activities is practical and workable if complete. In practice, unfortunately, some owners never give sufficient or complete authority to the office manager to accomplish tasks properly. The owner may insist on micromanaging every detail, no matter how small. As a result, the owner spends too much valuable production time on matters that an assistant can better handle.

Management Tip

An example of micromanagement in an agency is the owner who insists that he or she review every piece of incoming mail before it is routed to the proper person or persons. This activity may ensure good control and keep the owner aware of what's happening in the organization, but needless delays result in the proper information reaching the proper person, plus the owner loses valuable production time.

The advantage of the line organization is simplicity. Each employee knows who his or her superior is and who has the authority to give orders. The line organization makes it easy to determine how well the job is being done, and the ability to make a quick decision lends itself to prompt corrections of any problems. The line-only organization is an efficient one for a small business.

A disadvantage of the line organization is that it presumes the firm's owners or executives are competent in the many different phases of the business. They must deal with personnel, administrative office work, customer service, marketing, financial services, planning, and any research. If the owners are poorly educated or untrained in any one of these areas, that weak area is likely to be overlooked or ignored to the detriment of the agency's profit picture. In a smaller organization, the owner can cope with many problems, but, as the business grows, decisions become more difficult without the help of specialists. If the line executive does not have the expertise to handle a specialized problem, he or she may need to call in a consultant for assistance.

Perhaps the greatest potential disadvantage of line organization is the possibility of the owner's inability or unwillingness to cease being involved in activities better performed by other people. This is often the case when the business and the owner matured together, and he or she has difficulty ceasing being everyone's boss.

Functional Organization

An organization can capitalize on the strengths of line organization by dividing activities according to function. In Exhibit 2-4, for instance, the level below the owner can be redesigned into functions called "Administrative," "Finance," and "Sales." In a **functional organization** structure, the owner retains line authority but can staff each function with an expert in the respective area. The experts would each have some employees reporting to them, lengthening the line.

Exhibit 2-4
Simple Nonline Functional Organization

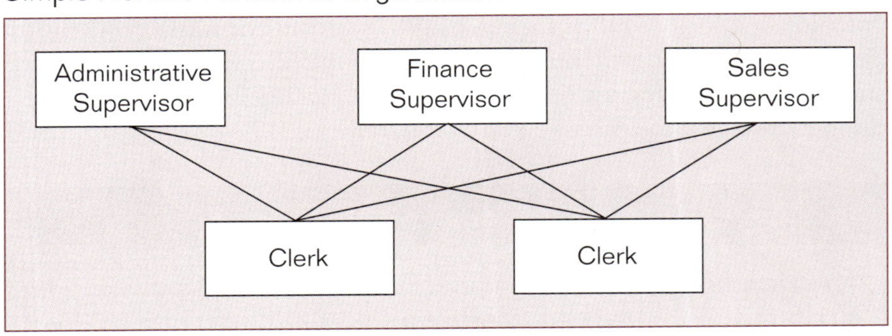

The greatest advantage of the functional division of authority is that the organization is built around experts in their individual fields. Such people have specialized training in a specific area and can presumably solve the special problems of the area more effectively than the line executives.

The effectiveness of this organizational structure depends on the behavior of the participants. If effective communication and negotiations take place among the functions, functional expertise within the firm can improve productivity. New employees can also receive specialized training much more effectively in a functional organization than in a line organization.

A disadvantage of functional structure is that authority is divided, and this may create problems if an employee must report to more than one person. "Too many bosses" has the tendency to introduce frustration and ultimately chaos, particularly when the functional specialists disagree, which is the natural result of specialists attaching too great an importance to their functions.

Functional organization can result in shirked responsibility, slow action on decisions, and considerable compromise before a decision is reached. As a result, many believe a functional organization without line authority is theoretically possible but practically unworkable because of the divided authority and responsibility. This form of organization is almost never recommended.

Line and Staff Organization

The nonline functional organizational structure generally uses individuals who are experts in specific fields. The line organizational structure tends toward people with more general skills who can generally execute and command in many different areas. The best of both types of structures can be achieved by bringing the two together. This type of organizational structure is called **line and staff organization**.

Meshing line and function enables plans to be executed effectively by line executives who have definite authority and responsibility. The functional or staff specialists can advise the line when their expertise is needed. The staff organization exists to serve the line functions, which are paramount. The specialist serves in an advisory capacity with no line supervisory authority.

Exhibit 2-5 is an example of an insurance agency organized on a line and staff basis. The exhibit shows relationships among various positions. The line authority and responsibilities are shown by solid lines. For example, the customer service representatives derive their authority from the policyholder service manager and are responsible to the same manager. The policyholder service supervisor has authority from and is responsible to the office manager. The office manager has authority for both accounting and policyholder service and is responsible to the principal for both activities. Similarly, the training and sales managers receive line authority from and are responsible to the principal. However, the training manager may only advise the office and sales managers. Hence, the training function is staff to the office and sales managers. This agency is functionally organized because different people are responsible for the functions of office administration (office manager), training (training manager), and sales (sales manager). The principal maintains simple line authority through a functional division of authority.

Exhibit 2-5
Hypothetical Line and Staff Organization

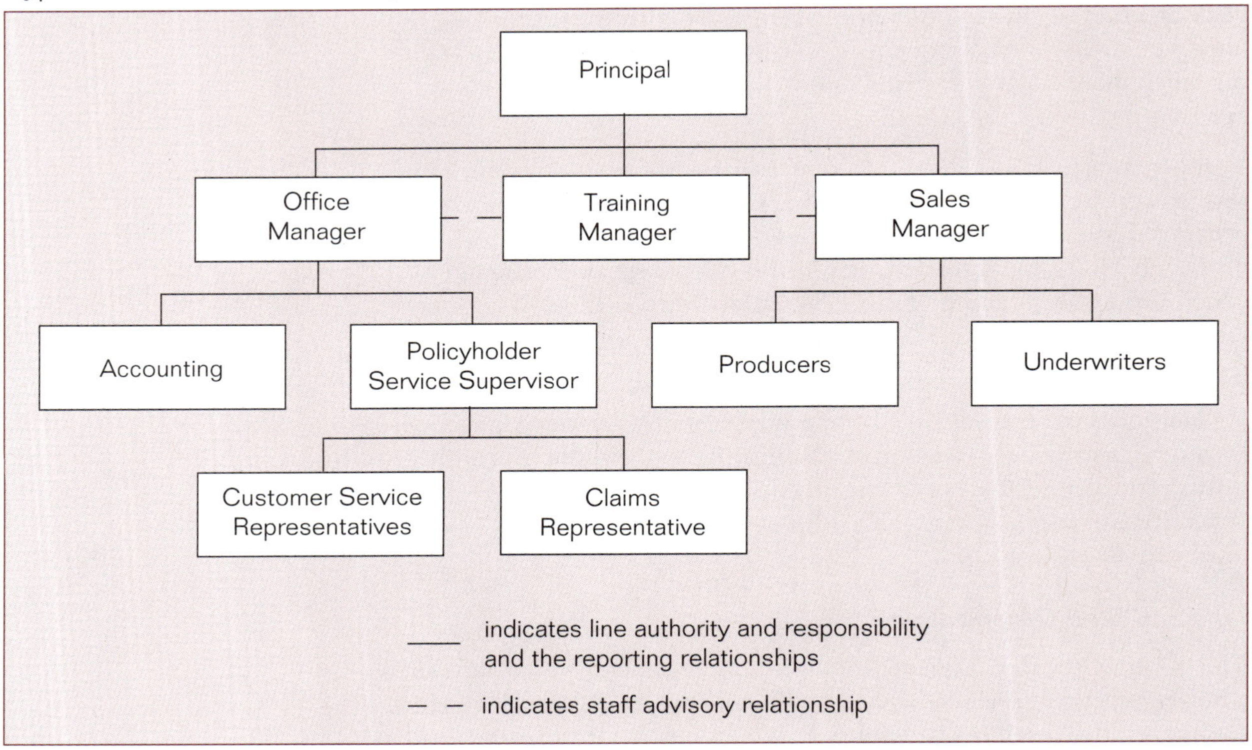

As a rule, the line and staff organization takes advantage of the strengths of both the line and functional structures. Each individual reports to only one person because authority and responsibility are fixed. If assistance is needed, specialists can be called on for help through the line executives. The line executives are not bound to take the staff recommendations, but they can profit from listening to their advice.

Accountability is definite and coordination is improved in a line and staff organization. In addition, the younger people in the firm can be given experience and training in both line supervision and staff problems in a line and staff organization.

The line and staff structure presents a few disadvantages. Staff people at times attempt to take over line authority because they want to see their ideas put into effect. On the other hand, line people may ignore the ideas of the staff. Both of these attitudes are mistakes.

Job Descriptions

Job descriptions are written summaries of a particular job in an organization. Each "box" in an organizational chart should have a job description written for it. A job description states the position of a job in the hierarchy of an organization, offers a summary of responsibilities, lists the primary accountabilities of the position, and states the nature and scope of the position:

- *Position in the organization.* Exhibit 2-6 is a job description for a commercial lines producer. The top portion locates the position in the organization. The title of the job generally appears first. Following the title is a reporting relationship. Finally, the department in which the position is located is listed. All of this information naturally flows from the organizational structure and acts as the defining document as to relationships among other positions within the agency.
- *Summary of responsibilities.* The summary of responsibilities is a one- or two-sentence paragraph that highlights the general activities of the person holding the position. The reason this short statement appears first is to provide a simple description of the job. A more detailed description follows, in which the manager logically develops the specific accountabilities of the job.
- *Primary accountabilities.* The heart of the job description is the section titled "Primary Accountabilities." Employees should know the responsibilities of a job and the basis on which their relative success or failure on the job is to be measured. For the manager charged with developing the job description, the accountabilities section is important for two reasons. First, the manager is establishing the performance expectations he or she will use to judge employees. Second, the accountabilities, if logically developed, will be essential in determining the qualifications for the job. More will be said about this in the following section on job qualifications.
- *Nature and scope.* The nature and scope section of the job description shows how the individual position fits within the department associated with the position. In Exhibit 2-6, the responsibility of the commercial lines department is delineated, and how a producer fits into the department is explained. In addition, a few of the most important skills and traits needed for the position are identified.

Job Qualifications

Writing a job description gives a manager an understanding of the nature of a job within the organization. The job qualifications allow the manager to set specific requirements necessary for success in the position. The qualifications should be written as though the perfect employee will occupy the position. Since the perfect employee will rarely if ever apply for the position, any qualification that the new employee does not possess becomes part of that person's individual training and education program. Therefore, careful attention must be given to developing the job qualifications.

The job qualifications begin with accountabilities from the position descriptions. Following the accountabilities, the tasks and knowledge, skills, and helpful personal traits necessary are listed.

Exhibit 2-7 is a sample blank form used to develop the job qualifications. The left-hand column includes a listing of the accountabilities from the job description. The middle column includes those tasks required to be successful in meeting the accountability.

II. Planning
III. Organizing
C. Job Descriptions
D. Job Qualifications
E. Hiring

Exhibit 2-6
Sample Job Description

Position: Commercial Lines Producer
Reports to: Commercial Lines Manager
Department: Commercial Lines Department

Summary of Job

This position is accountable for the production of new Commercial Lines business and the upgrading and retention of assigned Commercial Lines accounts.

Primary Accountabilities

Develop and maintain prospect file for new Commercial Lines accounts using personal efforts, agency marketing plans, and existing account referrals.

Develop, maintain, and document contacts with prospects in order to gain information on expirations, insurance needs, and receptiveness of proposals.

Conduct sales meetings with prospects using appropriate agency and company resources in developing surveys, gathering underwriting information, and making presentations.

Coordinate with appropriate agency personnel the underwriting, placement, and financing of all new and renewal business.

Maintain contact with insured so that on renewal appropriate coverages are in force.

Develop professional relationship with company personnel and insureds in order to maintain and expand relationship.

Maintain communication with other agency production units in order to forward and receive information concerning insureds that may affect new commercial or life business or indicate a change in insurability.

Nature and Scope

The Commercial Lines Department is charged with the development, placement, service, and renewal of all Commercial Lines accounts for the XYZ Agency. The producer is accountable for supporting departmental marketing activities as well as conducting his/her own individual marketing efforts at the direction of the Commercial Lines Manager.

In order to maintain systematic growth by the Commercial Lines Department the producer will be responsible for maintaining accurate and up-to-date files, documenting prospecting activities, account status, and sales and renewal activities.

The producer should possess strong written and oral communications skills, be well organized, exhibit a willingness to pursue professional studies, and maintain a familiarity with trends within the industry and new insurance products.

For most tasks, a particular type of knowledge is necessary. For example, data entry employees must have knowledge of the agency's software system in order to enter the relevant customer data.

Exhibit 2-7
Sample Job Qualification Form

<table>
<tr><th>ACCOUNTABILITY</th><th>TASK(S)</th><th>KNOWLEDGE/SKILL/TRAITS</th></tr>
<tr><td rowspan="3"></td><td></td><td rowspan="3"></td></tr>
<tr><td></td></tr>
<tr><td></td></tr>
<tr><td rowspan="3"></td><td></td><td rowspan="3"></td></tr>
<tr><td></td></tr>
<tr><td></td></tr>
<tr><td rowspan="3"></td><td></td><td rowspan="3"></td></tr>
<tr><td></td></tr>
<tr><td></td></tr>
<tr><td rowspan="3"></td><td></td><td rowspan="3"></td></tr>
<tr><td></td></tr>
<tr><td></td></tr>
<tr><td rowspan="3"></td><td></td><td rowspan="3"></td></tr>
<tr><td></td></tr>
<tr><td></td></tr>
</table>

In many cases, a skill is necessary in addition to knowledge. For the data entry position, the employee must have the typing skills necessary to enter the relevant client data efficiently.

Certain personal traits are helpful in certain jobs. For example, a surgeon must be able to concentrate over an extended period of time. A producer would find the traits of high ego drive and persistence very helpful. A data entry employee will be more productive with the trait of attention to detail. Finally, a person working in claims would find the trait of empathy helpful.

The right-hand column of Exhibit 2-7 would contain the knowledge, skills, and helpful personal traits associated with the tasks necessary to complete an assignment. The more detailed the delineation of the knowledge, skills, and traits, the more likely the person hired for the position will develop into a productive employee.

Check your understanding of the *Key Words and Phrases* found in the first part of this assignment.

Management (p. 4)

Planning (p. 4)

Organizational plans (p. 6)

Functional plans (p. 7)

Strategic business plan (p. 8)

Action plan (p. 8)

Mission statement (p. 9)

Strategy (p. 11)

Goals (p. 11)

Objectives (p. 11)

Forecasting (p. 12)

Budget (p. 14)

Policies (p. 15)

* Procedure (p. 15) – established routine for normal and recurring activities

Management by exception (p. 16)

Organizing (p. 20)

Activities analysis (p. 21)

Decision analysis (p. 21)

Relations analysis (p. 21)

Line organization (p. 21)

Functional organization (p. 22)

Line and staff organization (p. 23)

Review the concepts presented in the first part of this assignment by answering the following questions. **Note: Acceptable answers to all questions appear at the end of this segment.**

1. What activities are included in management? (p. 4)

Planning
Leading
Organizing
Controlling

2. Why is proper planning important? (p. 4)

– Improves chance of success
– reduces costs | increases profits
– minimizes mistakes

3. What are the characteristics of a plan? (pp. 5-6)

4. What are two areas of planning in an organization? (pp. 6-7)

- Organizational Plans – Survival – Independence – Public Image
- Functional Plans – Growth; Personnel; Product Line; Profit

5. How does a strategic plan differ from an action plan? (pp. 8-9)

6. What are the seven steps in the planning process? (p. 9)

- Mission Statement
- Strategy Development
- Goal Setting
- Objectives set
- Budgets developed
- Policies set
- Procedures established

7. What are the characteristics of a mission statement? (pp. 9-10)

4 criteria
- broadly stated
- desire to meet clients' needs
- generic
- directional

8. How do objectives differ from goals? (p. 11)

- goals – long term; final targets
- objectives – small stepping stones on way to goal

9. What are the characteristics of both goals and objectives? (pp. 11-12)

- time bounded
- stated results
- easily understood
- measurable
- not specific on way to accomplish

10. What are three types of short-term financial budgets? (p. 17)

Sales budget
Expense Budget
Cash Budget

11. What are the two types of long-term financial budgets? (p. 18)

- Summarized Sales & Expense Budget
- Capital Budget

12. What are three types of organizational structure in an agency? (p. 21)

- Line (Top to Bottom) ↑↓
- Functional (organization by function ie acctg.)
- Line & Staff

13. What are the four sections included in a job description? (p. 25)

1) Position in organization
2) Summary of Responsibilities
3) Primary accountabilities
4) Nature & Scope – responsibilities of dept; how the position fits in; skills & traits needed

Apply the concepts presented in the first part of this assignment by answering the following questions.

1. Determining the appropriate organizational structure for an insurance agency is a key business decision. Many agencies use either the line only structure or the line and staff structure.

(a) Describe the difference between these two types of organizational structure.

(b) Explain the advantages and disadvantages of each type of structure.

(c) Which is the better structure to use? Explain.

2. "This year," says Peter Principal, the president of an insurance agency, "we're really going to plan."
   (a) What must Peter do in planning for his agency?

   7 Steps in planning process

   (b) Explain whether he should develop a strategic plan or an action plan first.

   (c) Describe the characteristics of a good plan.

3. Draw an organizational chart for your agency.

   (a) Is this chart primarily line, function, or line and staff?

   (b) Explain how the different divisions shown in the chart interact with one another.

Read the definitions of the *Key Words and Phrases* that follow. Being familiar with these important words will help you better understand the second part of this assignment.

Career path A plan for employees to progress from position to position, including the education and training required for each step

Americans with Disabilities Act (ADA) Legislation prohibiting discrimination against qualified individuals with disabilities

Open probe A type of question that leaves its answer open to any response

Closed probe A question designed to elicit a short answer, often a simple "yes" or "no"

Leading Influencing others to work together to achieve the organization's goals, including creating a working environment to bring out the best in people to deliver high levels of performance and problem solving in order to achieve the expected business results

Delegating Getting things done through other people by giving them the authority and responsibility to do a job

Motivation The internal drive to satisfy one's needs

Controlling The process of determining what is being accomplished, evaluating results in terms of established goals, and taking steps to correct undesirable deviations from performance standards

Study the second part of this assignment, which includes the following sections:

III. Organizing, continued
IV. Leading
V. Controlling
VI. Other Management Methods

Hiring

In many organizations, little time is devoted to choosing the right employees. Consequently, people may be hired without sufficient consideration of what would best profit either the organization or the individual. Overworking or underworking the staff as the result of poor personnel decisions often leads to inefficient operations, low employee morale, excessive overhead, and ultimately, through poor service, the loss of the same clients the organization had worked so hard to obtain.

Management Tip

A good source for additional information on hiring employees is a publication called *Managing Your Human Resources,* produced by ACORD. This book has sample skills inventories, advertisements for employees, employment applications, and other useful tools for effective hiring.

Since hiring the right person the first time is desirable, managers should identify and extensively evaluate potential employees before inviting them to become a part of the organization. Selection is one of the most difficult tasks a manager must address, and also one of the most important, since without capable people to carry out the plan, the other functions of management have little meaning.

Although all new employees are hired to fill a particular job, a long-range goal could be to develop the new employee so that as other positions in the firm become available, current employees become the first source of prospective candidates. This concept is known as a **career path**. The career path shows employees how they may progress from position to position and what types of education and training are required for each successive step.

If an organization has a career path that indicates over the next few months a promotion might be in order, a training course may be consid-

II. Planning
III. Organizing
D. Job Qualifications
E. Hiring
IV. Leading

ered either to anticipate the promotion or to interest the employee in the promotion. For example, assume a salesperson is on a career path that allows him or her either to continue in sales or to move into a branch office management option. Assume a branch position will open in six months. It would be reasonable to send the employee to a management training program to see whether her or she is interested in the management option. It is far better to spend money on a short training program to find out if the person is truly interested rather than to promote the employee who later fails because he or she lacks interest or ability. The essential ingredient in this type of training and education decision is a viable career path showing all of the options so that the employee can factor into a decision education and training opportunities beyond the current job description.

Projected Growth of Staff

An organization should evaluate current personnel and project how much growth can be handled under the present organizational structure. Since production from existing staff may not be enough to attain a growth goal set during the planning process, a plan must be set up to obtain the necessary people and to revise the organization to help support projected growth. In the development of this plan, more immediate and specific personnel goals are set. Foresight in estimating these needs will help avoid a crash hiring program. Planned growth in personnel must also help answer other questions. What skills will these new people need to have? How soon will each of them be needed if the desired growth rate is to be maintained? What happens if these people are not found?

If plans include adding or changing automation systems during the next several years, including this consideration in personnel staffing plans is also important. Will new personnel be needed to help during any transition period? What training and qualifications will these personnel need in the new system as well as current agency procedures? What new permanent staff, if any, will need to be retained even after the transition period is completed to help manage, maintain, or fully exploit the potential of the new system?

Defining Staffing Requirements

As growth is projected, organizations should write job descriptions to outline the functions each position is to handle to ensure that the expanding organization will adequately cover all functions. Job qualifications and job specifications are then outlined to translate the job description into people specifications. What kind of experience, knowledge, personal characteristics, and emotional stability does a person need in order to perform the functions of the job as it has been described?

Take, for example, the position of computer programmer. In one firm this job may entail programming skills only, but the person may not be expected to deal either with computer repair or with software company personnel. In another firm, a person with the same basic job description may have to act as a network administrator. A manager needs to have a clear idea of what will be expected in the job to decide what characteristics a person filling that position needs to have. In this example, two different knowledge and experience backgrounds are required, although the personality necessary to handle the respective jobs might be similar. Defining staffing requirements is also vital if the training and development functions are to operate so that the organization always has existing staff ready to assume more responsibilities.

Employee Prospecting

To select the right person, management must have a pool of prospective employees from which to choose. Therefore, candidates should be obtained from as many sources as possible:

- *In-house.* The most obvious place to start looking is within the organization itself. People working in one position might be better suited to handle another type of job or might be in line for a promotion. Selecting a person of known quality, already familiar with the firm, takes some of the guesswork out of hiring and is less expensive than full-scale recruitment. Some people who have performed well in one job, however, may not do well in another. For this reason, the same selection criteria discussed later in this assignment should be used for prospective in-house transfer employees as for those recruited from outside.
- *Other organizations.* Another place to look for people is in other organizations. People who have proven to be good employees in one business are often good in another.
- *Recent graduates.* A third source of new employees is recent high school or college graduates. These prospects will require more extensive training since they rarely have any knowledge or experience in dealing with people in business situations. Hiring recent graduates, however, has at least two advantages. First, they may not have to be paid as much as a person with some work experience, thereby reducing entry-level financial risks; and second, they are generally enthusiastic and receptive to learning new things.

Management Tip

An excellent source for agency employees is Project InVEST. This program, sponsored by the Independent Insurance Agents and Brokers of America (IIABA), sets up an agency office environment in a high school. Participating students are given training to perform the various jobs in a typical agency. After completing this program, the students are ready to begin working in an agency and would require minimal additional training.

Depending on the resources available to assist in the training effort and the orientation of the organization, management must decide which of these sources to explore. If no time is available for training or if the manager is not so inclined, recruiting experienced people becomes the only alternative. Recent graduates are only going to be as good as the training they receive, and the employer must make the commitment to provide the necessary guidance for the good of the organization and the individual. Whether the employer has decided to seek experienced or inexperienced employees, the methods used to find these people are essentially the same.

Referrals from existing staff and other business sources are the best way to contact potential recruits. Relatives and friends of current employees not only provide good recruits themselves but are also excellent sources of leads. Two advantages of referrals are that finding people to interview is inexpensive and some pre-screening has been done.

High schools and colleges generally have placement offices that serve as clearinghouses for students and employers. Sometimes these offices administer tests and provide other screening assistance for the prospective employer.

An obvious advantage to using reputable employment agencies is their effectiveness in pre-screening applicants according to the agency's specifications. However, employment agencies may charge a fee, which increases the total recruitment expense. If the employment agency specializes in hiring for businesses similar to the organization, the amount paid may be less than the indirect costs of the manager's time in screening unsuitable applicants. Employment agencies should be evaluated carefully before they are used.

Newspaper or magazine advertisements provide another alternative. The media must be carefully selected, and the wording of the ad must be clear. Prospects should be able to get a clear picture of the type of person sought and generally what the job entails from the ad. Properly developed ads should reduce the number of time-consuming responses by unqualified applicants. Ads should be informative and may include the organization's name and salary range. Exhibits 2-8 and 2-9 present two sample ads.

Management Tip

One way to avoid spending time with unqualified applicants is to run a "blind ad"—one that asks prospects to send a resume to a post office box and does not list the agency's name. Only those with the required skills and experience need to be contacted.

Screening

The screening process for employees consists of initial contact, an application, a short interview, an in-depth interview, testing, and reference checks. It is tempting to skip some of the steps to save time. However, more time and money will be spent (and wasted) if the wrong person is hired. The disruption for the rest of the staff alone is costly.

The first step is to make initial contact with the prospect either over the telephone or in person. If the person does not have the necessary qualifications by this time, this should be communicated both verbally and in writing. Prolonging the screening process is neither fair to the applicant nor a worthwhile use of the manager's time. Those persons who satisfy the initial standards are invited to complete an application for employment.

Exhibit 2-8
Sample Notice for College Posting

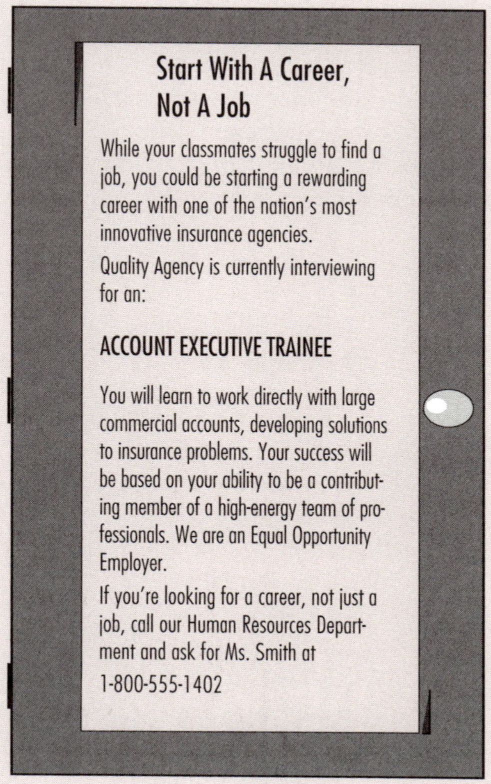

Used with permission. ACORD, *Managing Your Human Resources,* © 1994.

Exhibit 2-9
Sample Ad

Here We Grow Again

Quality Agency

We're looking for enthusiasm and commitment in our expanding insurance agency.

2 Inside Sales People

Entry level positions; excellent communication skills, positive attitude, desire to make the sale and work on a team to achieve goals.

2+ years large lines commercial property casualty sales experience required. Must be licensed.

Be part of a winning sales team committed to creating new business.

Call Ms. Smith by 5/20/9X.

Quality Agency
555 Main street
Smalltown, USA 12345
Phone: 213-876-5432 Fax: 213-876-4321
Equal Opportunity Employer

Used with permission. ACORD, *Managing Your Human Resources,* © 1994.

Although some initial screening occurs through the recruitment and short interview process, the job application serves as the primary screening device and frequently forms the basis for the in-depth interview. Most organizations have their own application form and may even have separate forms for each job classification, but certain characteristics are common to most applications: factual data such as name, address, educational background, and work experience; and questions pertaining directly to the job for which application is being made. Exhibit 2-10 presents sample questions an insurance agency might ask in each of these areas.

Exhibit 2-10
Elements of Application for Employment

Factual History	Education	Work Experience	Job-Related Questions

Full name
Phone number
Current address
Previous address
Height
Weight
General physical condition
Membership in social or business organizations and offices held
Outside interests, hobbies
	High school
	  Activities
	College
	  Major
	  Minor
	  Activities
	  Offices held
	  How financed
	  Degree obtained and when
	Post graduate
	  Major
	  How financed
	  Degree obtained and when
		For each of the Insurance-Related (more detail required) and Non-Insurance Jobs
		  Longevity with each
		  Functions performed
		  Salary history
		  Name of immediate supervisor
		  Reason for leaving
		Account for period of nonemployment
		Military service
			Why do you want this job?
			Why do you want to change jobs?
			How do you feel about being in the insurance business?
			What minimum income do you require?
			What do you want to be doing 5 years from now? 10 years?
			Are you willing to travel?
			Are you willing to be transferred?
			Are you willing to use your own car for business?
			Do you desire an ownership position in the business?
			What did you like about your last job? Dislike?

Legislation Affecting the Application Process

Civil rights legislation has significantly affected the questions asked of an applicant. Such legislation puts the burden of proof on the employer to prove that the application is not discriminatory on the basis of race, creed, sex, nationality, color, age, marital status, and so forth. Questions that may touch on these areas must be kept out of the written application.

The **Americans with Disabilities Act (ADA)** applies to firms with fifteen or more employees. The ADA focuses on prohibiting discrimination against qualified individuals with disabilities.

The ADA requires employers to base employment decisions on the ability of the individual, with or without reasonable accommodations to perform the essential functions of the job, not on whether or not the individual is disabled. Disability means a condition of an individual who has a physical or mental impairment that substantially limits one or more major life activities. "Major life activities" are those basic tasks which the average person in the general population can perform with little difficulty, such as walking, speaking, hearing, sitting, standing, lifting, and so forth. "Substantially limits" means unable to perform such an activity as the average person could.

Reasonable accommodations include any modification to the work facility, the application process, the job, or the manner in which the job is performed that do not place undue hardship on the employer. "Undue hardship" means the employer would incur significant difficulty or expense in making the accommodation. "Significant difficulty" is not defined in the law.

"Essential functions" are the fundamental duties required by the job. For example, the essential functions of an outside producer would include the ability to drive and the possession of the proper operator's license. Conversely, the ability to drive to the bank or post office would not be an essential function of a customer service representative's job if someone else could perform the task.

Given the requirements of the ADA, the following types of questions may not be asked *before* an offer of employment has been made:

- "Do you have any disabilities that would affect your job performance?"
- "How many days did you miss from work last year due to illness?"
- "Have you ever submitted a workers compensation claim?"
- "Have you had any major illnesses in the last five years?"

An employer is allowed to ask the prospect to show how he or she might accomplish a specific job task. For example, if a person with only one arm applied for a job as a data entry clerk, it would be permissible to have that person demonstrate how he or she will operate the computer with or without a "reasonable accommodation." A basic assumption of the ADA is how much nondisabled employers underestimate the ability of a disabled person to perform certain tasks. Rather than proving the disabled person is unfit for the job, asking for a demonstration often results in the disabled person's proving he or she has the ability to do the job.

Management Tip

After a tentative job offer, the ADA allows the employer to ask health-related questions and to require a physical examination, as long as such examination or questions are required of *all* job applicants for the same position. Never give the impression of discriminating by requiring such questions/examinations of some applicants but not of others.

II. Planning
III. Organizing
D. Job Qualifications
E. Hiring
IV. Leading

Because of the ADA, creating and reviewing job descriptions (discussed earlier in this assignment) are crucial. In order to be effective, these must include only essential functions, and must not include references to qualifications discriminatory to the disabled.

Interviews

Personal interviews can vary from patterned to informal or nondirect, depending on the dictates of management and the skill of the interviewer.

Patterned interviews are designed to overcome the problems many managers have in asking the right questions and properly interpreting the answers. Carefully designed questions are provided, and the interviewer must write down all the answers so they can later be evaluated by several people. Some critics believe that the patterned interview is inflexible and that standard questions do not elicit enough information. Also, recording answers in front of the applicant creates an additional emotional strain on the person being interviewed.

At the opposite end of the scale is a more informal, nonstructured interview, which encourages the applicant to talk freely, guided by questions from the interviewer. The theory behind this interview is that significant characteristics will come to light if the applicant is allowed to talk about past business experiences freely. A major problem with the nonstructured interview is that it requires much more interpretive skill on the part of the interviewer and more time unearthing some possibly irrelevant information.

Many organizations use a format falling between the two extremes with certain predetermined guidelines and questions that allow a degree of flexibility to the interviewer. In conducting an interview, the prospective employer should try to picture the applicant in the job and be honest and straightforward about the job and its responsibilities. Often the interviewer tends to become excited about a good applicant and to oversell the job rather than to use the interview to help determine whether the person is suited for the job.

Questions should be open-ended to encourage explanations that will give insight into the person's attitudes and desires. This type of question is called an **open probe** because it is open to any response. Asking "What did you like about your last job?" rather than "Did you like your last job?" will force the applicant to give answers of more than one word. Of course, interviewers must listen carefully not only to *what* is being said but also *how*, since the applicant is aware that he or she is being evaluated and thus may be trying to give the "best" answers.

If the interviewer has a good set of job specifications drawn from the job description and knows specifically what knowledge, skills, or personality traits are required, closed probes can be used to generate specific answers. A **closed probe** is a question designed to elicit a short answer, often simply a "yes" or "no." An example of a closed probe is, "Have you studied any insurance courses since you graduated from school?"

Management Tip

Most interviews should include both open probes and closed probes. The choice of style depends on the type of question asked and the type of answer expected.

The employer may conduct interviews in social situations to observe the person when he or she is more relaxed. Salespeople are frequently expected to entertain clients, so the interviewer may find it informative to include a social situation in the interviewing process to ascertain comfort and skills in that environment.

Management Tip

When holding such a social situation interview in a restaurant, observe the way the applicant treats those serving the food. An applicant often will treat support staff in the organization the same way he or she will treat anyone else in a service position, that is, the waiter or waitress. For example, the applicant who is gracious and charming to you (the potential employer) but treats the waitress with thinly disguised disdain or contempt will soon have your support staff planning his demise or tendering their resignations.

Thorough selection often involves several interviews before applicants are hired. Likewise, a more extensive process will provide the prospective employee with more information about the job and the employer and better prepare him or her to decide whether to accept the job if it is offered. Mistakes go both ways, and they are expensive for all concerned.

Testing

The application and personal interview are the two most commonly used tools in selecting new employees. A third tool, testing, and specifically the psychological test, is also used, particularly in the selection process for sales-related and management roles.

Typically, an organization uses one or several types of psychological tests:

1. Personality or interest tests to reflect positive or negative aspects of the individual's personality relating to the specific job and the other employees in the organization
2. Tests designed to measure the individual's aptitude for selling or for detail work or other basic functions of the proposed job
3. Knowledge tests set up to determine how much a supposedly experienced applicant knows about the technical aspects of the business
4. Intelligence tests intended to measure innate intelligence

Controversy surrounds the use of psychological tests. Many people believe that some questions foster discriminatory personnel practices. Testing in itself is not illegal, but the Office of Federal Contract Compliance stipulates that tests should be "professionally developed" and "properly validated" if they are to be used in the selection process.

Furthermore, as with the application and the interview, questions must be relevant to the job. Testing is perfectly acceptable when done correctly. The organization should keep records to show that the test is used to measure the person's ability to handle the needs of the job and does not screen out a segment of the population for the wrong reasons.

The purpose of testing is to identify more accurately certain traits and qualifications that cannot be measured adequately by other selection tools. Although tests should not be a substitute for judgment, they can lend a measure of objectivity to the selection process. They are also used to provide a basis for interviewing, since any questionable characteristics pointed out in the test results may be thoroughly explored at that time. Another reason for using validated tests is that they can help offset the high costs of hiring and training by increasing the chances of selecting people who will probably be more effective and content in the jobs they are hired to perform. Also, interpreting tests can identify an employee's personal growth needs and provide the manager with additional insights to assist with that individual's professional development.

However, problems are associated with reliance on test results. For example, most procedures compare the individual with a stereotype. Truly creative people, who may be perfect for the job, could be eliminated because they are outside the test's normal range. There is also the danger that good test scores will lull the manager into thinking that the person will succeed, and the manager will therefore cut back on training and support to the detriment of the organization and the individual. Although most tests have built-in mechanisms to minimize the chance of an applicant "rigging" the answers to achieve the desired results, those who have extensive experience with them can manipulate them. Finally, tests may assume a certain cultural background that will distort the results if the applicant is not from that environment.

As a safeguard, psychological tests should be used only in conjunction with other selection tools and not as the primary factor upon which a person should be hired or disqualified. Managers must be careful not to let test results overrule their own judgment. Instead, the tests should be used as constructive input for hiring and ongoing management direction.

Reference Checks

During the selection process, the employer may also check both personal and business references. A visit, a telephone call, or a letter can be used, although many references will hesitate to put their impressions in writing. There are no simple rules about who gives a good reference. Depending on the circumstances, former employers can be an invaluable source or grossly misleading. Former customers, teachers, and business associates may be good sources. Relatives are generally not objective references.

Management Tip

Don't limit yourself to the names given. Use the list as a starting point to get other names such as coworkers or clients who may be more willing to discuss the prospect.

Information turned up in references is seldom conclusive, but managers should not bypass this selection tool; a single significant fact uncovered may make the effort worthwhile. Some employers take the extra precaution of checking with a local credit bureau to get additional information on the applicant's background and financial condition, particularly if he or she is going to be involved with handling money for the organization.

The Employment Offer

Once the decision has been made to hire a person and the feedback from that individual indicates that he or she is seriously interested in the possibility of employment with the agency, the next step is to make a formal offer. It may take the form of a detailed employment contract, or it may be simply a letter outlining the offer. In all cases, the terms of employment should be described clearly in writing to protect the interests of all parties involved.

Leading

Leading is influencing others to work together to achieve the organization's goals. It includes creating the working environment that brings out the best in people and that facilitates the high levels of performance and problem-solving that are required to achieve business results.[2] Effective leadership involves more than simply plugging the best people one can find into predefined job slots and saying "go get 'em!" Employees need guidance and supervision to make them as productive as possible. An organization may have a clear-cut plan, an effective organizational structure, and a group of qualified employees, but unless the employees receive leadership, their activities may not track with the plan or may subvert the structure, thereby reducing their effectiveness. Successful leadership results in knowledgeable, dedicated employees working efficiently together to achieve the agency's goals and objectives.

Leadership in management theory and practice encompasses visioning, inspiring, motivating, influencing, and managing change. A complete discussion of the topic of leadership is complex and beyond the scope of this text. Some of the elements of leadership, however, are important in the preceding discussion of management and will be discussed next. These elements include delegation of authority and responsibility, motivation, and managing differences.

Delegating

Delegating is the art of getting things done through other people by giving them the responsibility *and* authority to do a job. Any organization in which more than one person is employed must practice delegation, yet it is one of the most difficult activities for many managers to handle effectively. Delegation is particularly difficult for managers who were promoted from a position within the department that they now manage. They are so accustomed to doing things themselves that the common tendency is to continue to do so.

Management Tip

A critical error often made by managers is only doing half of what's required for effective delegation. The errant manager freely dictates responsibility for tasks, but keeps all authority tightly clutched in his hands. The employee given more work without the authority to carry it out is being treated like a robot, with no brain of his or her own. Effective delegation means transferring the task *and* the power to see it through.

The key to effective delegation is communication. Expected results must be communicated and the scope of the authority and responsibility clearly defined. Since the manager does not delegate all authority or abdicate the ultimate responsibility, information must flow between the manager and the employee to ensure that the employee has enough information to make decisions and to use the delegated authority properly.

The chain of command must be understood. Employees must know who is delegating what responsibilities to them and to whom to refer matters beyond their authority. When the line of authority has not been communicated clearly, the process of delegation breaks down.

Motivating

Psychologists generally agree that motivation comes from within a person, not from an outside source. Effective leaders and managers, although not literally able to motivate employees, can influence them and lead them in the right direction—toward achieving the goals and objectives of the organization. Need is really the root of **motivation**. A desire to satisfy a need motivates action. If employees do not perceive that their needs can be satisfied, they have no incentive to act. To influence employees, the manager must be aware of these needs and must provide recognizable opportunities to satisfy them.

As used here, the word "need" includes both what a person must have and what a person wants. There are physical needs for food and shelter; security needs, both economic and psychological; social needs such as status and a sense of belonging; and self-expression needs, like personal accomplishment and opportunity to grow. To a certain extent, how intensely people want something depends on how much they already have and how much they want. The level of need of an individual will control the strength of the desire and the resultant action and hence will determine the capacity for motivation.

One of the more famous researchers into human behavior, Abraham Maslow, illustrated such a system of needs as *motivators* by setting up a hierarchical theory of needs in which all the basic needs are at the bottom, and the needs concerned with man's highest potential are at the top. The hierarchic theory is often represented as a pyramid, with the larger, lower levels representing the lower needs, and the pinnacle representing the need for self-actualization. Each of the five levels of the pyramid depends on the previous level. For example, a person does not feel safety needs until the demands of the physiological needs have first been satisfied. Maslow's hierarchy of needs is as follows, and Exhibit 2-11 shows their relationship:

1. *Physiological needs.* These needs are biological and consist of the needs for oxygen, food, water, and a relatively constant body temperature. These needs are the strongest, because if deprived, the person would die.
2. *Safety needs.* Except in times of emergency or periods of disorganization in the social structure (such as widespread rioting), adults seldom experience security needs. Children, however, often display signs of insecurity and their need to be safe.
3. *Love, affection, and belongingness needs.* People have needs to escape feelings of loneliness and alienation. They also need to give (and receive) love, affection, and feel the sense of belonging.
4. *Esteem needs.* People need a stable, firmly based, high level of self-respect and respect from others in order to feel satisfied, self-confident, and valuable. If these needs are not met, the person feels inferior, weak, helpless, and worthless.
5. *Self-actualization needs.* Maslow describes self-actualization as a person's need to be and do that which the person was born to do. It is his or her "calling." A musician must make music, an artist must create art, and a poet must write. If these needs are not met, the person feels restlessness, on edge, tense, and lacking something. Lower needs may also produce a restless feeling, but finding the cause is much easier. If a person is hungry, unsafe, not loved or accepted, or lacking self-esteem the cause is apparent. It is not always clear what a person wants when there is a need for self-actualization.

Exhibit 2-11
Maslow's Hierarchy

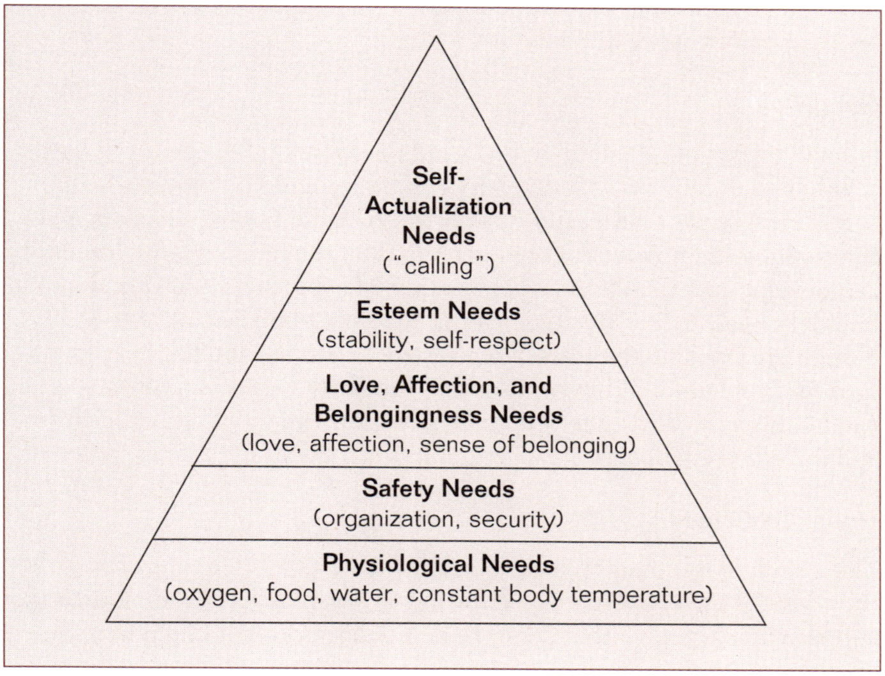

Any one of these levels of need may affect the motivation of an employee. The key to effective management is to recognize which needs apply to each individual employee at a given time and to structure a system that allows the employee to meet as many needs as possible.

Some of the more common needs emphasized in an employment setting are money, work, security, room to grow, a personal place, recognition, goals, and incentives.

Money

Money is an employee's most tangible need. Economically, an individual needs enough money to satisfy physiological needs such as food and clothing. Emotionally, he or she needs enough to have a feeling of self-respect and security. With few exceptions, people work to earn a comfortable living. This in itself is a motivator and will at least get the employees to the office or out into the field just so they will continue to receive their paychecks. The rate of pay should adequately reflect the difficulty of a job and should be comparable to what the person would be making in another firm. Money can also be a destructive, negative motivator if the salary level is perceived to be unfair with respect to that provided by other firms or, even worse, to other employees in the same firm.

Work Importance and Responsibility

People need to feel that their work is important and that they have been given enough responsibility to make a contribution to the organization. So much emphasis is placed on the importance of the producer in a sales environment that often the support personnel start to feel as though their jobs are worth little by comparison. Management must stress the importance of service in the production effort and must encourage the producers to do likewise. Support personnel given respect and recognition as full, crucial members of the production team will reach much higher levels of performance and job satisfaction.

Security

Human beings have a deep-seated need for security. An employee needs to know that good work and loyalty will be recognized. People who come to work every day fearing the sudden wrath of the boss or the collapse of the business exert more energy worrying than they do working. Insecurity can develop in a small office over the loss of a large account or a slump in sales that is adversely affecting agency income. Managers need to be aware that ignoring the fears of employees or attempting to cover up obvious problems will likely make the insecurity worse. Rumors are nearly always more frightening than fact. Consistent, stable leadership and informed employees are essential to satisfying the need for security.

Room To Grow

One of the most common reasons employees cite for quitting a job is that they did not have any room to grow in the organization. Communicating and proving to people that jobs will be filled from within help to retain them. If an agency adopts a career path, employees can be kept informed of the ways they can move upward in the organization and of the ways they can earn more money in the future. It is not enough that the opportunities exist; employees must be *aware* that they exist, and they must know what they should do to take advantage of the opportunities. An example of this problem is an ambitious account assistant who wants to work in production. No one in her firm had followed that career path before, so she believed that the path did not exist and left to join a competitor. That this opportunity was, in fact, available made no difference, because it was not communicated to the employees. With her went valuable training time and possible bad public relations for the firm.

Personal Place

Employees need a special personal place in the organization, both physically and mentally. An assigned office or desk or parking space, a telephone, a title, a territory to work, or a personal secretary can provide such a place. However, to some people these physical trappings of status are of no value. Instead, they find their own sanctuary in the respect and esteem of co-workers. To them, public praise for a job well done means more than ten private secretaries. As organizations grow, managers can inadvertently threaten an individual's place by shifting work around in the interest of increased productivity. An office worker who is responsible for certain tasks might feel a proprietary interest in handling these exclusively and may resent an offer of assistance even in times of heavy workload. This does not mean changes in assignments should not be made, but that the manager must be attuned to the possible reaction of the people involved and present the change in such a way as to reinforce rather than undermine the individual's feeling of place. The clerical worker, for example, could be made aware of how valuable extra time might be for pursuing larger, more complex duties, once that time is freed up by assigning some of the more basic tasks to a new associate.

Recognition

Recognition is a factor in creating the atmosphere for employees to motivate themselves. Giving a person a place is not enough. Too often a good job is taken for granted and employees become discouraged, thinking no one knows or cares about what they have done. Letting people know they are appreciated is not difficult; remembering to do so is hard. Recognition can take the form of a public announcement, a lunch, a bouquet of flowers, or even a pat on the back with a sincere "Thanks for doing a great job on that project!"

Goals

An individual needs direction—clearly defined goals and the way to achieve them. Goals must be stated in concrete terms, and actions need to be consistent with the goals. People have a natural desire to look forward to something. The manager needs to provide the target or expected result. It may be an organization goal (implementation of a new automation upgrade) supported by individual goals (converting the customer database to the new format) or more personal goals such as

III. Organizing
IV. Leading
B. Motivating
C. Managing Differences
V. Controlling
A. Developing Reporting Systems

completion of a professional designation. For the goals to be more effective, the length of time between the setting of the goals and their probable completion should be short enough for the individual to be able to visualize the result. Individual goal setting is thoroughly discussed in a later assignment in this segment.

Incentives

Incentives, as motivators that meet employees' needs, affect both hiring and retention of quality employees. Mangers can use incentives to influence employee performance, but only to the extent that the incentives meet the employee's needs. Incentives can be monetary or nonmonetary.

Monetary Incentives

The basic monetary incentive is salary, but more organizations are broadening monetary incentives to include individual- or group-based performance incentives. Bonuses based on team or department achievement of certain established goals are effective team builders. Each employee's efforts help or hinder all team members. Recognizing that frequent reinforcement is more effective than long-term reinforcement, many managers find that quarterly bonuses provide better results than a single year-end payment. Of course, to influence an employee, a monetary incentive must be viewed as both meeting a need and reflecting the work necessary to achieve it.

Nonmonetary Incentives

Money, beyond a certain level, is not an effective motivator of people. People reach a comfort level above which they become complacent and unwilling to work harder for more monetary rewards. This level differs for each employee since each has different basic needs. But when (and if) a person reaches this plateau, the prospect of more money will not produce more work.

Nonmonetary benefits include the following:

- *Benefits*. A benefits package is almost always provided for employees. Typical benefits include health insurance, life insurance, disability insurance, and a pension or retirement plan.
- *Ownership*. Some people are motivated by a desire to own their own business, either in whole or in part. For them, the opportunity for ownership in the agency might be the most important incentive. Ownership opportunities can come in the form of shares earned as performance recognition, employee stock ownership plans (ESOPs), or simply the sale of shares in the agency to important employees as a means of perpetuating the agency.
- *Fringe benefits*. Employees are motivated to a certain extent by fringe benefits or "perks" allowed in many organizations. Typical fringe benefits in insurance agencies include auto allowances (or a company car), expense accounts, and club memberships.
- *Time off*. Vacations, holidays, and flexible work hours (flex time) are all effective nonmonetary employee incentives.

- *Recognition*. Positive reinforcement and recognition of individual accomplishments can be effective incentives, and they usually cost little in relation to their influence on the employee. Posting the names of employees receiving a professional designation or even listing births of grandchildren have a positive influence on an employee's self esteem.

Management Tip

Some of the more creative—and popular—incentives now offered by some organizations focus on child care. Many employees are single parents, or part of a two-income household, and caring for preschoolers or sick children can cause a great deal of mental as well as financial strain when the parent has to take time off from work to care for the child. One business turned an upstairs room in the building into a nursery/clinic staffed by a medically trained child-care worker. Another offered vouchers for a local home nursing service to send someone to stay with the sick child at home while the parent came to work. Ask your employees with children what you can do to help, and try it!

Although management must take the initiative in setting the stage for people to motivate themselves, the employees must participate in creating a favorable work environment. Executives need to recognize the efforts of support personnel, who in turn must recognize each others' contributions. People need to know they are instrumental in the group effort, and this feeling can be communicated only by a sense of teamwork and mutual respect on the part of all employees.

Managing Differences

Sometimes a manager has to act as a mediator in managing differences between employees. These differences can arise because of different personalities, different opinions on how to do something, and a variety of other factors. A manager should be objective when dealing with the inevitable differences that arise between employees. A manager who loses impartiality will also lose the respect of the other people and, as a result, will become a less effective manager. Some disagreements are temporary and can be resolved favorably, but sometimes two individuals just find it impossible to co-exist in the same organization. Unpleasant but necessary action, such as probation or even termination, may have to be taken for the benefit of everyone in the agency.

Controling

Control is the function of monitoring and regulating activities to bring the desired result of the organization's planning. **Controlling** includes the process of determining what is being accomplished, evaluating results in terms of established goals, and taking steps to correct undesirable deviations from organization performance standards. The control function involves six activities. The first two activities are the establishment of reporting systems and developing a standard or basis for measuring performance. A standard is a yardstick or benchmark such as a producer's sales goals. The third control activity is measuring results against the standard; for example, comparing the producer's actual sales with the sales goal. The fourth activity is to correct deviations from the standards if deviation is undesirable. The final activity is rewarding. For example, a producer who did not meet the sales goal might be offered a sales training course to help improve sales. A producer who met the goal, however, would be rewarded with a bonus or some other incentive. Sales management control is addressed at greater length in Assignment 3 in this segment.

Some managers believe the controlling function is limited to checking on a person or activity, but control involves considerably more than "checking." Control is used to influence the outcome and will always be present where good management exists. Control is the vital follow-up to planning, organizing, and leading.

Developing Reporting Systems

Reporting systems gather and present information in a form useful for measuring performance. These systems should be simple and geared to allow easy comparison. Reports that are excessively time-consuming to prepare may lose their value because of the adverse effect they have on employee or manager productivity. Reports should always be in writing, particularly when dealing with the individual performance evaluation of employees.

Control reports should contain only key comparisons. They are meant to present a comparison of performance against a standard and to reveal whether the situation is getting better or worse. Reports should be developed to measure key areas of agency operations for which measurable standards can be developed. They usually involve employee performance results (individually and as a group), financial results, and sales results.

Developing Standards

The first step in developing standards is to identify which characteristics determine good performance. In the second step, the manager must determine how high a level of achievement is desired for each characteristic. For this reason, establishing standards depends heavily on previous decisions made in planning and organizing.

Measuring all financial and personnel performance results in an organization would be burdensome. The aim is to keep track of what is happening without going to the expense of watching everything. Performance should be measured only at strategic points such as year end, anniversary date, end of each quarter, and so forth.

Measuring Results

The third step of the control function is to measure results against the standards that have been established. This activity actually serves two purposes. First, it provides an objective comparison of the employee's performance compared to what was expected. It also provides an opportunity to evaluate the standard. The manager might ask the following questions about the standards:

- "Were the standards set so high that they were unattainable?"
- "Were the standards set so low that they were too easily accomplished?"
- "Did changes outside of the employee's control (such as changes in the law or available insurers) prevent achieving the standards?"

Depending on the answers to these and similar questions, the standards may need to be revised.

Correcting Deviations

After measuring the results of employee performance and asking the questions above, if the manager believes that the employee did not meet an achievable standard, he or she may need to take corrective action, the fourth step of the control function.

The manager must first determine why the employee did not meet the standard. The reason for not meeting the standard will dictate what corrective action should be taken. Failing to meet a sales standard, for instance, might have been due to insufficient training or a lack of calls on prospects. To correct these problems, the manager might require additional training or establish specific goals for weekly prospect calls.

Rewarding

When standards have been achieved, rewarding the employee (the final step in the control function) is appropriate. The reward should be commensurate with the achievement and further influence employee motivation. Consequently, the reward might be money or some other incentive that meets the employee's needs or desires. The manager should also realize that the reward will most effectively reinforce the desired behavior when it is given soon after the accomplishment.

Evaluating Employees

Anyone who manages or supervises employees has the responsibility to provide them with an evaluation of their performance. Whether it shows success or failure, the evaluation must be produced in an objective, accurate manner. The following article, which appeared in previous editions of the AAI 83 course guide, gives managers and supervisors tips on how to provide employees with a realistic performance evaluation.

How to Evaluate Employees in a Realistic Way[3]

Although developing an employee evaluation program may be distasteful, it remains a vital ingredient in a well-run organization. Unfortunately, many managers and supervisors are ill prepared for the task and consider employee reviews one of the most difficult aspects of their jobs.

Regardless of how well prepared a manager is, however, many things can "go wrong" during the process.

By definition, the term "evaluation" means "to judge or determine the worth or quality of." In dealing with an employee evaluation, the employer becomes involved with two conflicting yet complementary processes—criticism and praise. Seldom are we faced with the "model" employee or with the polar opposite—the total failure. Instead, employees are consistently inconsistent, making it impractical and unfair to "vote on a straight ballot" when conducting a performance appraisal.

Reluctance to Evaluate

Even though most managers admit to the benefits of employee evaluations, they often resist becoming involved in the process. They do so only to fulfill a legal or organizational requirement, and they view the task as bothersome and time consuming. Reasons for these negative feelings vary but some common ones follow:

- The roles of "judge" and "counselor" are often viewed as incompatible when attempts are made to fulfill them simultaneously.
- Lack of formal training in personnel administration may make it difficult for a manager to understand fully how performance appraisal fits into an organizational system.
- Ethical objections may arise when managers feel they are assuming a role that makes them appear to be "playing God."
- Negative appraisals may serve to alienate employees and cause tension between employees and managers.

10 Rating Errors

In any evaluatory procedure the possibility for error exists. The supervisor should be particularly aware of the 10 Typical Rating Errors.

- *Halo Effect.* This term refers to a rater's tendency to rate all aspects of performance based on the observance of one trait. For instance, if you observe that a certain employee is a meticulous and thorough worker, you might rate the employee high on all characteristics. This is a very common error among evaluators.
- *Horn Effect.* The opposite of the "halo" effect, horn refers to a supervisor's tendency to let one poor rating influence all other ratings—resulting in a lower overall evaluation than is really deserved.
- *Error of Central Tendency.* This is both the most common and most serious type of error. The error of central tendency describes the tendency of an appraiser to cluster appraisals around a central point—usually an "average" or "middle" point on a scale. This can result from the fear of rating too high or too low. It may seem safer to cluster all scores toward the center to lend greater "validity" to the appraisal.
- *Latest Behavior.* We have a tendency to forget about past problems or past accomplishments and to focus, instead, on what's been happening recently. This is most likely to be a problem when an employee is evaluated only once every six months—or once a year.
- *Leniency or Generosity Error.* This attitude involves high ratings for most employees, perhaps because of a reluctance to "rock the boat" by seeming too critical. A harried

manager may find it much easier and certainly more pleasant to offer unconditional praise to employees than to bring up instances of substandard performance.

- *Strictness.* The opposite of leniency; this is the tendency to be overly harsh when rating employees.
- *Stereotyping or Initial Impression.* This may be the hardest type of error to deal with. Stereotypes may be either conscious or subconscious—often we may be unfairly biased toward an employee without actually being aware of the bias. First impressions really *do* make lasting impressions. Because of this, it is extremely important to base any evaluation on observable, objective behaviors rather than subjective opinions.
- *Projection or Similarity Error.* "Birds of a feather flock together..." It's easy to realize that we tend to like people who are like us and to dislike people who are unlike us. This can become a problem in the rating process when we give high scores to employees because they either consciously "remind me of myself when I was just starting out," or low scores to other employees who "just don't have the ambition that I have."
- *Spillover Error.* Allowing past evaluations to reflect—either positively or negatively—on the current rating, even though actual behavior during the current rating period has not been the same.
- *Inter-individual Error.* Basing each employee's evaluation on a comparison with other employees. This can be especially unfair since one employee may have received very high marks because of favorable circumstances rather than actual performance.

Steps to Error-Free Evaluations

Investigators have found little relationship between ratings generated by evaluators and actual on-the-job performance. In addition, when the same employee is evaluated by two or more evaluators, assessments vary widely.

The evaluation process is, by its very nature, quite subjective, leaving many areas open to bias and error. Being aware of the possibility of errors occurring is one of the first steps toward becoming a fair evaluator.

Before conducting an evaluation or appraisal, consider several points—steps that can make this somewhat difficult task a little less awesome.

- Be prepared.
- Clarify standards among raters. Make sure that everybody agrees on what "good" means or what "5" represents on a scale of 1-5.
- Identify desired behaviors on observable, rather than subjective, terms. For instance, "sales over the next quarter should increase by 5%" rather than "increase sales." Consider using management by objective techniques.
- Keep a running log of employee performance to review before the formal evaluation. This will help avoid the possibility of the "latest behavior" error.
- Be aware of your own personal biases and work to overcome them—don't overcompensate, though, and become a victim of "leniency error."
- Try using more than one assessor and compare results to determine possible bias.
- Don't assume that excellence in one area implies excellence in all areas. Observe each employee's performance objectively for each factor on the rating form.
- Base judgments on *demonstrated* performance, not *anticipated* performance.
- Base judgments on written, observable standards, not on a comparison with other employees.
- Always conclude the review with a summary and a plan for the future.

Other Management Methods

The preceding management discussion revolved around what is often referred to as the "command and control" method. The reasons for focusing on this particular style of management were detailed at the beginning of this assignment. But major changes have been suggested to this method, largely because of the growing influence of the "quality" and "best practices" movements. The best practices movement will be discussed specifically as it applies to insurance agencies in the next assignment. However, a brief introduction to the quality movement is in order.

Total Quality Management

The concepts of total quality management (TQM) were first given public notice through the dramatic turnaround in post-war Japan's manufacturing capabilities. By the late 1970s the Japanese techniques and processes seemed poised to overwhelm the rest of the industrialized world, particularly the United States. When American firms sought to study the Japanese methods to learn the secrets behind their success, they were astonished to find the Japanese giving full credit to the teachings of an American statistician, Dr. W. Edwards Deming.

Dr. Deming had originally developed his ideas on quality before and during World War II for use by American engineers during the war effort. Following the war, however, with a booming American economy based less on quality and more on getting the most production possible out of the factories, American manufacturers disregarded the concepts. Visiting Japan in 1947, Deming was struck by the war-ravaged country's need to rebuild and found eager pupils for his theories in the Japanese engineers and scientists. Their success in not only recovering from the war but also becoming a world economic power within a few decades gave credence to their willingness to learn and confirmation to the effectiveness of Deming's ideas.

Although Deming's work formed the foundation, TQM was revised and enhanced by others into primarily a two-part system: (1) a focus on developing a system of tools and procedures that, if used systematically, would enhance the quality of both the process and products; and (2) a focus on meeting and exceeding customers' wants and expectations. Many companies took on TQM with an obsession; they told skeptics simply to "look at the Japanese and what they've accomplished."

Unfortunately TQM has recently faltered for a myriad of reasons, but two stand out: (1) many companies followed TQM advocates' advice that the only real quality lay in "zero defects" and "get it right the first time every time," two goals that proved not only elusive but extremely expensive; and (2) the Japanese economic juggernaut appears to have fallen on hard times.

Return on Quality (ROQ) and Continuous Quality Improvement (CQI)

Deming himself stressed the need to "improve constantly." In reaction to the growing sense that true "zero defects" was either unattainable by many businesses or not worth the often exorbitant investment of time and resources, two main variations of the TQM concepts have evolved. Both seek to keep the fundamental focus on quality that Deming advocated, but to develop ways of gaining much of the benefits of TQM while making the costs reasonable. In this way, companies that might otherwise have simply dropped the entire quality focus may still be encouraged to stay the course.

Return on quality (ROQ) focuses on what the company can expect to gain from a given investment in quality concepts. Although zero defects may be unacceptable or unattainable as a goal, major improvements may still be available at a reasonable investment. In this method, management's focus shifts to the most gains given the amount of time and resources invested.

Continuous quality improvement (CQI) says, "Although the journey to perfection may seem impossibly long or expensive, let's start down the road and see where it leads." Also referred to as process improvement or work flow analysis, CQI has emerged as an extremely effective method for analyzing and improving the quality and efficiency of business operations. It is especially suitable for sales and service industries (such as insurance), whereas the concept of zero defects seemed targeted specifically at manufacturing processes. With CQI, improving quality is an ongoing goal, rather than a specific point at which the goal is achieved. In other words, no matter how good an organization is, it can always get better.

Both ROQ and CQI retain the focus on the customer. No business can expect success in today's economy without such a focus. Customers are more aware of their options for demanding quality service and value for their money, and are unafraid of exercising them. CQI has become for many businesses their method for eliminating unnecessary costs so that the product or service can be delivered to the customer at an attractive price while still enabling the business to make a profit.

Check your understanding of the *Key Words and Phrases* found in the second part of this assignment.

Career path (p. 33)

Americans with Disabilities Act (ADA) (p. 38)

Open probe (p. 40)

Closed probe (p. 40)

Leading (p. 43)

Delegating (p. 44)

Motivation (p. 44)

Controlling (p. 49)

Review the concepts presented in the second part of this assignment by answering the following questions.

14. What are three sources an agency can use to prospect for employees? (p. 35)

15. What steps are included in the screening process of hiring a new employee? (pp. 36-38)

16. What type of answer is expected when using an open probe? (p. 40)

17. What are the levels of needs identified in Maslow's hierarchy? (p. 45)

18. What nonmonetary incentives are frequently used to influence employee motivation? (pp. 48-49)

19. What five activities are included in the control function? (p. 50)

20. What are three management methods that focus on quality? (p. 54)

Apply the concepts presented in the second part of this assignment by answering the following questions.

4. Explain how written job descriptions and job qualifications help in the hiring process.

5. Identify the basic human needs and describe their importance in motivating agency employees.

6. Good communication is vital in managing an insurance agency. Illustrate examples of good and bad communication relative to the following:
   (a) delegating authority and responsibility for a task

(b) influencing employee behavior

(c) measuring results

7. How might changes in an agency's automation system affect staffing changes?

8. How does the Americans with Disabilities Act (ADA) affect hiring practices?

Summary

Although there are many management approaches, the traditional "command and control" approach is still in widespread use in insurance agencies. In this system, managers use activities such as planning, organizing, leading, and controlling to achieve their organizational goals.

Planning involves setting an organization's goals and devising ways to achieve those goals. Managers must implement several types of plans. These include organizational plans (which address survival, independence, and public image); functional plans (which address profit, growth, product line, and personnel); strategic plans (which address long-range goals); and action plans (which address short-range goals).

Planning includes seven steps—setting a mission statement, developing strategies, setting goals, setting objectives, developing budgets, setting policies, and establishing procedures. After the various plans have been implemented, managers must monitor the results of the agency's activities and make any revisions and adjustments that are warranted.

Organizing is the process of determining how work will be divided into manageable units. The process includes establishing an organizational structure, defining relationships with appropriate authority and responsibility, creating job descriptions, establishing job qualifications, and hiring the right people.

An agency can choose three basic forms of organizational structure: line organization, functional organization, or a combination of the two known as line and staff organization. This last form is the most common in mid-size and large size agencies, and it represents the best of the other two types of organization.

Leading is the management function of influencing others to work together to achieve the organization's goals. Leadership encompasses visioning, inspiring, motivating, influencing, delegating authority and responsibility, managing differences, and managing change. Effective agency managers learn what factors motivate employees and use these factors to influence employees to achieve the agency's goals.

Controlling is the function of monitoring and regulating activities to bring about the desired result of the organization's planning. Controlling includes determining what is being accomplished, evaluating results in terms of established goals, and taking steps to correct undesirable deviations from the organization's performance standards. The five activities involved in controlling are establishing reporting systems, setting standards to measure performance, measuring results against the standards, correcting undesirable deviations from those standards, and rewarding activity that meets or exceeds the standards.

Many new management systems have evolved from the traditional command and control system. These new systems include total quality management, return on quality, and continuous quality improvement among others. Most of these systems focus on quality and "best practices" and can be used effectively in insurance agencies.

Notes

1. Peter F. Drucker, *People and Performance: The Best of Peter Drucker on Management* (New York, NY: Harper's College Press, 1977), pp. 176-193, and *Managing the Non-Profit Organization* (New York, NY: Harper Collins, 1990), pp. 121-129.
2. Reprinted with permission from Independent Insurance Agents of America, Inc., and Woodgate Partners from *Five Practices of Highly Effective Leaders* by Doron (Bud) Antrim, ©1996, p. 8:3.
3. Lin Grensing, reprinted with permission from Communications Briefings, November 1985. All rights reserved. Communications Briefings, 806 Westminster Blvd., Blackwood, NJ 08012.

Agency Management

Assignment 3

Assignment Objectives

After completing this assignment, you should be able to:

1. Given an insurance agency case, design a sales management planning system that would improve the agency's performance.

   In support of the assignment objective listed above, you should be able to do the following:

   a. Describe a system that would indicate when an agency could afford a full-time sales manager with no production responsibilities.

   b. Describe the types of sales management planning systems and the producer's role in each.
2. Explain how to modify a traditional income statement to change the statement into a planning document and control device.
3. Explain how sales planning logically follows from agency planning.
4. Explain how to organize sales management in an insurance agency.

   In support of the assignment objective listed above, you should be able to describe the steps in organizing sales management.
5. Describe the seven key producer accountabilities.
6. Explain the sales management of people.
7. Explain how to develop sales performance standards and controls.
8. Describe the objectives of and rules for sales meetings.
9. Define or describe each of the Key Words and Phrases for this assignment.

Assignment Outline

- I. Agency Management and Sales Management
  - A. The Need for Sales Management
  - B. Sales Management Systems
  - C. Sales Management as a Bottom Line Expense
  - D. The Seven Planning Phases and the Sales Management Process
  - E. Sales Management Organization
- II. Sales Management of People
  - A. Staffing the Agency
  - B. Adding New Producers
  - C. Producer Orientation, Training, and Development
  - D. Producer Compensation
  - E. Sales Performance Standards and Controls
  - F. Sales Meetings
- III. An Argument for Change
- IV. Summary

Assignment 3

Agency Management

Orient yourself to this assignment by reading the following introduction.

Agency Management and Sales Management

Insurance agencies are primarily sales organizations. Because managing sales is so crucial to the effectiveness of the agency, this assignment will be devoted to applying the management process to the sales process.

Sales management activities must not exist separately from an agency's overall management. A sales plan must fit into the agency's business plan and work in concert with it rather than at cross-purposes.

Read the definition of the *Key Words and Phrases* that follow. Being familiar with these important words will help you better understand the first part of this assignment. *Key Words and Phrases* appear in bold in the text when they are defined.

Sales management Includes managing all activities designed to put the producers in touch with the right customers and prospects at the right time

Marketing Includes finding, identifying the needs of, selling to, and providing services to insureds

Top-down system Management sets the long-range and year-to-year sales goals for the organization and determines how they will be achieved

Bottom-up system Each producer outlines what he or she expects to achieve during the year in new sales, retention, and personal and technical development. Management then compiles these plans into an agency plan.

Controllable sources of revenue Include property and liability commissions, life insurance commissions, health commissions, and perhaps fees for services rendered pertaining to insurance operations

Noncontrollable sources of revenue Types of revenue not directly related to insurance sales such as contingency commissions and interest income

Seven key producer accountabilities The functions necessary to sell and retain clients: prospecting, fact-finding, preparing proposals, physically presenting understandable proposals to the client prospect, closing, initial service, and long-term service

Study the first part of this assignment, which includes the following section:

I. Agency Management and Sales Management

The Need for Sales Management

Sales management includes managing all activities designed to put the producers in touch with the right customers and prospects at the right time, in the right place, and with the right product or service. Sales management involves directing the production force through the seven sales accountabilities that must be performed in a sales job: prospecting, fact finding, preparing proposals, presenting proposals, closing, providing initial client service, and providing long-term service. The agency's sales management system determines the amount of support that the organization will give the producer in each of these areas.

Sales management is considered part of the broader field of marketing. **Marketing**, as the AAI program uses this term, includes finding, identifying the needs of, selling to, and providing service to insureds. Agency personnel responsible for marketing management must make both broad-range decisions that determine the framework for the agency's marketing activities and frequent short-term decisions that implement those planned marketing activities.

The job of the sales manager is to coordinate selling (distribution of the product) with the other elements of a total marketing program. Although he or she is responsible for the general administration of the sales force, a sales manager is also involved in setting year-to-year sales and marketing goals, planning a program to achieve those goals, and evaluating results.

Insurance agencies have two primary functions: selling insurance policies and servicing insureds. If a policy is not sold, it cannot be serviced; and likewise, if it is not serviced, it will become some other firm's sale. Success in both of these functions is crucial to the ongoing success of the agency, effective sales management is important.

The cost of managing and operating a sales force is typically the largest single operating expense in an insurance agency. No matter how great the premium volume and commission revenues are, the revenues are only valuable if the sales expense incurred in generating them is reasonable. Management is the key to keeping the expenses in line by planning and directing the sales activities to reduce or eliminate wasted time and expense because of duplication of effort, inadequate staffing or training, and misdirected energy.

Reluctant Producer-Sales Manager

Too often, a good producer ends up as a reluctant sales manager. An outstanding employee becomes a mediocre supervisor. The producer or employee may neither want nor enjoy this role, yet often must assume it. How?

Consider the following sad but often true tale. In a small agency, the agency producer-principal is acting as the informal sales manager. The agency needs little management because of its size, so the principal can continue to sell. With a small, motivated staff, this loose management system works well for a time.

Then an ambitious new producer causes agency sales to increase, and the agency needs new staff to handle the new business. The increase in staff eventually forces the principal to spend more time managing and less time selling. When another new producer is added, sales increase again, and the principal has even less time for selling.

So the agency principal makes the potentially wise decision to hire a sales manager. But rather than seeking out a person who has the training and ability to focus on the sales management position, the principal takes what appears to be the quick and easy solution. What better choice than choosing the agency's current top producer, who clearly knows both the agency and successful production? Plus, it will be a feather in the producer's cap, as she is recognized for her outstanding achievements by a promotion to management!

So the promotion is given, and the producer is now a sales manager, a position for which she has no training or inclination. But within a few short months, sales are down (largely from the new manager's drop in production), and the other producer has become surly and is threatening to quit, citing the new sales manager's overly critical attitude and "interference" in his activities. The principal must now make a decision about this deteriorating situation: whether to keep the sales manager in this position and risk further problems or to remove the sales manager and take back the management function. Neither decision represents a positive outcome of the producer's promotion.

This agency principal could have avoided this situation by hiring a full-time sales manager who has management training and no production responsibilities. Many agencies would not make this choice, however, because the sales manager's salary would be an expense not offset by that person's sales. The agency principal can decide about this new person by evaluating the costs involved.

First, assume that a principal or producer can generate $200 per hour in commissions in selling. If that principal or producer is spending fifteen hours a week on management activities, the agency is deprived of $3,000 a week in additional revenue that could be used to pay the sales manager's salary. Secondly, agency principals should recognize that the two functions of sales and management require different talents.

The best solution is for the agency to hire a full-time nonproducer manager to take care of the sales management functions and free the best producers to carry out their primary function—selling. Many agencies immediately point out two things: first, if an agency is trying to maximize production without increasing expenses unreasonably, the addition of another nonproducing staff member seems to be moving in the opposite direction; second, in the above example, the total hours assigned to sales management are only fifteen, and waiting to hire someone until the need is full-time is wisest.

Let's consider both objections. First, as a nonproducer, the new employee could affect profitability. In the above example, if the new manager freed up fifteen hours of production time for the current manager, the agency will have $3,000 *more* revenue coming in per week. Assuming the agency's current expense level (before commission to producer) is 50 percent, then $1,500 per week is available to pay the new manager without the agency's giving up any current profits. If a sales manager can run the agency for a total compensation of less than $1,500 a week, the agency would be better off hiring the manager.

As to the second objection, if a full-time manager can be hired for the amount by which the agency can profit by the current manager returning to full-time production, the decision is simple. If not, can a part-time manager be found just to unburden the producer of those fifteen hours? If so, hiring the manager is an advantage.

But both of these "commissions earnable versus salary of sales manager" arguments may greatly underestimate the true potential value to the agency of hiring a full-time sales manager. For example, Paige Proctor, an experienced agency consultant on sales management, cites three costly producer failures that a competent sales manager can help an agency avoid.[1]

- *Hiring the wrong producers*. Often an agency hires in a "crisis" without properly checking and testing. The costs in lost salary and benefits, lost time, and stress on staff (and possibly clients) can be substantial. And this situation assumes the agency actually fires the failing producer, whereas some agencies hang on to such producers as long as possible, hoping the producer will turn things around, but end up losing more money.
- *Improper management*. Some producers are reasonably successful but never achieve truly outstanding production. Proctor reports that some moderately successful producers, when held accountable by a focused sales manager, have doubled their production.
- *Inadequate training*. Since the producer is improperly managed, adequate product knowledge and up-to-date sales training is not provided. The typical closing ratio for a properly trained producer can double compared to an improperly trained producer, once again adding significant revenue to the agency's bottom line.

Other possible gains from a full-time sales manager may include training CSRs for account development and helping the sales manager in planning (and meeting) agency goals and budgets. Each agency should determine, based on its own makeup, personnel, sales potential, and current management, just what the potential gains are in its unique situation.

Sales Management Systems

Since the unique characteristics of the individual agencies mold each sales management system, there are almost as many sales management systems as there are agencies. In some agencies, no one person is responsible for sales management; the responsibility rests with general management personnel or the individual producer. Other firms, particularly exclusive agencies, have highly sophisticated sales management systems to support individual producers. State Farm, for instance, has Agency Leadership teams that work with about thirty local agencies. These teams consist of an Agency Field Executive (the leader of the team), an Agency Field Consultant, an Agency Field Specialist, and additional support personnel. These teams have no direct management authority over the agents (who are independent contractors), but support those agents' efforts with administrative and technical information and guidance. The leadership teams are located in the field and report to that office's Vice President—Agency in the regional office.

Sales management systems, like management systems in general, are divided into two groups: those that plan from "the top down" and those that plan and monitor from "the bottom up."

Top-Down Systems

In a **top-down system**, management sets the long-range and yearly sales goals for the organization and determines how they will be achieved. Salespeople are given specific objectives (for example, $50,000 in new business commissions over the next year, 90 percent retention rate on renewals, and twenty-five new expiration dates per week) to help the agency reach its goals. In large organizations, the goals will work their way down through several levels, as illustrated in Exhibit 3-1. Producers and branches are then monitored periodically to ensure that they are on target. In smaller organizations, the one or two producers will have to meet the agency's goals, but those goals can be relatively simple to administer and control: "We want to grow 20 percent this year; if each of us increases our book of business by 20 percent, we will reach our agency goal."

Bottom-Up Systems

Other agencies have approached sales management from each production unit in order to reach overall goals for the agency. Each producer in a **bottom-up system** outlines what he or she expects to achieve during the year in new sales, retention, personal and technical development, and so forth. At every level managers compile the plans, discussing and reviewing them as necessary, until the agency creates one overall plan. This approach gives individuals and departments more involvement in and control over their work, often increasing motivation. The bottom-up system will not work, however, unless the agency first establishes strategic

Exhibit 3-1
Sales Management From Above—XYZ Agency, 1998

General Corporate Sales Goals

Property-Liability Agency Commissions	—Reach a total of $1,000,000, including $150,000 in new commissions
Prospects	—Increase prospect file to 500 names
Life and Group Premiums	—Add $50,000 in new life commissions and $15,000 in new group commissions

Main Office	Branch Office
$120,000 in new property-liability commissions	(One Producer)
$30,000 new life commissions	$30,000 new property-liability commissions
$15,000 new group commissions	$20,000 new life commissions
400 new prospects	100 new prospects

Producer A	Personal Lines Department
$30,000 new property-liability commissions	$30,000 new property-liability commissions
$10,000 new group	$10,000 new life commissions
150 new prospects	100 new prospects

Producer B
$60,000 new property-liability commissions
$20,000 new life commissions
$5,000 new group commissions
150 new prospects

long-range goals, since the salespeople will need some idea of preferred agency growth patterns to fit the individual goals into the whole. A simple example of conflicting goals occurs when the producer outlines a plan to increase personal lines volume by 25 percent next year, but the agency has agreed to terminate contracts with several personal lines insurers because writing personal lines is no longer a long-range agency goal.

Sales Management as a Bottom-Line Expense

In the preceding discussion of the benefits of hiring a full-time sales manager, a simplified formula was suggested for determining when the cost to the agency would be justified. But this discussion ignores the simple fact that an agency is always paying a cost for management, whether the principal or someone else is doing the job. The reason this cost is often overlooked when the principal is acting as the manager is simply that no management expense appears on the agency's income statement. Thus, the principal concludes mistakenly that sales management is "free," and many principals object that the agency just cannot afford to hire someone to be the sales manager. The fact is, the agency has already hired a sales manager—the principal! The "salary" is being paid in lost time and opportunity to the principal and the agency.

Can this management expense be separated from the agency's income statement as a starting point to determining how much an agency can afford to pay for the sales management position? One way to answer this question is to examine an agency's income statement. Exhibit 3-2 presents a traditional income statement.

The traditional income statement was developed over a long time by accountants in order to have a standard for comparing one organization to another. Although the statement is traditional, it does not always serve the needs of the producer who is required to spend some time in management activities because the statement does not reflect management as a direct expense. Identifying the amount of money lost, in some concrete dollar term, because of management activities would benefit the agency.

In order to determine the cost of management, the producer-sales manager must record his or her time spent in sales and management activities. Once the time distribution is determined, the producer will be able to develop an idea of the amount of time required for sales management of the agency. The principal must begin viewing the day-to-day management and sales management functions as a pure expense item.

Exhibit 3-2
Traditional Agency Income Statement Format

I. Revenue
   A. Property and casualty commissions
   B. Life commissions
   C. Other income
   Total Revenue
II. Sales Expenses
   A. Auto
   B. Advertising
   C. Commissions paid
   D. Etc.
III. Office and General Expense
   A. Rent
   B. Postage
   C. Repairs
   D. Office salaries
   E. Employee benefits
   F. Etc.
   Total Expense
IV. Profit or Loss

Management Expense Modification

In order to isolate the amount of the management expense, a new item could be added to the income statement entitled "Management Expenses." To determine the amount of management expenses, the producer need only multiply the average number of hours spent in management by the average commission income generated from sales activities. Exhibit 3-3 shows the revised income statement.

Exhibit 3-3
Revised Profit or Loss Statement

I. Revenue
II. Sales expense
III. Office and general expense
IV. Management expense
V. Profit or loss

Changes in Revenue Format

The change in the income statement will help the principal determine when full-time management expertise is affordable. However, further changes in the income statement would allow the producer to make more effective use of sales time. One suggested change is in the portion of the profit and loss statement called "Revenue." Often, all agency revenue is lumped together into one figure. In reality, agencies have two sources of revenue—one *controllable* and one *noncontrollable*.

The **controllable sources of revenue** include property and liability commissions, life insurance commissions, health commissions, and perhaps fees for services rendered pertaining to insurance operations. Other types of revenue, not directly related to insurance sales, are called **noncontrollable sources of revenue**. Contingency commissions, for instance, are usually based on some relationship to the agency loss ratio, and are generally not directly controllable. Additionally, interest income may come from investing the cash float generated through agency billing. There may also be other sources of revenues, such as countersignature commissions, service fees from accounts receivable, rent, and so forth. The important point is that revenue can be divided into its controllable and noncontrollable elements.

The biggest controllable item is commission revenue. The more the producer sells, the more commission revenue he or she generates. Most other sources are noncontrollable. For instance, there is little that a producer can do to increase the rate of return received on the cash float or the amount of interest charged on accounts receivable. The return from these last two sources of revenue is outside the agency's control, and therefore good management dictates that a producer should not spend time trying to change things he or she cannot control.

If the income statement were revised to show the differentiation between controllable and noncontrollable revenue, the sales manager could more easily develop a sales plan. The plan would generate the greatest revenue effect for the amount of effort and time available. Exhibit 3-4 shows the revised revenue portion of the income statement.

Exhibit 3-4
Revised Revenue Format

I. Revenue—Controllable
   A. Property and casualty commissions
   B. Life commissions
   C. Health commissions
   D. Fees
   Total Controllable
   Revenue—Noncontrollable
   A. Contingent commissions
   B. Countersignature commissions
   C. Interest income
   Total Noncontrollable
   Other Revenue
   Total Revenue

Changes in Expense Format

The agency may also make some changes with the traditional sales expense items. Again, the purpose of the revision in the traditional income statement is to redirect the producer's sales management time so that the producer is concentrating on those items that will produce the maximum revenue for the agency. Exhibit 3-5 shows the division suggested for sales expenses—direct sales expense and indirect sales expense.

Exhibit 3-5
Revised Sales Expense Format

II. Sales Expenses
   Direct
      A. Compensation to producers
      B. Commissions to others
      C. Bad debts
      D. Entertainment
   Indirect
      A. Advertising
      B. Auto expenses
      C. Goodwill payments

Direct sales expense items include all of those expenses that flow directly from client-oriented sales. This information will allow the agency to know its cost of the sales operations in direct expense dollars. Knowing the cost of sales expenses, the agency can develop figures that determine the actual costs incurred to develop new sales and to handle renewal sales. Furthermore, if the agency has producers compensated on a split of commissions, the additional information will help the agency develop the proper commission-sharing arrangement with producers. Finally, the revised management information is also useful for developing an agency budget.

Percentage Conversion

With the changes suggested thus far, the agency can also modify the income statement into a percentage format that will relate total direct sales expense to total sales expense and total agency expenses. The revised income statement, reflected in percentages, lends itself to budgeting. In fact, a budget could be a reformatted income statement converted into percentage figures as shown in Exhibit 3-6. The right-hand column indicates the percentage, in this case, of controllable revenue and management expenses planned (budgeted) for the year. The center column shows actual results.

Exhibit 3-6
Income Statement Converted to Percentages Instead of Dollars

		Currently	Budgeted
I.	Revenue		
	Controllable		
	A. Property and casualty commissions	75%	60%
	B. Life commissions	10	15
	C. Health commissions	10	15
	D. Fees	5	10
	Total Revenue	100%	100%
II.	Management expense	25%	25%

What if the agency in Exhibit 3-6 had a goal to diversify by means of shifting controllable revenue away from property and casualty sales into life and health commissions and fee revenue? Additionally, the agency had planned to begin to control management expenses. Given the results shown in Exhibit 3-6, the agency might institute the following sales strategies:

1. Solicit current property and casualty clients for life sales
2. Solicit group major medical sales from current commercial clients
3. Assign office management tasks to supervisors so that agency principals may have more time for selling

Another advantage of showing the income statement in percentages is that the agency does not have to disclose dollar figures developed in the budget if these are confidential. Principals may use the percentage figures as a communication tool to involve employees in the budgeting and goal-setting process without compromising the confidentiality of accounting records.

Year-to-Date Change

The traditional income statement tends to give a distorted view of agency operations. The traditional income statement is a view of agency activities through a predetermined chronological period. Since most agencies generate income statements monthly, each statement is just one portion of a twelve-month year. The first monthly report reflects the first month. The second monthly report is added to the first followed by a year-to-date column. Nowhere in the traditional report does an agency get to view twelve months of transactions. For that reason, an additional column could be added to the income statement that shows the last twelve months of activities. Exhibit 3-7 shows dollar figures, but the dollar figures can be converted to percentages.

Exhibit 3-7
Abbreviated Comparative Income Statement—Sales Management Tool

	Current Month	Year to Date	12 Month Cumulative
January 1998			2/1/97 to 1/31/98
Premiums	$100,000	$100,000	$1,000,000
Total revenue	15,000	15,000	150,000
Total expenses	10,000	10,000	100,000
Net income before taxes	5,000	5,000	50,000
February 1998			3/1/97 to 2/28/98
Premiums	$100,000	$200,000	$1,000,000
Total revenue	15,000	30,000	150,000
Total expenses	10,000	20,000	100,000
Net income before taxes	5,000	10,000	50,000[1]
March 1998			4/1/97 to 3/31/98
Premiums	$50,000	$250,000	$950,000
Total revenue	7,500	37,500	142,000
Total expenses	10,000	30,000	100,000
Net income before taxes	–2,500	7,500	42,500[2]
April 1998			5/1/97 to 4/30/98
Premiums	$66,000	$316,600	$950,000
Total revenue	10,000	47,500	142,500
Total expenses	10,000	40,000	100,000
Net income before taxes	0	7,500	42,500[3]
May 1998			6/1/97 to 5/31/98
Premiums	$200,000	$516,600	$1,050,000
Total revenue	30,000	68,500	157,500
Total expenses	10,000	50,000	100,000
Net income before taxes	20,000	18,500	57,500[4]

1. February: No relative change.
2. March: Operations for month were lower than last year or lower than planned. Overall agency size was reduced as a result.
3. April: Traditionally a low sales month. No change over previous year and therefore no relative change in agency.
4. May: Very good sales month. Agency met or exceeded sales for previous year's same month. Overall agency size exceeded $1 million mark.

Sales Activity Control Report

The revised income statement is now a sales management tool because it indicates to the sales manager general areas where efforts should be concentrated. However, the sales manager will have to directly control the activities of the salespeople. A reporting system will allow the sales manager to gather information on sales activities so that he or she may either redirect producers' efforts or identify problems and provide solutions. The sales activity control reports should indicate all of the important producer accountabilities in the sales function. Additionally, the report should and review the relationship between actual performance and goal.

Exhibit 3-8 is a sample weekly sales control report for a producer. In this report, the producer has a goal of contacting ten prospects per work day, obtaining five X-dates, presenting three proposals, and closing one sale. Room is also allowed for other activity such as training and so forth. The preprinted weekly sales report contains daily and weekly goals in each of the goal categories. To the right of the slash, the producer would indicate the actual number. For instance, on Monday, if the producer contacted twelve prospects, in row one the report would read 10/12. If, on that same day, the producer presented only one proposal the report for proposals would read 3/1.

Exhibit 3-8
Weekly Sales Report of ________________

Goal/Actual	Mon	Tues	Wed	Thurs	Fri	Total
1. Prospects contacted	10/–	10/–	10/–	10/–	10/–	50/
2. X-dates	5/–	5/–	5/–	5/–	5/–	25/
3. Proposals	3/–	3/–	3/–	3/–	3/–	15/
4. Sales	1/–	1/–	1/–	1/–	1/–	5/
5. Other activity (training, planning, vacation, etc.)						

The weekly sales control report indicates to the sales manager where producers are spending their time. If producers are successful in reaching their goals, the sales manager does not have to invest additional time in managing those producers. Only when the producers do not succeed in attaining their sales goals must the sales manager become more involved in the sales management process with the producer.

The weekly sales report enables the sales manager to identify the failing producer's major problem. If the goals and objectives have been agreed upon, and if certain goals are not being reached, the problem of the particular producer becomes obvious. For example, if the producer is not prospecting enough, the sales manager can introduce training or direct supervision to help the producer prospect. If the producer is not making enough proposals, the sales manager will have to identify the reason and take corrective action. Not closing enough sales might indicate that the producer needs additional sales training, possibly including communicating, listening, and closing, or that he or she is simply trying to sell to the wrong prospects. Finally, if the producer is not spending enough time X-dating, the manager will notice eventually. Without correction, the producer will eventually run out of things to do, because X-dating provides next week's, next month's, and next year's prospects. Without some sort of organized report, however, the sales manager will not immediately know why the producer is not successful and cannot provide the leadership required to correct the situation.

Collecting X-dates, contacting prospects, making proposals, and closing on sales will eventually lead to commission income. The weekly sales report should be converted to a dollar-based monthly sales report. The monthly report will give an overview of all sales activities and has the additional benefit of being a communications tool to continually remind all the staff members that the agency is a sales organization. Exhibit 3-9 is an example of such a report.

Exhibit 3-9
Monthly Sales Report

Producer ____________________
Month ____________________

	Current month premium/ commission	Year to date premium/ commission	Cumulative last 12 months premium/ commission
Total new business	/	/	/
Total renewal	/	/	/
Combined total	/	/	/

In addition to the traditional current month and year-to-date information found in most sales reports, a cumulative column reflects annual activity of the producer. The sales manager can now monitor whether the agency is growing or shrinking. This type of information should eliminate the fear caused by the fluctuations of business throughout the year.

Another distortion in sales activities is the delay between ordering and delivering a policy. With agency-billed business, an agency cannot record sales and commission income in the month in which the sales take place. For example, if a commercial account renews in February, but the agency does not receive the policy until April, the sale and commission revenue are usually not recorded until April, even though the sale took place in February. When this happens, the sales manager cannot review the real sales activity that took place in February. The only alternatives are either to use the cumulative twelve-month running column, as in Exhibit 3-9, or, preferably, to have the agency prebill and record the income in the month in which the sale or transaction took place.

Management Tip

Although production and agency volume have traditionally been measured in premium dollars, agency budgets are expressed in commission dollars and other income. Thus, the best method for the agency manager to compare actual income to budgeted income is to use commissions on the production reports. The percentage of commissions paid on different types of policies varies greatly. Since life commissions may approach 90 percent and workers compensation commissions may be as low as 2 percent, measuring only premium dollars is neither accurate nor useful.

The success of a producer or another agency employee making a transition to sales manager and using forms similar to those in Exhibits 3-8 and 3-9 depends on a commitment to require the producers he or she supervises to complete and submit a weekly sales report. The sales manager must also commit to recognizing deficiencies and taking corrective action if the reports indicate that a particular producer is not meeting his or her goals. These two commitments sound easy, but they can be extremely difficult to fulfill. However, without the commitment to correct, gathering the information to prove financial results and agency performance merely wastes time.

The suggested modifications to the agency's financial information will help a sales manager not trained in management to isolate problem areas and to find solutions. Using the modifications suggested, the agency can meet its overall goals. The modified documents may be used as a form of communication to the production staff and support staff to work toward the same goals, which enhances the team spirit within the agency.

The Seven Planning Phases and the Sales Management Process

Once the sales manager is ready to develop sales plans, the same seven phases in the overall agency planning should be followed: (1) mission statement, (2) strategies, (3) goals, (4) objectives, (5) budgets, (6) policies, and (7) procedures. A complete description of these planning phases was presented in a previous assignment in this segment.

Sales Mission Statement

The sales manager need not develop a mission statement. The agency principals should draw up the mission statement. However, the duty of the sales manager is to help convert the agency's sales strategies into producer sales goals, objectives, budgets, and policies and procedures.

Sales Strategies

Typical sales strategies for an insurance agency could involve volume, business mix, specialization, and so forth. Volume strategies would be designed to have the agency's volume grow to a planned level. Business mix strategies involve a conscious plan to change from some given percentage of sales in an area (such as commercial) and increase some other area, such as life insurance. Specialization strategies may include growth in narrowly defined areas such as professional liability or growth from a predetermined market such as current customers.

One large West Coast agency has developed several related sales strategies. One is to expand its base of operation by acquiring branch offices and establishing regional centers in key cities throughout the western region of the United States to better serve its clients in that area. Another strategy is to develop loss control and risk management services since the agency's market will consist of firms doing $2 million to $50 million in sales, firms not large enough to have their own risk management departments. A third strategy is to establish and maintain good relationships with insurance companies that can provide the necessary coverages and services.

This agency's fourth strategy is to establish an organized method of obtaining prospects. All insurance buyers of the defined size operating in the western United States are suspects. To turn these suspects into prospects with policy information and expiration dates, this firm is expanding its existing newsletter follow-up call procedure. The informational newsletter, which gives the reader a synopsis of business and insurance news, is sent to a wide spectrum of businesses. The newsletter provides agency recognition and allows the agency to establish and maintain an identity. Each newsletter includes a reply card, used in conjunction with a telephone solicitation program, to obtain prospect information. Producers use these cards and calls to make appointments with these qualified leads.

Sales Goals and Objectives

The agency defines the size of accounts it wants to pursue, and all businesses within this size in the western United States are considered suspects.

Agency planning begins with broad missions and narrow strategies that are consistent from year to year. Modifications in both mission and strategies should be made as conditions change, but both are characteristically stable. Goals and objectives, on the other hand, usually do change from year to year. Goals and objectives should be narrower in purpose than strategies and are the final target for a one-year planning period. In contrast to mission statements and strategies, which are broad and general, goals and objectives are specific, measurable, time-bounded, controllable, and oriented to results. They should be meaningful, challenging, and committed to writing.

Agency Sales-Related Budgets

Although the most common use of budgeting is to allocate *money* in such a way that it will best serve the agency's goals, the allocation of *people* and *time* is also an important aspect of the budgeting process. Just as the sales manager should allocate available money, he or she must also allocate the producer's and CSRs' time. Finally, as sales grow, a budget for allocating support staff should be planned.

Policy Statements

Following are some examples of common policy statements used in property and liability agencies and brokerages:

1. A 25 percent down payment (minimum) must accompany all new business applications.
2. All commercial accounts generating premiums under $5,000 annually will be handled by the Small Accounts Unit.
3. Renewals for Personal Lines V.I.P. accounts are handled by the producers; all other renewals are the responsibility of the personal lines CSRs.

These and other policies tell personnel what to do in certain situations and define the general rules of work. They help to smooth out work flow and speed up processing by eliminating the need to make decisions on certain processes.

Procedures

The importance of written procedures is something that a growing agency often overlooks. Pressures of daily work always seem to take precedence over such administrative tasks as creating procedures to follow. The result is duplication of effort and inefficient processing, which affect both the sales and servicing functions. Consequently, producers spend less time selling and more time trying to solve problems or find out where something is.

Agencies with well-structured sales management systems provide written guidelines for producers. Step-by-step procedures facilitate training and help maintain quality control in the field. When calling on prospects to quote, producers sometimes get "yes" answers and sometimes get "no" answers. Written procedures are helpful in responding to either answer. Sample procedures for producer activity are illustrated in Exhibit 3-10 for either a "yes" or "no" prospect response.

Sales Management Organization

An effective sales organization provides the framework for producers and support personnel to interact effectively.

Sales organizations are not static. They must be able to adapt to changes. At various stages in its life, a business will have to alter its organizational structure to accommodate growth or changes in the market. The organization needs to be flexible enough to handle change and yet stable enough to withstand the inevitable trauma that accompanies organizational change.

Theoretically, an agency could be set up in almost any organizational structure a manager could think of, but certain structures have proven to be more effective than others. Usually, work between sales and support personnel will be distributed in one of the following ways:

- By line of business

- By production unit
- By volume
- Alphabetically by account
- A combination of more than one of these

The first step in organizing sales management is establishing a structure. This structure includes isolating activities and functions, combining activities and functions, and determining job interrelationships.

Exhibit 3-10
Sellsmore Agency, Inc., Sample Procedures and Forms

Position: Commercial Accounts Producer
Function: Initial Call on Prospect
Date of this revision: June 1, 19__
Replaces revision of: January 1, 19__

1. Make presentation that reviews the programs available through the agency, loss control emphasis, billing plans, stability of the agency and/or insurance companies.
2. Response from prospect is:

Yes

a. Gather information on prospect
   - Current coverage and policies
   - Expiration dates
   - General info needed for quoting

b. Set time to return for presentation
c. Submit information to Commercial Accounts Assistant for preparation of proposal and marketing
d. Maintain suspense to contact prospect every two weeks until proposal has been prepared

No

a. Thank prospect for time
b. Obtain expiration dates
c. Make notes on exposures
d. Update prospect system
e. Suspense for re-solicitation
f. Determine plans for a second attempt by discussing situation with Sales Manager
g. Re-solicit as planned

3. When proposal has been prepared by the Commercial Accounts Assistant, proceed according to the guidelines in the procedure on Presenting Proposals.

Isolate Activities and Functions

In establishing a structure for an agency, management must define and isolate the major marketing and selling functions. For a firm producing property and liability insurance, these activities include sales management, property-liability sales, business placement with insurance companies, rating and quoting, policy processing, accounting, word processing, filing, and perhaps reception. When establishing a structure for an

I. **Agency Management and Sales Management**
D. The Seven Planning Phases and the Sales Management Process
E. **Sales Management Organization**
II. Sales Management of People

existing agency, management must forget the current structure and list the functions performed without regard to the existing positions or persons now handling that activity.

A good place to begin isolating sales activities is the producer's job description. **Seven key producer accountabilities** or functions are necessary to sell and retain clients: prospecting, fact-finding, preparing proposals, physically presenting understandable proposals to the client/ prospect, closing, initial service, and long-term service.

Prospecting

The sales process begins with prospecting. Producers must build and maintain a bank of potential clients to have a readily available group of people to call. In most property and liability agencies, each producer is responsible for prospecting. In some agencies, however, prospecting is the responsibility of the agency, and special staff is hired to mail information, call for expiration dates, and arrange appointments for the sales staff. This type of prospecting, commonly known as telemarketing, is becoming more common.

Since producers should be as free as possible to sell, agency principals should look for ways to maximize their producers' selling time. Many agencies have shifted prospecting duties to a telemarketer within the agency or have even hired outside services that can produce leads. Generally, market segmentation here is by Standard Industrial Classification (SIC) codes, ZIP Codes, or other preferences of the agency.

Fact Finding

Most insurance sales are based on matching an insurance product or service with a specific need of the prospect. Fact-finding involves mainly exposure identification. A prospect may then be interested in a proposal for insurance based on his or her needs. The fact-finding process may simply be a physical inspection of the various operations or premises or may involve using preprinted survey forms, drawing flowcharts of operations, or even researching financial statements to determine which items of value need protection. All of these techniques (and others) are discussed in greater detail in other assignments in the AAI program.

Preparing a Proposal

When the needs of the prospect have been identified, the producer prepares and discusses the proposal. A copy of the formal proposal is maintained in the agency files or database of an errors and omissions problem and can be used for call-backs if the prospect does not purchase. If the prospect does buy, the proposal goes into the client's file so that coverage not sold may be presented again in future calls.

Preparation of a proposal involves contacting insurers to see whether coverage is available, rating or pricing the coverage, and listing coverage alternatives such as different deductibles or limits of liability, separately priced. The format of a proposal is discussed in another assignment of AAI 83.

Presenting the Proposal

Clarity is important in the actual presentation of the proposal to the prospect—the prospect must be able to understand what the presenter is saying. Using insurance jargon such as "ACV," "products liability," or "coinsurance" can be confusing to many prospects. Liberal use of illustrations, examples, and the simplest possible language are essential when presenting a complex technical insurance proposal. In addition, presenters will use their sales skills; some producers are good salespersons naturally, but others benefit from sales training.

Closing

Closing, or asking for the sale, is considered part of proposal presentation. Many agencies, however, use inside technical or support people to present part or all of the proposal and leave closing to the producer. Either way, closing is vital—few people will buy if they are not asked to buy.

Initial Service

Initial service includes completing and signing applications, collecting money, perhaps issuing a binder along with a binder bill, and so forth. Sometimes the producer handles only the first of these tasks, with others in the agency taking care of the rest. In any event, the initial service is essential in establishing a healthy, long-term relationship with a client.

Long-Term Service

Once the policy has been issued, it must be delivered, audits may be arranged, and mid-term contact with the client should be planned. Before renewal, new information on operations should be gathered. Claims may require follow-up action. Duties associated with long-term service, such as audits and claims, should be carefully allocated and supervised in order to meet (and possibly exceed) the client's expectations, which will help maintain and perhaps increase the client's business.

The support staff must do any of the seven accountabilities not assigned to producers. For example, if an agency has decided that the accountabilities of the producer include only fact finding, presentation of proposals to prospects, and closing, some other employee or employees are charged with prospecting (a sales center), proposal preparation (underwriting), and initial and long-term service (customer service representatives). In another agency, the producer may be charged with all seven of the accountabilities.

Combine Functions or Activities

If the agency is still relatively small, some of these functions will have to be consolidated into multi-function job positions since any one of the functions would not keep a person occupied full time. For instance, the same position may encompass both sales and sales management. On the other hand, very large agencies can afford to have specialization within a major function. Salespeople, for instance, are frequently divided by line of business (such as surety specialist) or type of account (such as school accounts). In general, the larger the agency, the more it lends itself to specialization.

Deciding how far to go in dividing or consolidating the functions is not a simple matter. Since the manager or sales manager wants the new structure to be applicable for some period of time without major revisions, the temptation is to create more positions than is practical, hoping the agency will grow to fit them in several years. The problem with this approach is that the agency will have a difficult time growing unless the people working there can operate efficiently and capably. Creating twenty-five different job descriptions for an agency currently employing ten people defeats the purpose of setting up a formal structure in the first place.

A manager must determine the optimum number of jobs. Experience helps, but many agency managers and principals have had little management experience. Lacking that, many have relied on rule of thumb measurements to determine the number of people and positions required. One of the most commonly used measurements is the "average revenue per employee" guide. Given total projected revenues for the next year, a manager can estimate the number of people needed to sell and service that business by figuring an average of between $80,000 and $100,000 in revenues per employee—counting everyone in the agency, not just producers. An agency expecting substantial growth in the next several years would use the low end of this guide, and an established agency that is not expecting to expand much would use the upper end in planning personnel and job requirements.

Management Tip

A danger in using this type of measurement is that a manager might try to adhere to it too closely without taking into account the unique features of the agency. For instance, a firm handling mostly personal lines might generate a lower revenue per employee. A highly automated agency with nearly all business on direct bill should expect higher average revenue per employee. As with any tool, the "average revenue per employee" figure should be adapted to the particular agency.

Determine Job Interrelationships

Once the major functions have been assigned to job positions, the next step is to decide how these positions should relate to each other. There are many possible configurations, so no one way is right. Each organization has its own needs, and the manager must take them into account. However, the jobs are related, and the relationships must be clearly communicated to everyone concerned. Reporting relationships need to be defined, and responsibility must be granted with requisite authority.

One of the most frequently debated issues is the relationship between producers and support personnel. A producer's primary function is selling. Should this position also have the responsibility of seeing that the policy gets issued accurately and on time? If so, does this mean the producer should be given management authority over the service personnel? A person who is sales-oriented and who was hired to sell may now be spending time as a manager. Is this shared time the best way to maximize the skills and abilities of all the personnel? Some agencies have created a structure in which the producers all report to the sales manager and the support personnel are responsible to an administrative manager. In smaller agencies, it might be more practical to have both sales and service personnel reporting directly to the president.

Regardless of the structure, all personnel involved must still understand that each is important to the overall success of the agency-client relationship. If the producer, for example, only does fact finding, proposal presentation, and closing, he or she must work closely with those who obtain the prospects, those who prepare the proposals, and those who are introduced to the client at the sale close as the service representatives of the agency.

Management Tip

In a quality management environment, the focus on managerial authority is shifted to "teams." In an effective team approach, the sharing of time between sales and management can be minimized, as both producer and support staff are individually responsible to the team. Both have responsibility *to* the other and support *for* the other, but neither has authority *over* the other.

Management must communicate the interrelationships between jobs in an organization to all employees. The number of agencies in which the employees do not have a clear understanding of how they fit into the whole or even to whom they report is surprising. Inadequately communicating reporting responsibilities can result in confusion, which will consequently affect productivity and may cause dissatisfaction and morale problems. Management should provide an organizational chart to help minimize misunderstandings. These charts can include job titles or names or both, and they may be basic or detailed. The previous assignment presented representative organizational charts

Check your understanding of the *Key Words and Phrases* found in the first part of this assignment.

Sales management (p. 2) — to put producers in touch with the right customers & prospects at the right time, right place, right product or service.

Marketing (p. 2)

Top-down system (p. 5)

Bottom-up system (p. 5)

Controllable sources of revenue (p. 8)

Noncontrollable sources of revenue (p. 8)

i.e. - interest income
- contingency

* Seven key producer accountabilities (p. 18)

prospecting
Fact-Finding (needs, APPS)
preparing proposals
presenting proposals
closing
initial service
long-term service

Review the concepts presented in the first part of this assignment by answering the following questions. **Note: Acceptable answers to all questions appear at the end of this segment.**

1. What is a sales manager's job in an insurance agency? (p. 2)

- general administration of sales force
- year to year sales & marketing goals
- planning a program to achieve those goals
- evaluating results

2. What are the two primary functions of insurance agencies? (p. 2)

1) - selling insurance policies
2) - servicing insureds

3. Why should an agency hire a nonproducing sales manager? (p. 4)

to take care of sales management functions like hiring and training and allow producers to sell.

Indirect expenses - Administrative salaries

4. What are two types of sales management systems? (p. 5)

Top-Down - management sets long range & yearly sales goals & determines how to achieve

Bottom-Up - producers set individual goals and a agency creates an overall plan from them.

5. What are three sources of controllable income? (p. 8)

- property & liability commissions
- life insurance commission
- health commissions

& possible fees

6. What types of expenses can be considered direct sales expenses? (p. 9)

- Commission to Producers
- Commissions to Others
- Bad Debts
- Entertainment

7. How can a traditional income statement be revised so that it becomes a sales management tool? (p. 12)

8. What steps should management take in establishing a structure for sales management? (p. 14)

Sales Mission Statement
Sales Strategies
Sales Goals & Objectives
Budgets
Policies
Procedures

Apply the concepts presented in the first part of this assignment by answering the following questions.

1. Two producers are talking about their agencies. One says that each year he is given his sales goals without the benefit of any discussion. He does not like this approach. The second producer says that she develops her own sales goals after her annual performance evaluation.

   (a) Explain the types of sales management system each producer works within.

   He is in Top-Down

   She is in Bottom-Up

   (b) Describe how each approach is coordinated with agency planning and budgeting.

   Top Down - Mgt sets goals & sales force must meet them

   Bottom-Up - Producers set goals & agency develops plan

2. When promoted to management, an agency's best producer often becomes known as a reluctant producer-sales manager.

   (a) Why might such a producer not want this promotion?

   —Doesn't like managing
   —Decreases sales, negatively affecting earning ability

   (b) Explain how analyzing an agency's income statement will help a reluctant producer-sales manager know when he or she can go back to full-time sales.

   (c) Why might an agency be better served by choosing someone other than the top producer to fill this position?

   —someone with better management skills
   —won't decrease commissions earned

3. What changes could an agency make in its traditional income statement that would help with sales management?

   —percentage conversion
   —year to date—compare to budget

4. Agency revenues may be either controllable or noncontrollable.

   (a) What are the major sources of controllable revenue?

   Commission — property & liability
   life ins
   health
   fees

   (b) What are the major sources of noncontrollable revenue? Why are they considered noncontrollable? How should they be treated when establishing an agency budget?

Read the definitions of the *Key Words and Phrases* that follow. Being familiar with these important words will help you better understand the second part of this assignment.

Judgment and experience standards	Frequently used standards employed by agencies that are based on the judgment and experience of management
Historical standards	A performance standard either from internal or external sources, based on past performance
Engineered standards	A performance standard based on an objective quantitative analysis of a specific work situation and designed to measure the potential output of individuals

Study the second part of this assignment, which includes the following sections:

II. Sales Management of People
III. An Argument for Change

Sales Management of People

Sales management of people involves staffing the agency appropriately, adding producers effectively, compensating producers to meet agency objectives, setting performance standards, and implementing sales management controls.

Staffing the Agency

Finding the right people is often the most difficult task that a manager faces, but it is also one of the most important because without capable people to carry out the plan, the other functions of management have little meaning. According to the *IIABA Best Practices* study, no high-achieving agency could exist without obtaining and retaining the best, most capable people.

Positions

The AAI program refers to producers and support personnel, the people who perform the sales and the service functions, respectively. There are actually several different types of sales and servicing positions. Some agencies are large enough to have a person occupying each of them, and some are so small that the one or two people perform all the necessary functions. Following are typical agency positions:

- The sales manager's primary job is the management of the sales function and the people who perform it. The job entails market analysis, sales planning and organization, and recruiting, selecting, training, and leading salespeople. In some agencies, the person responsible for sales management also directs the advertising and public relations efforts and encourages sales consciousness among nonsales staff members.

I. Agency Management and Sales Management
II. Sales Management of People
  A. Staffing the Agency
  B. Adding New Producers
  C. Producer Orientation, Training, and Development

- Salespeople in the property and liability insurance business are usually referred to as "producers." In some organizations, the term refers only to those people whose job is to "produce" new business. The people who service accounts and "sell" renewals are called account coordinators, account executives, customer service agents (CSAs), or customer service representatives (CSRs). In other firms, all of the people who deal with clients are called producers or account executives, and the various sales or service functions they perform are not distinguished.
- The term "support staff" can refer to all of the positions that help service the business, from account coordinators to data entry. In other organizations, the "support staff" means the group of people working directly with the producers, clients, or insurance company underwriters.
- The technical staff consists of those people who underwrite, rate policies, provide loss control and claims services, or perform other duties requiring a certain skill or level of technical expertise in the insurance business.

Management Tip

As it grows, an organization can distribute the sales, technical, and support functions among more levels of jobs. Nontechnical personnel can perform routine or administrative tasks, freeing the more highly trained technical people and producers. The productivity of the entire agency will increase if technical staff can exercise their training and salespeople can sell.

Job Descriptions in the Agency

Job descriptions describe the basic functions that each job is expected to handle. Written job descriptions should be provided to the employees when they are hired or promoted to a new position. See Appendix A at the end of this assignment for sample CSR job descriptions, one for commercial lines accounts and one for personal lines accounts.

Compensation of Support Personnel

How much support personnel should be paid (producer compensation will be discussed later in this assignment) depends on cost of living in the area, level of expertise required for the position, experience, responsibilities of the job, industry standards, and the agency's profit margin. Frequently, salary ranges are established for each job classification, and employees are paid according to their own performance and experience within this range. The position in the salary range may be determined by points assigned in the performance evaluation.

Two ways to pay employees are salary or commission, with several combinations of the two creating other options. Servicing and support personnel are usually paid a salary, but many may be compensated at least partially by commission or bonuses based on new sales. Either method has advantages. People on salary tend to be more agency-oriented and to be team players. People on commission tend to be more aggressive and sales-oriented.

Servicing and support personnel are most often salaried, but they may share in their production team's success or the agency's profitability with an incentive bonus at year end. Bonuses are more common in the independent agency system, but the other production systems offer incentive bonuses, too.

Agencies sometimes use bonuses not tied directly to production and not meant to be a part of the person's normal remuneration incentives to do something extra. Particularly if based on total agency profit and goals rather than individual achievement, bonuses are effective in developing teamwork and cooperation. Nonproduction personnel may, for instance, be given a flat amount for every X-date they acquire. Sometimes agencies pay employees a flat sum for referring other potential employees. Holiday bonuses of varying amounts may be given out. Although some people may stay enthusiastic for an entire year after receiving a year-end bonus, many agencies find that paying a quarterly bonus has a greater effect on employee performance.

Positive feedback is extremely important on both the agency and the individual level. When people perform well, they need to be rewarded with recognition and more tangible feedback. The key is *not* the reward itself, but the giving of it to recognize and positively reinforce a job well done.

Adding New Producers

Because sales are the heart of the agency, it makes good sense to find out what makes a good producer and how these people can be attracted to the insurance business.

Some estimates claim that 80 percent of the people recruited and trained by large companies were no longer with the company that recruited them after three years. The small agency or brokerage firm cannot afford this kind of turnover. As a result, the firm must plan and proceed carefully to avoid spending unnecessary dollars increasing the sales force.

Reasons for Adding Producers

One major reason for adding a producer is to ensure perpetuation of the firm. Unfortunately, some agency owners have added a producer with the intention of retiring immediately. There is nothing wrong with adding producers for the purpose of perpetuation of the agency, but it must be done a number of years before retirement if it is going to be successful. Another mistake is hiring someone close to the agency principal's own age, which does not help solve the perpetuation or continuation problem. If the reason for adding a producer is perpetuation, the added producer should be someone substantially younger than the principal. The addition should be made early enough to give the individual adequate training so he or she can take over the firm when the appropriate time comes.

Another reason for adding a producer is to stimulate the agency's growth. This growth does not necessarily mean getting "big," but means at least increasing the agency's size to the point where increased commission income exceeds the increased overhead. With the downward pressure on commission percentages, premium volume must often be increased (and the agency better managed) just to maintain profits.

There are other reasons why principals might wish to add producers, but perpetuation and growth are probably the soundest reasons. Agency principals adding producers should be sure they understand the objective and the cost in time and effort necessary to achieve that objective. A look at the procedure for adding producers may help with this process.

Planning for a New Producer

Planning for a new producer is more than just recognizing that additional sales growth is needed. Crucial to the planning is developing a job description for the new producer. Most agency principals, consciously or unconsciously, want to hire a new producer "just like me." Principals may forget that it took them a long time to be a profitable part of the operations. Consequently, new producers are hired with great expectations, and disappointment rapidly follows. On the other hand, some principals have no definite expectations for a new producer. When this is the case, the new producer may be placed behind a desk with a stack of files. He or she may gradually absorb enough knowledge or may, unfortunately, become bored and quit. Properly establishing a job description for the new producer clearly gives both the principal and prospective producers a logical path for growth.

A producer need not be held accountable for all seven sales functions described earlier. In fact, some agencies have found that removing some of the functions from the producer not only improved production but also allowed the agency to reduce the commission split paid producers. For example, some producers hate to prospect. They want to hand over prospecting to someone inside the agency. The sales center or telemarketing idea is basically this approach. Naturally, since the producer does not prospect and the agency does, the agency retains a portion of the normal commission split. Producers generally like the idea despite the reduction in their split because it allows them to concentrate on the tasks they are good at—such as presentations and closing. They find their income actually rising because they are spending more time selling and less in what they consider unproductive prospecting. A similar argument can be made for the long-term service function.

The major planning effort in hiring a new producer is to set the job qualifications. First the principals or sales manager must determine which of the seven sales functions the producers will be responsible for. These become the job accountabilities. Each accountability represents certain tasks the producer must accomplish—such as completing a survey for the fact finding accountability. The tasks are then separated into the required knowledge, needed skills, and personal traits needed to accomplish them. Once all of these are known, the sales manager may begin prospecting for new producers.

Prospecting for Producers

The traditional sources for producers are employees of insurance companies or producers in other agencies. Generally, employees of insurers have been attractive because their technical knowledge is good and the agency personnel know about their people skills. Producers from other agencies can be successful, but their success is not guaranteed.

Other sources of potential producers include noninsurance sales-related organizations and organizations that hire people and develop their interpersonal skills. Such organizations include banks, schools, real estate agencies, and so forth. An often neglected source is the agency itself. Many times support staff make excellent producers with little additional training. These people already know the organization and can become productive rapidly.

Another source is advertising. With a properly written job description, a newspaper advertisement can be generated with sufficient detail about the job of producer to attract those who would otherwise not know or find out about the job opening. Essentially, any good source of employees, such as referrals or those mentioned above, can help the agency prospect for producers.

Project InVEST

One organized effort to interest and educate high school and community college students in the insurance business is Project InVEST, a course sponsored and promoted by the Independent Insurance Agents and Brokers of America. When participating in the program, students create a total insurance environment, complete with agencies, insurers, underwriting, coverages, rating, selling, claims adjusting, and bookkeeping. "Insurance" is sold by "agents" to other students and "underwritten" by the "insurers." While learning what it takes to run any type of successful business, students specifically acquire training that can become the basis of a future in the insurance industry. It is estimated that one third of InVEST graduates pursue various insurance careers.

Screening Out Potential Producers

Any attempt to locate employees will generally bring applicants who are not qualified or suited to the job. Three steps help to quickly eliminate or screen out those obviously not right for the job of producer: the initial contact, an application for employment, and a short interview.

The initial contact may be in person, by mail, or on the telephone. A few questions should be devised that can be asked or checked against any written information the candidate sends in. The questions are based on the major qualifications for the job that are considered essential for the job of producer. Each agency will have different qualifications, so describing them all here is impossible. Anyone rejected following the initial contact should be notified in writing immediately. Those meeting this first qualification are invited to a short interview.

Obtaining an application is another process that can be used to screen out applicants. The application is studied, and if the applicant continues to qualify, he or she is invited for a short interview.

A ten-to-fifteen-minute interview allows applicants to see the job description and agree to proceed further or decide that the job is not right for them. The short interview also allows the interviewer to obtain information on the applicant's background to see whether the agency is further interested. If there is mutual interest, an in-depth interview is scheduled.

Screening-In

The screening-out process eliminates those not qualified for the job; screening-in attempts to find those remaining applicants who will fit into the organization. Screening-in involves an in-depth interview, testing, checking references, and making the hiring decision. The previous assignment discussed complete details on both the screening-in and screening-out processes.

Agencies often use standardized tests before offering employment. One such test used by agencies is administered by Personality Dynamics, Inc., of Princeton, New Jersey.[2] Both the Independent Insurance Agents and Brokers of America and the Professional Insurance Agents have endorsed it. Its main thrust is to measure the qualities most often found in successful sales personnel and managers. Traits such as empathy, ego-drive, leadership, and delegation ability are measured in the test and related to traits of individuals who have been successful in similar positions. Other testing services are available and may provide similar information about prospective employees.

Employment Contracts

A characteristic of the independent agency system is that expirations are a property right owned by the agency. As a result, the customer lists and expiration date information are important items of proprietary information. A condition of employment with many agencies is that producers sign agreements not to compete on accounts of the firm for a specified period of time after leaving the firm. These nonpiracy and noncompete agreements (discussed earlier in this text) are included in an employment contract. Direct writers and exclusive agency companies generally have new producers sign contracts that stipulate that the producer may not write business for other insurance companies during the term of employment. All distribution systems may limit the access to client files for both producers and support personnel.

Management Tip

As more client contact responsibilities are delegated to support personnel, agency employers should consider having nonpiracy and noncompete agreements drawn up for all such employees. When a good CSR leaves the agency, he or she can take along far more valuable and abundant client information than many producers may possess, and thus cause far more damage if another agency uses that information to take those customers away. Such contracts provide protection for the employer and reinforce for the employee the importance of the job and the confidentiality of the information.

Producer Orientation, Training, and Development

When a producer is hired, he or she must be oriented to the agency. The procedures and work flow of the agency can be explained. The producer may, for instance, trace a new piece of business from its inception to its conclusion. All production people outside of the agency, such as marketing representatives and company underwriters, should be introduced.

Training the new producer is easy if the job description and job qualification have been properly drawn. If the accountabilities from the job description have been translated into duties on the job qualifications form, there may be certain knowledge, skills, and helpful personal traits that the new producer did not bring to the job. These constitute areas for training.

Ideally, an agency could hire someone new to the insurance business and train the new producer according to the desires of the agency. Most agencies, however, hire someone already familiar with the business, but this person is also familiar with the way that his or her former employer did business. A new person does not have to forget old and bad habits and then learn the new ways of doing business.

Agency Training and Development

Whether for new employees just brought into the agency or for veterans who have filled a position for years, insurance is a dynamic and rapidly changing business, requiring ongoing training and development if all employees are to adequately perform their assigned tasks at a high level.

Employees can turn to many sources for continuous education. Trade journals, industry newsletters, insurance sites on the Internet, and participation in groups such as Young Agents or The National Association of Insurance Women provide valuable opportunities for new and experienced employees to gain additional knowledge. So many resources are available, in fact, the employee can become overwhelmed by the amount of information. The key is to balance the educational pursuits with the employee's needs. Quality, not quantity, of learning is the goal.

Management Tip

Don't confuse the term *continuous education* with *continuing education*. Many states now require licensed individuals to earn certain numbers of continuing education hours in order to renew their licenses. This should not change the goal of education—to gain knowledge and skill. If the focus becomes "getting the hours," the courses taken may be a total waste of valuable employee training time. Focus on the *content*, not the *credits*.

Sources of Training and Education

With few exceptions, independent insurance agencies are relatively small businesses and lack the resources to develop or administer an in-house training program. Agencies will provide on-the-job training but usually must turn to outside sources for formal training for new and existing employees.

Many organizations offer education, training, and development courses. Insurance companies, producer trade associations, the Institutes, and other educational institutions and organizations are sources of low-cost, high-quality programs. Insurance company programs, educational institutions, agent-association-sponsored programs, and other courses provide both basic and specialized instruction in many topics related to production. But they do not provide a structured goal-oriented program of training for agents and support personnel. All of the elements of a top-notch program may be available, but the producer or service person still needs a plan to follow. The individual agency must provide educational assistance and training. Creative principals who recognize that they must take qualified inexperienced personnel and turn them into insurance professionals need to develop training programs using these outside programs combined with on-the-job instruction and experience:

- *Insurer training*. In response to the need for formal training, many insurance companies operating through independent agents and brokers have programs that train production personnel.

  Typically, these insurance company schools consist of several weeks of in-depth study in commercial property and liability coverages, with each of the companies emphasizing the products they are particularly interested in selling. In most cases, the schools are meant for persons who have been in the business for some time and have perhaps been selling for a year or two. Some insurance companies do have correspondence courses that cover terminology and concepts of insurance.

  In conjunction with their training courses, some insurance companies actively assist agencies recruiting new producers. Agencies that cannot afford to subsidize a new person during the time it takes him or her to become productive can benefit from this assistance. Examples include a referral system of prospective employees and no-interest financing for new producers' salaries.
- *Producer associations*. Local, state, and national agents' associations have developed seminars, correspondence courses, and workshops to address the training needs of producers for the different stages of their professional development. Both the Independent Insurance Agents and Brokers of America and the Professional Insurance Agents offer their members insurance and management courses.
- *Private vendors*. Many basic and some advanced training programs are available from private vendors. Companies such as the Merrit Company, the National Underwriter Company, Pictorial Publishers, and Insurance Marketing and Management Services (IMMS) have developed self-study materials used extensively for training both producers and staff members.

- *The Institutes.* The American Institute for Chartered Property Casualty Underwriters (AICPCU) and the Insurance Institute of America (IIA) have educational and development programs to prepare both new and experienced personnel to better handle their jobs. Offering courses such as *How Insurance Works* (INTRO), the Program in General Insurance (INS), and courses in more specific areas, as this Accredited Adviser in Insurance program, the Institutes have done much to standardize the instruction for independent agency, brokerage, and exclusive or direct writing insurance company producers.
- *Other educational organizations.* Numerous other educational programs are related to insurance. The American College has the Chartered Life Underwriter (CLU) professional designation for those with careers in life insurance and related financial services. The College also offers a Chartered Financial Consultant (ChFC) professional designation emphasizing financial planning.

  The College of Financial Planning offers a Certified Financial Planner (CFP) designation. The Society of Certified Insurance Counselors has a lecture program leading to the CIC designation.

Simple Sales Tasks

An agency might hire a producer to train him or her to handle the complex risk management of large commercial accounts. However, to reach that level of expertise most efficiently, the newly hired producer will concentrate on small commercial lines, beginning with businessowners policies and "niche" products. The agency often turns over a group of customers to the producer, and the producer looks for new accounts. The sale of a new policy requires the producer to be persuasive; but the renewal may only require delivery of a new policy. New producers will not require extensive technical knowledge to maintain these accounts, so the agency will not have to provide much training at this stage. Most duties will be routine. Renewals are processed and mailed. Prospects are mailed letters, and phone calls are made to obtain appointments.

Complex Sales Tasks

After three to five years, when the producer is ready to address the risk management needs of large commercial lines accounts, the situation changes. The sales task becomes a problem-solving exercise, perhaps involving many noninsurance techniques. The importance of transmitting information about the treatment of exposures to the client increases dramatically. Essentially, the producer is now addressing the more complex needs of clients and prospects. Premiums or fees become higher, as do potential profits per account. Because the market for large commercial accounts is significantly smaller than for businessowners policies, customers are fewer. The producer must get the necessary training to do all these complex sales tasks.

Commitment Necessary for New Producers

No organization would spend time and money to recruit a new employee expecting to see that employee fail. However, too many times employees are hired and are then allowed to drift, making launching a successful career difficult, if not impossible. Agencies and producers are not immune. Sometimes producers fail because they are in the wrong business, but too often they fail because they lack commitment to their success in the agency.

The commitment necessary to promote a producer's success requires production-oriented duties, with or without supervision, to generate business. The person who hires the producer must make sure that any areas of knowledge, skill, and education in which the producer is weak are covered in the training process. The producer must draw up a personal production plan based on the production responsibilities in the job description and the agency's plan. Jointly, the sales manager of the agency and the producer agree on the producer's plan. Both must also use control, sales, or activity reports to ensure satisfactory progress. Finally, both the producer and the sales manager must note if the producer becomes bored with the type of sales. When the producer becomes competent and wants to sell more challenging and profitable insurance, both parties should attempt to increase the responsibilities of the producer.

Increasing Job Responsibilities

Few people are happy to accept a position in an organization and remain in that same position for long. Initially, the responsibilities of a job exceed the competence of the individual for that job. As illustrated in Exhibit 3-11, the shaded area represents the need for training, but this need changes as the individual is trained and becomes more familiar with the job. Essentially, the job assigned remains static, and the duties and responsibilities of the job are constant. But through training and on-the-job experience, the area of ability of the employee grows. At some point, the producer's ability exceeds the job responsibilities.

Because the area of ability grows, the sales manager must acknowledge that the producer may begin experiencing job dissatisfaction, perhaps felt by both the producer and staff. To eliminate problems from this dissatisfaction, changing the job's dimensions and responsibilities, or moving the producer to more demanding and complex sales, will help to develop the producer.

As the producer grows in ability, the markets the producer sells to tend to change, thus automatically providing growing job responsibilities as the area of ability grows.

Certain producers, however, may honestly not want to change. Management should decide whether they can or should develop these people further. A semi-retired producer, for example, may be perfectly happy with the current book of business, and no further development is necessary. But for most people, growth is a natural process that can and should be encouraged with continual development of job duties and responsibilities.

Exhibit 3-11
Map of Responsibilities and Areas of Ability

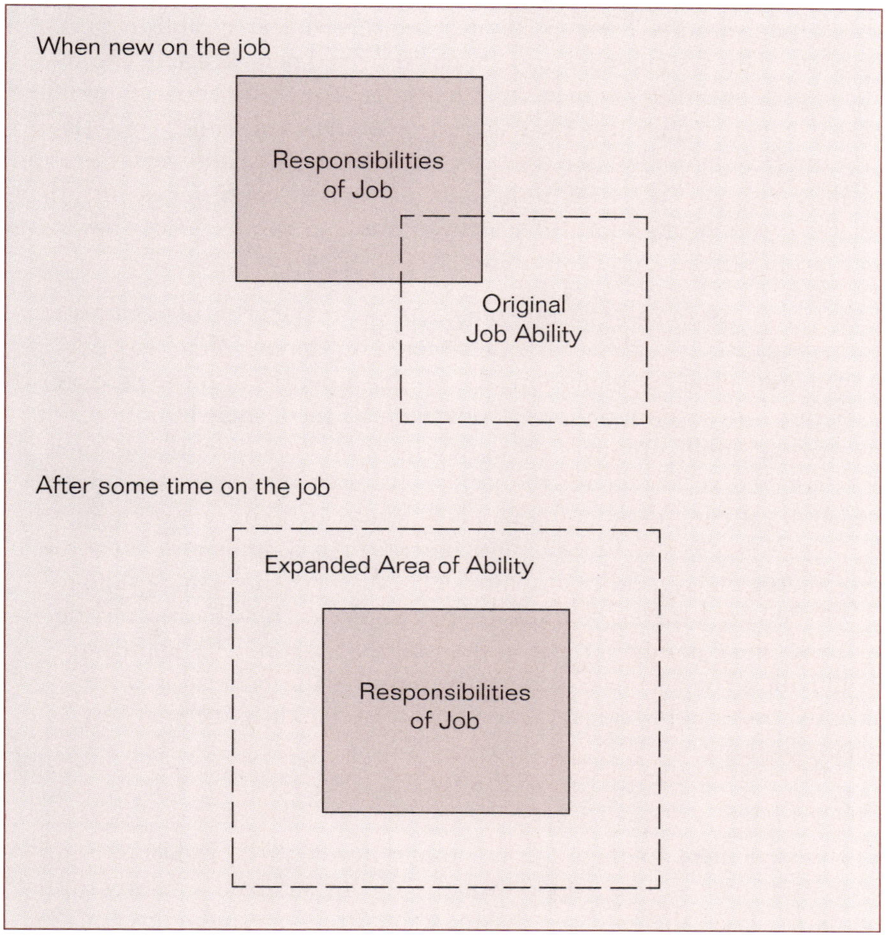

Producer Compensation

Perhaps no area in agency operations causes more discussion than producer compensation. Producers who are paid based on commission receive a percentage of the commission that the agency receives from the insurer. Currently, producers often receive compensation of 35 percent of commissions or lower. No guidelines establish compensation because each agency requires different accountabilities of its producers. Only an analysis of the duties of each producer, the desires of the principals, and the financial resources of the agency can determine appropriate compensation. Generally, the fewer of the seven sales functions for which the producer is accountable, the lower the compensation.

Compensation Systems

The three producer compensation systems are commission only, salary only, and salary and commission.

Commission Only

Many agencies compensate producers only on commission. Generally, this system works well with veteran producers with an established book of business. This system may be as simple as a fixed percentage of commissions on all business produced. But many agencies have intricate systems that pay higher splits for new business versus renewal, large versus small accounts (as defined by the agency), and property/casualty versus life and health. Although these multiple splits may appear confusing at first, they focus the producer's efforts into areas that the agency feels need emphasis or that increase agency profitability.

In the commission system, generally 20 to 40 percent of the commissions the agency receives goes to the producer. The amount often depends on how many of the sales functions the producer performs. If the producer is to perform all seven functions, sooner or later he or she will not be able to produce significant amounts of new business because of the demand of the service functions. The producer's percentage of commission tends to be toward the high end of the range. Producers who have fewer responsibilities generally receive a smaller percentage of commission, but those producers generally earn more money because they have more time to sell. Allowing a higher commission percentage on new business while reducing the commission split at renewal is common. This approach would allow the agency to service the business (probably at a lower overall cost) and provide an incentive for the producer to seek new business.

Salary Only

This system most commonly compensates newly hired producers. Some level of income is agreed upon by management and paid regularly to the producer. Then the salary is adjusted at quarterly or annual intervals to reflect the individual's level of production. After a producer has reached a level of sales that results in the producer's commission split exceeding the salary, the agency will begin to pay the producer based on the commission split in place of salary.

Salary and Commission

Some combination of salary and commission is appropriate for a producer responsible for producing new business but who still extensively services existing accounts. Salary is paid for servicing renewals, and commission is paid for new business.

Fringe Benefits

Any of these compensation plans may include various fringe benefits beyond what would be called "normal fringe benefits" (like health insurance or a retirement plan). Such benefits are club memberships, trips the agency wins from insurers, agency ownership, automobiles, or liberal expense accounts.

Considering the different ways to compensate producers, principals must make choices. What works in one agency will not work in another agency. Most agencies have found that new producers who are also new to insurance sales need to be treated differently from producers who have insurance sales experience. Further refinement of an agency's producer compensation system is beyond the scope of this text.

Sales Performance Standards and Controls

Once capable staff are in place, they still need to know where they fit on the agency team. What are their goals? Who are they responsible to or for? How will their activities lead to desired results? Is the organization functioning properly? Have the right people been put in place with the proper direction?

An organization is made up of a group of individuals. Each of these individuals has skills and desires that must be directed so that each employee is striving to achieve personal goals that are coordinated with the goals of the organization. As discussed in the previous assignment, this coordination requires the agency manager to delegate to others, motivate all employees, manage differences, and manage change. These processes are the same for management in general and sales management, so they will not be discussed here.

Some elements of control, however, are different in sales management. Controlling the activities of an agency's sales force is the sales manager's most important function because these activities determine whether the agency will succeed (or survive) financially. The sales manager must therefore concentrate on two areas of control—setting performance standards and measuring the achievements of the sales force in those standards.

Without a method of measuring actual results against plans, the agency risks being a triumph of motion over meaning: much activity with no results. Benchmarking, the process of comparing the agency's results with standards of performance, is an effective method of agency control.

Setting Performance Standards

Performance standards agencies can employ include judgment and experience performance standards, and historical, engineered, financial, sales, and individual performance standards:

- *Judgment and experience standards.* **Judgment and experience standards** are the most frequently used and involve little measurement. These standards are not scientific or quantitative; they are based simply on the judgment and experience of management. An example of this type of standard for personnel could be "I guess it is time to add another employee." This decision can be precipitated either by employees failing to do their job or by the need for an additional employee. Many agencies have excess personnel capacity as a result of the judgment method, since people are often added considerably before actual needs. Some managers have extremely good intuitive skills, but for the most part quantified standards are needed for comparison purposes to supplement their judgment and experience.

- *Historical standards.* **Historical standards** can come from internal or external sources. The internal source is the most readily available standard because it is what has been done in the past. If an employee leaves, he or she is replaced because that is the historical staffing requirement. Nothing is wrong with this technique if the staffing base was correct from the start. Unfortunately, an overstaffing error is frequently perpetuated because "that is the way we have always done it."

  The Rough Notes Company years ago recognized the need for a quantified standard and publishes the book *What It Costs*. This survey requests data from agencies country-wide and then tabulates the answers from respondents into averages for firms of various sizes. The purpose of the survey is to provide an average agency benchmark with which to compare an agency's performance. This book is an excellent external source for an insurance agency.

  Rough Notes presents several benchmarks, including the number of personnel by premium volume, total office payroll as a percentage of income, and premium volume per employee. All of these measures vary widely among agencies, depending on the efficiency of the management techniques in an agency. For instance, agencies that do not process their business efficiently spend a considerably larger percentage of revenues on office payroll. Exhibit 3-12 illustrates benchmarks for agency owner compensation as a percentage of their agency's total revenue.

Exhibit 3-12
Owners' Compensation as a Percentage of Total Revenue

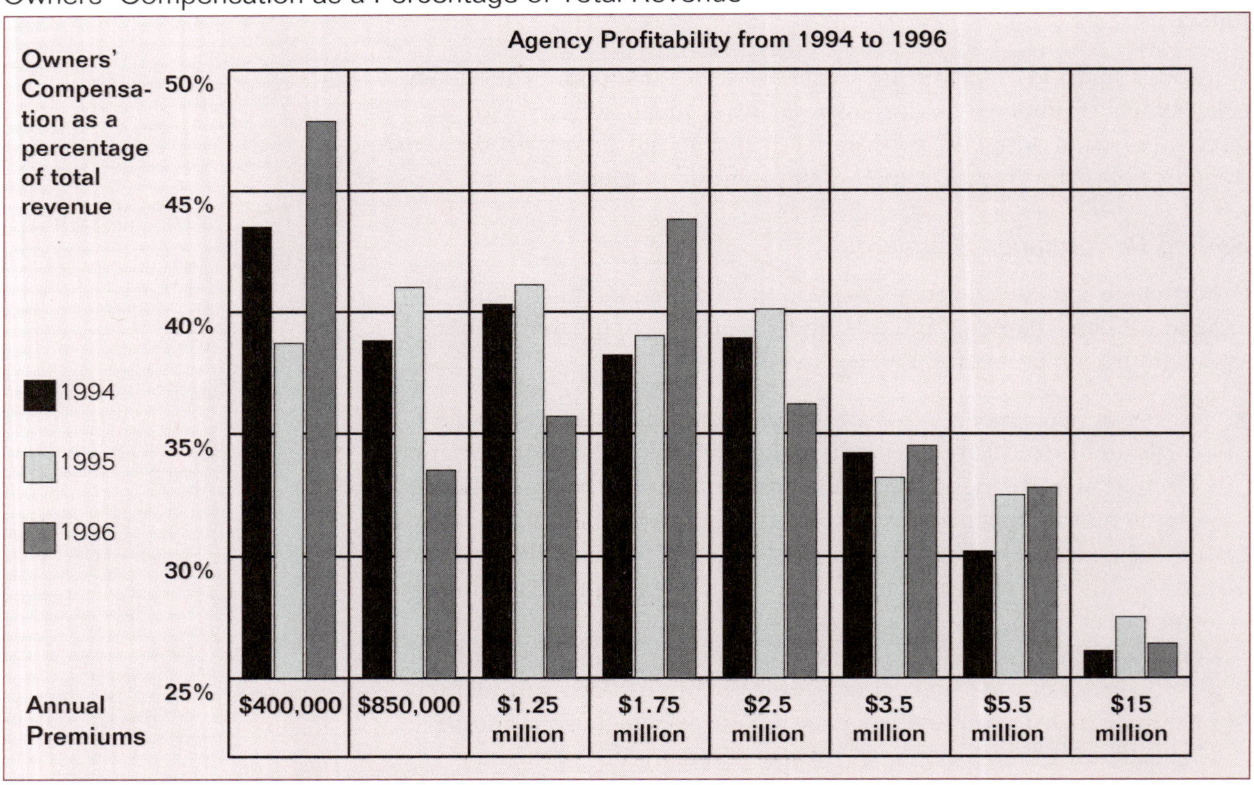

Reprinted with permission: *What It Costs*, The Rough Notes Company, Inc., 1997.

One of the most recent quantified standards is the IIABA *Best Practices* studies. Rough Notes bases findings on the information supplied by agencies willing to respond to a random survey of many agencies differing size and profitability. The IIABA study seeks the top 25 percent (based on certain performance criteria) of all independent agencies. The annually published findings thus provide the agency with benchmarks to compare its results to those of the best. Exhibit 3-13 is an example of the Best Practices benchmark for revenue per employee.

Exhibit 3-13

Revenue per Employee

Agency Size (by net revenue)	Average Agency	Top 25% Profitability	Top 25% Growth
Under $250,000	$57,714	$46,123	$66,142
$250,000-500,000	58,599	63,790	50,784
$500,000-1,250,000	67,835	76,615	76,180

Adapted from the 1995 *Best Practices* study, ©1995 Independent Insurance Agents of America, Inc., and Reagan & Associates.

Management Tip

When using the *Best Practices* information, be careful. If you find yourself getting depressed over how badly you seem to compare, remember these are the top achievers. If the gap between your agency and theirs is large, and until now you were feeling good about yourself, don't panic. Think how much better you'll be doing when you start closing the gap! The study is *not* designed to frustrate you. Its goal is to inspire you to keep improving.

- *Engineered standards.* **Engineered standards** are based on an objective, quantitative analysis of a specific work situation. These standards measure the potential output of individual workers or groups of workers.

  An example of an engineered standard a number of management consultants use is the measurement of the number of premium transactions per administrative employee. This standard determines on average how much work each administrative employee does each working day. A premium transaction is any transaction that produces an invoice, either direct billed or agency billed. An administrative employee is anyone working at inside servicing. By setting an engineered standard, agency management can evaluate how much work is being done and whether the results indicate increasing or decreasing employee performance trends.
- *Internal financial standards.* Internal financial standards come from past performance and budgets. Past performance standards are most frequently used, comparing the current period (usually quarterly or monthly) with that same period in previous years to determine how the firm is doing. Although it is the most commonly used quantitative standard, past performance may be a weak standard because of changing economic conditions.

I. Agency Management and Sales Management
II. Sales Management of People
D. Producer Compensation
E. Sales Performance Standards and Controls
F. Sales Meetings

The second internal standard is the agency's budget or plan. A well-designed budget and plan give the guidance necessary to meet objectives and represent the best standard to use for comparisons. Agency management can use this standard to easily and quickly evaluate the agency's performance relative to projections. Changes to the budget or plan necessitated by lagging performance or changes beyond the agency's control can be made immediately; thus, this type of standard is a useful management tool.

- *Sales standards*. Individual and agency sales standards are integral to planning. Sales standards determined by the top management level include sales volume, product mix, commission income, and profit.

Sales Volume

A common measure of sales activities is comparing prior years' premium volume, yet that may be the worst possible choice. Inflation and rate increases can easily lead to a 10 to 15 percent increase in volume when the agency may in reality be losing ground to its competition. For example, one agency was showing an annual sales premium volume growth of 10 percent and believed it was progressing satisfactorily. Since rates had increased substantially, new business was growing at a rate of 10 percent. But the new sales volume did *not* show that the agency was also experiencing a lapse rate of 19 percent. Its policyholder base was decreasing, but the agency believed it was increasing. Unfortunately, a year later it became a candidate for acquisition, and management could not understand what went wrong. The use of an incomplete standard gave the principals a false sense of security.

Similarly, a decrease in volume resulting from declining prices in a soft market does not necessarily indicate that an agency is doing anything wrong. The number of new agency clients may actually increase as the volume falls.

Product Mix

A balance of commercial, personal lines, and financial products (life, health, and disability) based on the business available in the agency's territory and the sales objective of the firm are appropriate sales objectives. The desired percentage of each type of product line will vary by agency based on its expertise and profit goals.

Commission Income

As previously discussed, premium volume can be a misleading and inappropriate measure of growth or profit. A far better measure is commission income. After all, commission is the real income of the agency, not premium. Premium volume could be high but commission income low (a large volume of workers compensation, for example). The agency should adopt an appropriate average commission standard in the planning stages and then determine how to reach its target for commission income.

Profit

The bottom line standard for any agency is profit. The overriding standard in sales objectives should be to write profitable business. (Contingent commissions, although not controllable income, are more likely when an agency sells profitable business.). Also, the premium payment pattern of an account, the amount of service required, and the stability of the account should all be considered in examining the profit standard.

Individual Performance Standards

Performance standards should be set for each employee. An individual should not be compared with group averages but with his or her own standards as set at the beginning of the review period. These standards should be negotiated with the employee and documented in writing to underlie the performance evaluation at the end of the review period. The list of standards should include qualitative items (such as a low loss ratio) and quantitative items (such as commissions or numbers of new policies), as well as job-related goals such as training and education.

Measuring Results

Once standards have been adopted, actual operations and individual performance can be compared to those standards to determine how well everyone is doing. Most agencies will measure results as a whole, looking at financial aspects as well as productivity for each individual employee.

Measuring Agency Performance

The best method for measuring agency performance is to compare actual financial results to the budget or to goals. This comparison alerts the financial manager to cost and income trends, and it highlights specific areas that need attention. Something out of line in comparison to the selected standard is not necessarily good or bad. For example, assume an agency has a lower office payroll than the standard. This may appear "good," suggesting that the office force was extremely efficient and able to process more work than the standard. The office may, however, be understaffed, or it could mean wages are lower in the agency's community compared to a national average.

Perhaps the agency is overstaffed or understaffed based on the amount of work to be performed. If the "normal" average transactions per day per employee have been determined to be 3.25 by an engineered standard, and if the employee has a transaction count of 6.5, then the manager can conclude one of two things: the employees are very efficient or the agency is understaffed. The latter can be determined by the timeliness of the work, whether or not a backlog of work exists, and employee morale. A low transaction-per-day count of 1.5 per employee would indicate either inefficiency or overstaffing. Standards require constant attention since changes will be necessary as an agency's efficiency changes.

Particularly in the case of external standards, the organization creating the benchmarks will often provide tools for the agency to use in making meaningful comparisons. Exhibit 3-14 is a worksheet provided in the *Best Practices* manual. By filling in the blanks with the agency's actual results and adding the benchmarks for agencies of similar size, the agency will clearly see how its performance compares to a long list of external benchmarks.

Exhibit 3-14
Worksheets for Four Phase Planning

Understanding Your Current Position

Revenues:	Your Results __/__/__	Percent of Total Rev.	Best Practices Benchmark
1. Commercial P&C Commissions	$______	______%	______%
Account Retention-CML P&C	______%	______	______%
Average Rev. per Acct.	$______	______	$______
New Business-last 12 months	$______	______%	
Percent Growth-last 12 months	______%	______	______%
2. Personal P&C Commissions	$______	______%	______%
Account Retention-PL P&C	______%	______	______%
Average Rev. per Account	$______	______	$______
New Business-last 12 months	$______	______%	
Percent Growth-last 12 months	______%	______	______%
3. P&C Service Fees	$______	______%	______%
4. Contingent/Bonus	$______	______%	______%
5. Group-Life & Health	$______	______%	______%
Percent Growth-last 12 months	______%	______	______%
6. Individual Life & Health	$______	______%	______%
Percent Growth-last 12 months	______%	______	______%
7. Investments	$______	______%	______%
8. Miscellaneous	$______	______%	______%
9. Total Revenues	$______	100%	100%
10. Brokerage Commission Expense	$______	______%	______%
11. Net Revenues	$______	______%	______%

Compensation Expense:			
12. Total Payroll	$ ______	______ %	______ %
13. Employee Benefits	$ ______	______ %	______ %
14. Total Compensation	$ ______	______ %	______ %

Selling Expense:			
15. Travel & Entertainment	$ ______	______ %	______ %
16. Automobile	$ ______	______ %	______ %
17. Advertising & Promotion	$ ______	______ %	______ %
18. Total Selling	$ ______	______ %	______ %

Operating Expenses:			
19. Occupancy	$ ______	______ %	______ %
20. Telephone	$ ______	______ %	______ %
21. Postage	$ ______	______ %	______ %
22. Supplies/Printing	$ ______	______ %	______ %
23. Dues/Subscriptions/Contrib.	$ ______	______ %	______ %
24. Taxes/Licenses	$ ______	______ %	______ %
25. Insurance	$ ______	______ %	______ %

Operating Expenses:	Your Results __/__/__	Percent of Total Rev.	Best Practices Benchmark
26. Professional Fees	$ ________	________ %	________ %
27. Equipment Rental/Maintenance	$ ________	________ %	________ %
28. Bad Debts	$ ________	________ %	________ %
29. Outside Services	$ ________	________ %	________ %
30. Data Processing	$ ________	________ %	________ %
31. Education/Training	$ ________	________ %	________ %
32. Miscellaneous	$ ________	________ %	________ %
33. Total Operating Expenses	$ ________	________ %	________ %
Administrative Expenses:			
34. Amortization	$ ________	________ %	________ %
35. Depreciation	$ ________	________ %	________ %
36. Officer Life	$ ________	________ %	________ %
37. Interest	$ ________	________ %	________ %
38. Other	$ ________	________ %	________ %
39. Total Admin. Expenses	$ ________	________ %	________ %
40. Total Expenses	$ ________	________ %	________ %
Profitability Analysis:			
41. Pretax Profit	$ ________	________ %	________ %
42. Pro-forma Profit	$ ________	________ %	________ %
Productivity Analysis:			
Number of Employees	________		
Revenue per Employee	$ ________		$ ________
Compensation per Employee	$ ________		$ ________
"Spread" per Employee	$ ________		$ ________
Balance Sheet Analysis:			
Current Ratio	________		________
Receivables to Payables Ratio	______ %		________ %
Receivables Aged Greater than			
60 Days (% Total Receivables)	______ %		________ %
90 Days (% Total Receivables)	______ %		________ %
Tangible Net Worth (% Net Rev.)	$ ________	________ %	________ %

Adapted from the 1995 *Best Practices* study, ©1995 Independent Insurance agents of America, Inc., and Reagan & Associates.

Measuring Individual Performance

The primary method for evaluating individual performance is the written performance evaluation. Employees should receive feedback from their manager or supervisor regularly, but they should also have at least one formal review each year.

The formal review should involve a meeting with the individual employee to review the written evaluation that the manager or supervisor has already prepared. A good practice is for employees to "sign off," indicating that they have seen the document and have noted any disagreements with the evaluation. This is particularly important if the employee is being put on notice that his or her performance is not satisfactory.

A common practice in many agencies is to have the employee complete a self-evaluation and then to use this analysis and one completed by the manager as a basis for the oral evaluation. Employees are forced to think about their performance rather than simply to react to praise or criticism from someone else.

Reporting Systems

Reporting systems include financial reports that compare budgeted income and expense items with the actual income statement for the period being reviewed and producer reports that record and compare actual sales volume results with predetermined goals and quotas.

> **Management Tip**
>
> Automation has made detailed reports available to agencies of all sizes, but many sales managers have yet to learn how to extract the most important information and to come up with meaningful guidelines for planning. Master the art of interpreting computer output by selecting and comparing the information that is most important to the agency, and you'll discover that the bulk of your time can now be spent rectifying mistakes rather than trying to figure out what happened in the first place.

Financial Reports

Financial reports interest sales managers particularly in commission revenue and selling expense. Variations from budget expenses, either up or down, need to be analyzed carefully. Often logical explanations will account for differences. Landing a big account in another state will increase commission income and will understandably affect travel expenses. Lowering premium rate levels because of intense competition among insurance companies during the soft market cycle may reduce commission income even if all the new business sales goals are met. When the financial statements reflect differences that cannot be readily explained, the production management reports may be needed to analyze the make-up of the business written and the transactions processed to determine why results were not as expected.

Producer Reports

Producer reports are most often handled manually, although more agencies are automating them. Producers or their managers keep track of calls, proposals, number of sales, and volume (premium and commission) on specially designed forms. The larger insurance companies and agency consultants have sample forms that producers can use or revise to suit their own purposes, and many agencies have developed their own forms and systems after trial and error. An example of one of these forms is shown in Exhibit 3-15.

Exhibit 3-15
Monthly Production Record

Month	New Prop. & Cas. Comm.	New Life Health, Group Comm.	Total New Comm. for Month	Monthly New Comm. Objective	Cumulative New Comm. Year to Date	Cum. New Com. Objective Year to Date	$ + or – Cumulative Objective
January							
February							
March							
April							
May							
June							
July							
August							
September							
October							
November							
December							
TOTALS							
OBJECTIVE							

Reprinted with permission from George Nordhaus, IMMS of California, 1992.

Performance Reviews

Evaluation and control take on a new dimension when applied to the performance review of individual salespeople since management is engaged in counseling rather than cold statistical analysis. This evaluation should serve as the basis for the producer's development and as a basis for the agency's program for guidance and training of sales personnel in general. For instance, performance evaluations may uncover the need for improvements in technical training necessitated by a change in a law or the introduction of a new policy form.

Evaluation of Performance

Many agencies lack an effective, complete procedure for evaluating the performance of salespeople. Establishing and administering such a program takes time. Also, many of the factors that have to be evaluated cannot be quantified, and people tend to shy away from making subjective judgments. Once management does get a performance appraisal system installed and operational, however, conducting the reviews becomes less averse.

Performance evaluation systems all have some basic characteristics in common although many different approaches can be used. Essentially, a system for evaluating sales performance must have the following components:

I. Agency Management and Sales Management
II. Sales Management of People
D. Producer Compensation
E. Sales Performance Standards and Controls
F. Sales Meetings

1. Bases for the evaluation
   a. Quantitative—premium, commission, new prospects, accounts sold, and so on
   b. Qualitative—self-organization, knowledge, customer relations, appearance, attitude, and so on
2. Standards against which to judge the performance
3. Comparison of performance against standards
4. Discussion of the evaluation with the individual and method to establish a plan for the coming review period

Traditional standards for comparison almost always involve identification of the achievements of the agency's best salesperson to indicate realistically what *can* be done. The other salespeople are reflecting the differences between what *can* be done and what *is* being done. The sales manager strives to develop all of the producers so that they are eventually producing at the level of the top person. Performance evaluations provide the means to achieve this objective.

Management Tip

The downside to this producer comparison method is best summarized by the question, How do we know the *top* producer is a good salesperson? Two benchmarks may offer answers. First, Is the top producer meeting or exceeding the agency's sales goals and objectives as to revenue, profitability, loss ratios, and so forth? Second, an external source of standards such as IIABA's *Best Practices* should be used to compare the producer with his or her best peers. Measuring other producers against the top person is fine once the top person is determined to be a good benchmark. Otherwise, the agency risks conferring "outstanding" rankings on producers who have simply mirrored mediocrity.

Taking Corrective Action

A vital step in the control process is corrective action. Taking corrective action is the mark of an effective manager. Knowing about a problem is one thing, but doing something about it is another. Without corrective action, there is no control. There may be too much or too little control, and the personality of the manager as well as the organization's structure will influence the amount of control.

Agency Correction

The judgment or experience standard is likely to be used by a person exercising too little control. The attitude may be, "Just relax, it has always worked out." Many managers with this attitude point to profitability as support for this style of operation. Unfortunately, they may be using mediocrity as their standard rather than an optimum profit level.

If by comparison the agency is overstaffed, the decision may be made to control the situation. This may mean terminating an employee or increasing production to a point that excess capacity no longer exists. It may be difficult to terminate an employee or wait until the staff is reduced through attrition. It is much *better,* but not necessarily *easier,* to examine the systems being used, streamline them, and raise the premium volume and transaction count by upgrading the existing accounts. Taking action to correct a problem offers many creative opportunities. In the scenario above, one choice could have been to fire someone, but other often better solutions do exist.

Individual Correction

If by comparison of actual performance to expectations an employee is not performing up to the established standards, the manager must determine whether this is caused by a lack of training or education. If so, corrective action can take the form of a training plan. If personality clashes with other co-workers, low morale, family problems, or other emotional or psychological traits cause poor performance, the manager has a more difficult task correcting the problem.

Management Tip

Sometimes improving performance sufficiently is not possible. The employee may not be suited to the job or may not fit into the agency environment. If this is the case, the employee should be terminated. Many agency managers find it difficult to terminate employees, tending to keep people who are not performing well rather than fire them. This, in turn, causes morale problems among the other employees and agency productivity suffers. It is better to deal with the situation head on and build a staff with everyone pulling his or her weight.

Rewarding

Rewards for above-average performance may include any of the compensation possibilities previously discussed, but special care should be taken before offering promotion as a reward to a producer. Promoting a successful salesperson to a management position is not as simple as promoting someone from one level of management to another. The ability to sell is different from the ability to manage. Some people have both talents, but many more do not. The result of promoting a good salesperson may mean the loss of a highly productive producer and the gain of a mediocre manager, and once someone has been promoted, taking a step backwards by a return to selling may be difficult or impossible.

Many experienced managers have learned about promotion problems the hard way—by losing good people. They have therefore devised methods of rewarding producers that keep these people satisfied without a shift to management. If the agency is large enough, various levels of sales jobs can be established so that a certain amount of merit promotion can take place within the confines of the sales function. Examples of this technique include giving titles, such as Assistant Vice President, or by naming the producer as a production team leader. Another approach is to design the incentive compensation plan for the producers in such a way that they have the potential to earn much more money in sales than they ever would as a manager. The thought of being promoted to a management job is less appealing if it means a cut in pay.

Sales Meetings

The hatred of wasting time in seemingly useless and lengthy meetings is universal, particularly among producers. Consequently, there has always been some question as to whether or not sales meetings are a necessary component of the managerial process for an insurance agency. Most people in sales management strongly believe that sales meetings are beneficial to their sales forces if conducted properly. These managers also believe that these meetings are necessary and support having them regularly.

Successful sales meetings require hard work and thought to accomplish the goal or goals management sets for them, such as communicating information, providing continuous education and training, or creating enthusiasm and team spirit among the producers. This section will examine the benefits of holding these meetings, the frequency with which they should be held, and several techniques used to achieve the objectives of the meeting.

Benefits

Sales meetings can accomplish several objectives that are useful both to the salespeople as well as to the sales manager.

One benefit of a sales meeting is providing a channel of feedback through the meeting itself. A feedback mechanism allows producers to express their attitudes toward certain subjects, such as new agency procedures, which in turn allows the manager to identify problems and to take necessary corrective action. This feedback also provides the manager with a better understanding of the producers' status and direction, as well as providing the opportunity to present technical information or changes to which producers can respond immediately.

The sales meeting can also provide the vital and necessary function of communication and information sharing among peers. In many instances, the producer works alone; therefore, the sales meeting provides interaction. Producers can share their accomplishments and learn from one another how to improve their marketing and sales performance.

Management Tip

No producer closes 100 percent of his or her prospects. This inevitable rejection by at least a few prospects can steadily wear the producer down unless balanced by a positive agency support system. A sales meeting is an excellent place to enhance personal esteem, which often takes a beating from the rejection that all insurance salespeople encounter. The meeting also presents an opportunity to recognize producers for their successes, to establish relationships with their peers, and to rekindle enthusiasm.

The necessity of using a meeting for sales training has been questioned. Many managers believe that if they do not attempt to train at sales meetings, no training will ever occur. Some, however, believe that sales training must be addressed individually, depending on each person's needs and circumstances; it does not lend itself to group dynamics.

The training problem is approached in various ways by different agencies, depending upon their organizational structure. For many, the idea of using the sales meeting for training the producers would fit in comfortably with the other aspects of their operations.

E&O Alert!

Training in a group context has the advantage of confirming that everyone is getting the same information from the same source. Many misunderstandings that lead to E&O claims arise from a person acquiring important information not from an expert source but rather from the mistaken recollections of a fellow staff member. Hearsay is not accepted as evidence in court and should not be accepted as adequate training in an agency.

Although feedback and communication are necessary in most sales meetings, they are not always the most important reasons for holding the meeting. Different firms use sales meetings for different purposes. Items such as continuous education, coverage review, new product introduction, motivation, and sales training are often on the sales meeting agenda.

The argument has often been made that small agencies do not need sales meetings, especially when the entire office consists of one large room and communication between management and salespeople is easy. Often in these situations, no formal sales meetings are scheduled, but when everybody happens to be in the office at the same time, they might sit down and have a brainstorming session. When all the salespeople and management sit down and discuss their ideas, they are in reality having an informal sales meeting. But such brainstorming sessions may be rare in the hectic pace of daily business. If effective sales meetings are to have benefits, a formal time should be set aside and emphasized as an important part of the agency's successful operation.

Even if the office personnel have no trouble communicating information through other means, they still need to get together simply to establish their self-image as a professional, organized firm that works as a team.

Even the smallest offices could benefit from formal sales meetings, because nobody is infallible—everybody can use someone else's advice and opinions.

Frequency

Small agencies may not need frequent meetings if enough informal communication keeps the sales staff informed. Larger agencies, however, find regular meetings helpful, often weekly or even daily.

One very profitable agency insists that daily meetings are a key to their success. Exhibit 3-16 discusses this agency and its meeting system.

Exhibit 3-16
Example From a Best Practices Agency

Exceptional communications and follow-up.

This agency (26 Associates, $25 million in premiums, all commercial) has a record of exceptional performance that goes beyond financial results, and includes awards from both their State and city governments for quality leadership. Their Associates are a model of client-focused teamwork and *inter*dependency. Their culture is founded on quality, stability, professionalism, and a commitment to and respect for individuals. This culture is exemplified in their communications. And the cornerstone of their communications practices is their daily meeting.

The meeting starts at 8:15 sharp, and usually lasts for an hour to an hour and a half. One focus is on current business, e.g.: client service issues; significant activities and issues from the previous day and those that are anticipated for the present day; technical issues, trends, and educational items.

A second focus of each meeting is this team's process for identifying and following-up on improvement opportunities. Central to the process is a "Covey Board," (named for Stephen Covey, the author of "The Seven Habits of Highly Effective People").

The "Covey Board" is a 4-foot by 8-foot lightweight foam board that is marked into four equal quadrants and a strip at the top. Attached to the board are self-stick notes that outline change/improvement needs and projects. Each note is placed in one of the five sections that are marked as follows:

New Items	
Important/Urgent	Important/Not Urgent
Less Important/ Urgent	Less Important/ Not Urgent

The process starts when an Associate recognizes a need/opportunity, jots it down on a sticky note, and attaches the note in the "New Items" section of the board. Then, at the next day's morning meeting, the Associate describes the Need/opportunity. During the subsequent discussion the group decides how to proceed and with what priority. Volunteers are sought for the individual who will have overall responsibility for ensuring that the "project" is completed, even if it will be a team project. A due date is added to the sticky note, which is then placed in the quadrant that reflects its priority.

Items in the first quadrant, the highest priority, may be reviewed during the meeting each day. Others are reviewed on a schedule that fits their due-date and priority. The point is that all items are always visible, as is what is to be done, by whom and by when. When these obligations are subject to regular, if not daily review, things tend to get done. They also get done with cooperation and teamwork.

Reprinted with permission from Independent Insurance Agents of America, Inc., and Woodgate Partners from *Five Practices of Highly Effective Leaders* by Doron (Bud) Antrim, ©1996.

Once the desired frequency of meetings is agreed upon, they should be held during a time (1) that is convenient for the staff, (2) that does not interfere with their work, and (3) that will not be interrupted. It is best to choose a schedule and adhere to it rather than have each meeting at a different time. Thus, if Monday morning at 8:00 A.M. is satisfactory, the time should be adopted and kept. Once it becomes habit, attending the meeting becomes automatic, and those attending might be more receptive to regular meetings.

Sales Meeting Rules

Although the success of any agency meeting depends on the skill of the person who plans and conducts it, sales meeting specialists suggest certain rules. Each sales meeting should have an objective, have an agenda, stay on schedule, and be a proper length.

The first rule is to have an objective and to meet it. A meeting is a means, not an end in itself. If the meeting does not have an objective, it should not be held.

A second rule is to have an agenda, that is, a written list of literally "things to be done." The purpose of an agenda is threefold. First, it forces those holding the meeting to think about what they want to accomplish. Second, it informs those attending the meeting what is to be discussed. Thus, they can think about it before the meeting and have a clear understanding of what is being discussed. Third, an agenda gives the meeting a track to run on. The track helps accomplish the objectives by keeping the meeting headed in the desired direction.

The third rule is to keep the meeting on schedule. If a meeting is to be held every Monday morning starting at 8:00 A.M. and ending at 9:15 A.M., it should start and end on time. If it starts late each time, the staff will either resent being on time or will get into the habit of arriving late. If the meeting does not end on schedule, the people cannot plan their work for the balance of the morning properly. If they know they will be out of the meeting at a specified time, they can arrange their work schedules accordingly. Insisting upon keeping the meeting on schedule requires the kind of planning and leadership that creates meetings that are good in other respects as well.

A final rule is that agency meetings should not be too long. Long meetings can be tiresome, boring, and inefficient.

An Argument for Change

This assignment began by stating that the focus would be on applying to insurance agencies the basic management system described in the previous assignment. Most agencies operate on these principles and the producer must understand them.

But this is not to suggest this basic system of management has no alternatives, or that there are not even better approaches to take. Many have been suggested over the years, varying in acceptance or practical application. As stated in the last assignment, the astute manager will continuously keep his or her eyes open for new possibilities for improving the operation, morale, and profitability of the agency.

Appendix B provides one eloquent argument for change in the way a typical agency is managed. This discussion was originally included in the text *The Five Practices of Highly Effective Leaders*, one of the publications making up the IIABA's *Best Practices* program. Because it summarizes so well many of the management ideas suggested by the continuous quality improvement process (described in the previous assignment), it provides an excellent ending to the agency management discussion and is reprinted here in its entirety.

Check your understanding of the *Key Words and Phrases* found in the second part of this assignment.

Judgment and experience standards (p. 37)

Historical standards (p. 38)

Engineered standard (p. 39)

Review the concepts presented in the second part of this assignment by answering the following questions.

9. What types of standards can be used to measure an agency's performance? (pp. 37-38)

- Judgement & Experience
- HISTORICAL
- Engineered - objective, quantitative analysis

10. What is the best method for measuring an agency's performance? (p. 41)

- Compare actual financial results to the budget or to goals

11. What components should be included in an employee performance review? (pp. 43-44)

12. What are the benefits of sales meetings? (p. 48)

Share information

13. What are the rules for a successful sales meeting? (p. 51)

Objective
Agenda
Start Time / End Time
Not Too Long

Apply the concepts presented in the second part of this assignment by answering the following questions.

5. (a) How can an agency develop sales performance standards?

   (b) What types of standards should an agency owner use to measure performance?

   (c) How can the standards identified in your answer to (b) above be used to control an agency's performance?

6. Explain ways to eliminate the following negative comments about sales meetings:
   (a) "I have worked for several different agencies, and in some agencies the meetings were great, while in others they were a total waste of time."

   Objectives

   (b) "The boss always gets way off track when he holds these sales meetings, and it seems as though we get nothing accomplished."

   STICK TO AGENDA

   (c) "Because of these 8:00 A.M. sales meetings, I never know when I can schedule my first appointment."

   SET END TIME

Summary

Although insurance agencies may face many unique situations, general management principles that apply to other businesses still apply to operating an effective agency.

Sales management is the application of the process of management to the sales function in the organization. The cost of managing and operating a sales force is usually the largest single expense in an insurance agency's budget. The job of the sales manager is to ensure that this expense is not out of line with the commission revenues produced by the salespeople.

Many producers become sales managers because they were good at production. Because management and production differ, some producer-sales managers do not really know how to manage. Developing a sales management report through modification of the agency income statement can give the producer-sales manager a good start. Modifying the income statement for a direct charge for "management expense" gives the agency an idea of when it can afford full-time sales management and allow the producer to sell. Other modifications to the income statement can indicate to the sales manager the types of sales activities producers should be involved in. Finally, the modifications to the income statement help establish important sales control forms and procedures.

Staffing the sales organization with good people can be a lengthy process, particularly because finding potential candidates with sales and insurance experience is difficult. The recruitment and selection process may take months, and orientation and training take up a significant portion of the sales manager's time. Vital to staffing is the producer's job description and job qualifications, which establish job functions for others and set the training and development of producers .

Management must provide direction by delegating responsibility and authority, motivating the salespeople with monetary and nonmonetary factors, coordinating, and managing difference and change.

Sales management control involves establishing reporting systems, setting performance standards, measuring results, taking corrective action, and rewarding producers. It provides the mechanism to ensure that the producers are acting according to the general sales plan.

Sales meetings can be productive for agencies since they provide feedback to producers, increase communication, and foster self-esteem. Sales meetings should have an objective, have an agenda, stay on schedule, and not be too long.

New management ideas and concepts are always being developed that may help the agency manager improve on the management process. One source for such ideas is the IIABA *Best Practices* study, several excerpts of which have been used here to illustrate why the manager must never assume only one way to perform the management functions is correct.

Notes

1. Adapted with permission of ACA *Insider*, vol. 2, no. 3, November 1992.
2. Personality Dynamics, Inc., P.O. Box 2050, Princeton, NJ 08540.

Appendix A

Sample Job Description
Client Service Agent, Commercial Lines

Title: Client Service Agent, Commercial Lines

Reports to: Commercial Lines Manager

Job Summary: The Commercial Lines Client Service Agent performs the essential functions of the position, which include aiding clients with service needs and making changes to existing accounts. Specific service and marketing responsibilities are required in this position. Meets service and sales delivery standards and performs essential functions to the quality and service standards developed by the agency.

Primary Responsibilities:

New Business

- Pre-qualifies own new business according to agency standards.
- Assists clients with making coverage changes in an automated environment supported by transactional filing; determines if delayed or advanced billing is appropriate and invoices accordingly; uses each contact with the client as an opportunity to review the whole account, round it and market.
- Informs and educates clients about policy coverage, changes, exclusion, and insurance coverage needs.
- Provides technical support to producer(s) to benefit clients and to reach agency's strategic business goals.
- Prepares proposals and completes application in coordination with producer(s); submits applications to eligible and appropriate carriers; obtains client signatures on all applications; follows up to ensure timely receipt of quotations and policies.
- Explains to clients' needs by producing binders, certificates, policies, endorsements, and other related items; verifies their accuracy.
- Actively seeks referrals from current client base; follows up to generate new business by using prospect data base and automated marketing tools.

Retention

- Prepares summaries of insurance, schedules and proposals as needed for account review.
- Remarkets renewals, contacts clients, creates renewal proposals, and handles other renewal activities in coordination with the producer(s).
- Renews policies following agency standards; verifies each renewal's accuracy; ensures that all renewals are produced.
- Reviews audits of policies; verifies accuracy and facilitates corrections, as needed, between client and carrier.
- Maintains and updates electronic and transactional files.
- Verifies policy and policy change information, facilitating corrections when necessary.
- Processes incoming mail requests, responding promptly and appropriately.
- Verifies accuracy of all direct billed cancellations and takes appropriate corrective action when needed.

- Uses agency credit and collection policy in invoicing and pursuing prompt payments; requests cancellations from the carrier according to agency standards.
- Determines reasons for requests for cancellations; acts to save accounts; notifies producers) according to agency standards.
- Processes and follows up on cancellations requests to carriers to ensure accurate and timely resolution; maintains agency in financial equity whenever possible.
- Reviews walk-in payments and verifies acceptability; processes, as appropriate, providing receipts to payers or directing the receptionist to do so.
- Assists clients in submitting first reports of claims, obtaining adjustors or visits from agency staff; facilitates prompt response from carrier staff and follows up on claims status to keep insureds informed and to work toward settlement of all claims; uses each claim contact as an occasion to review coverages and market as needed.

Marketing

- Actively solicits increases in coverage and rounds out accounts through sales to clients; leaves good documentation of all contacts.
- Refers current and prospective clients to Life/Benefits Department and to Personal Lines for solicitation of those lines of business; assists in profiling the commercial book of business for marketing purposes.
- Assists in design of, or independently designs, insurance plans for clients as assigned and directed by the agency management.
- Assists or completes other tasks as directed by agency management.

Personal and Organizational Development

- Sets priorities and manages workflow to ensure efficient, timely, and accurate processing of transactions and other responsibilities.
- Maintains a cordial and effective relationship with clients, co-workers, carriers, vendors, and other business contacts.
- Keeps informed regarding industry information, new product information, legislation, coverages and technology to continuously improve knowledge and performance.
- Interacts with others effectively by utilizing good communications skills, cooperating purposefully, and providing information and guidance, as needed, to achieve the business goals of the agency.
- Maintains up-to-date technical manuals and understands how to perform technical tasks to expedite client service.
- College education or equivalent insurance experience.

Knowledge, Skills and Abilities:

- Ability to communicate orally and in writing with others to explain complex issues, receive and interpret complex information, and respond appropriately.
- Ability to understand written and oral communication, and interpret abstract information.
- Property, Casualty, Life and Health License.
- Full knowledge of insurance products and usages.

- Adequate knowledge of rating procedures, coverages, and industry operations to effectively manage, maintain, and write assigned client and prospect lists.
- Full knowledge of insurance markets and reference to markets.
- Knowledge of insurance rating and underwriting procedures.
- Ability to carry out complex tasks with many concrete and abstract variables.
- Ability to add, subtract, multiply and divide whole numbers, and to accurately perform simple calculations involving decimals and fractions.
- Ability to utilize computer programs and understand functionality.
- Ability to perform 70% sedentary work, exerting up to 10 pounds of force occasionally and exert negligible force frequently or constantly to move objects, including the body. May be asked to exert up to 20 pounds of force periodically, as needed.
- Field of vision must be adequate to observe up and down or right to left while eyes are fixed on a given point.
- Ability to process written and other materials visually.
- Physical efforts required include fingering, repetitive small motor activity, grasping, verbally communicating detailed and important information to others quickly and accurately, stooping, reaching, standing, lifting light objects under ten pounds frequently, and climbing occasionally.
- Requires ability to receive detailed information through oral communication, perceiving the nature of sounds with no less than a 40 dB loss at 500 Hz, and 2000 Hz without correction.

Working Conditions

High-pressured, fast-paced environment with significant telephone and personal disruption. Large number of multiple steps in complex system performed with accuracy and speed is essential to the successful completion of tasks.

This job description is intended to describe the level of work required by the person performing the work. The principal duties outlined are the essential responsibilities and duties. Other duties may be assigned as needs arise.

This description is not intended as a contract and is subject to change. Any written contractual agreements supersede this job description. All requirements may be modified reasonably to accommodate physically or mentally challenged staff members.

Sample Job Description
Client Service Agent, Personal Lines

Title: Client Service Agent, Personal Lines

Reports to: Personal Lines Manager

Job Summary: The Personal Lines Client Service Agent performs the essential functions of the position, which include supporting the service needs of clients. Specific service responsibilities are assigned. Marketing activity is required in this position. Meets sales, service, and quality standards adopted by the agency.

Primary Responsibilities and Duties:

Sales

- Prequalifies and analyzes prospects' personal lines coverage needs. Recommends coverages and prepares rating quotes and proposals to sell new accounts.
- Actively solicits increases in coverage or rounding out accounts through sales to clients at every service contact.
- Recommends excess and surplus coverages, as needed to meet client insurance needs. Educates clients as to coverage limitation and documents on the system.
- Completes applications for insurance and has insured sign them. Submits to eligible and appropriate carriers, and follows up to ensure timely receipt of policies or quotations.
- Actively seeks referrals from current client base to solicit for new business prospects; follows up to generate new business using prospect data base and system.
- Actively refers clients to Life Benefits and Commercial Lines department for solicitation of new business.

Retention

- At each service contract, reviews current client coverages and recommends changes in coverage and in markets, as needed to ensure high quality coverage.
- Processes renewals and remarkets, as needed.
- Assists clients with making coverage changes and completes all service requests for clients.
- Informs clients of policy changes, exclusions of coverage and insurance coverage needs. Explains coverages and exclusions to clients. Uses every service contact as opportunity to review and market appropriate coverage.
- Handles direct-billed "walk-in" payments. Verifies coverage status processes, as appropriate. Provides receipt, or directs receptionist to handle.
- Generates documents and produces correspondence to satisfy client service requests or to provide automated information, as needed by client.
- Prepares summaries of insurance, schedules and proposals, using computerized system.

- Assists clients in submitting first reports of claims. Obtains adjusters or visits from agency staff, facilitates prompt response from company staff and follows up on claims status to keep insureds informed and to work toward settlement of claims.
- Maintains orderly electronic files and information, following agency standards.
- Verifies accuracy and coverage adequacy of policies. Requests changes to correct errors and follows up.
- Surveys insureds' loss exposures and recommends coverage at every service opportunity.
- Processes incoming mail requests and responds promptly and appropriately.
- Works with manager to schedule and plan visits to clients.
- Verifies accuracy of all direct bill cancellation notices, and takes appropriate action.
- Implements agency credit and collection policy in regard to agency billed personal lines clients.

Personal and Organizational Development

- Sets priorities and manages workflow to ensure efficient, timely, and accurate processing of transactions and other responsibilities.
- Keeps informed regarding industry information, new product information, coverages, and technology to continuously improve knowledge and stay current.
- Interacts with others effectively by utilizing good communication skills; cooperates positively and provides information and guidance, as needed, to contribute to the business efforts of the agency.
- Maintains and updates technical manuals, and understands its use to perform technical tasks and expedite customer service requests.
- Performs other miscellaneous duties as assigned by agency management.

Knowledge, Skills and Abilities

- College education or equivalent insurance experience.
- Ability to communicate orally and in writing with others to explain complex issues, receive and interpret complex information, and respond appropriately.
- Ability to understand written and oral communication and interpret abstract information.
- Property, Casualty, Life and Health License.
- Full knowledge of insurance products and usages.
- Adequate knowledge of rating procedures, coverages, and industry operations to effectively manage, maintain, and underwrite assigned client and prospect lists.
- Full knowledge of insurance markets and reference to markets.
- Ability to carry out complex tasks with concrete and abstract variables.
- Ability to add, subtract, multiply, and divide whole numbers, and to accurately perform simple calculations involving decimals and fractions.
- Ability to utilize computer programs and understand functionality.

- Ability to perform 70% sedentary work, exerting up to 10 pounds of force occasionally, and exert negligible force frequently or constantly to move objects, including the body. May be asked to exert up to 20 pounds of force periodically, as needed.
- Field of vision must be adequate to observe up and down or right to left while eyes are fixed on a given point.
- Ability to process written and other materials visually.
- Physical efforts required include fingering, repetitive small motor activity, grasping, verbally communicating detailed and important information to others quickly and accurately, stooping, reaching, standing, lifting light objects under ten pounds frequently, and climbing occasionally.
- Requires ability to receive detailed information through oral communication, perceiving the nature of sounds with no less than a 40 dB loss at 500 Hz, 1000 Hz, and 2000 Hz without correction.

Working Conditions

High-pressured, fast-paced environment with significant telephone and personal disruption. Large number of multiple steps in complex system performed with accuracy and speed is essential to the successful completion of tasks.

This job description is intended to describe the normal level of work required by the person performing the work. The principal duties outlined are the essential responsibilities and duties. Other duties may be assigned as needs arise, or as required.

This description is not intended as a contract and is subject to change. Any written contractual agreements supersede this job description. All requirements may be modified reasonably to accommodate physically or mentally challenged staff members.

Appendix B

Needed: A New Paradigm for Management

First, let's clarify what we mean by "paradigm." Unfortunately, the term has become a buzzword, and is used with inconsistent meanings. The dictionary definition is simple; "A paradigm is a model, pattern, example." We prefer the expanded definition that Joel Barker offers in his book *Paradigms:*

> *"A paradigm is a set of rules and regulations (written or unwritten) that does two things: (1) it establishes or defines boundaries; and (2) it tells you how to behave inside the boundaries in order to be successful."*

A new paradigm for management/leadership, then, will define the rules, regulations, and behaviors that managers/leaders will need to adapt to be successful.

The Old Management Paradigm

To build the case for a new paradigm let's go back a few decades, back into the Era of Smooth Sailing. There was little talk of leadership then. Business was run very successfully (in financial terms) by *managers*. Basically, managers were responsible for accomplishing key business results through others. Managers performed such tasks as:

- ☐ **Goal setting, planning and budgeting;** setting goals for the business, action plans and timetables, and allocating resources.
- ☐ **Organizing and staffing;** establishing the organizational structure for accomplishing the goals, staffing the structure with competent people, delegating responsibility for and authority for plan implementation, providing policies and procedures to guide Associates, and creating methods or systems to monitor implementation.
- ☐ **Controlling and Problem Solving;** monitoring results vs. plan in some detail, identifying deviations, and then planning and organizing to solve the problems.

Management's overall goals were an organization than ran smoothly and predictably, and made good money. The organization was like a machine. Managers both designed the machine to produce specific outputs, and ran the machine to make sure that it produced those outputs.

The key challenge to managers was less designing the machine than running it. The reason, of course, is that most of the "parts" that comprised the "machine" were people. People had to be either hired with the necessary knowledge and skills to do their jobs, or they had to be trained. So selection and training were management issues (and remain issues). Ensuring that the people had the right tools and technology to do the job was also an issue. But the most difficult issue, by far, was motivation.

Since managers were also responsible for the productivity of their people, they needed to be concerned about their people's motivation, for how hard they worked. And managers did not lack for guidance. Countless studies on worker motivation have been conducted over the past decades; a library could be filled with the books and articles that offer sound observations and advice on the subject; millions of managers have received training in motivation techniques. But, despite all of this guidance, ask managers what their toughest job is, and most will respond, "managing people." Decades of research and training on motivating workers have produced only incremental gains, at best.

The old paradigm, then, was a *management paradigm*. The model was mechanistic and controlling. The following table illustrates the sharp division of responsibility:

Managers	Workers
Develop strategies, goals, plans	Implement strategies and plans
Define organizations, jobs, tasks	Perform jobs/tasks
Set rules, procedures, regulations	Follow rules, procedures, regulations

Organizations that use this paradigm are hierarchical, like the military. Everyone knows their "rank," and the privileges and rewards that it brings them. And in most such organizations, there is a broad gap between the privileges and rewards that accrue to managers and those received by the workers. Managers in these organizations justify the gap with the belief that management bears a much larger share of the responsibility for the growth and profitability of the business.

The management paradigm has been with us for a long time. Its roots are in the industrial revolution. And it has flourished along with American business ever since. With a hierarchical, command and control paradigm of management, America's managers and workers have produced an incredible variety of goods and services, together with a standard of living that was the envy of the world.

Why do we need a new paradigm now?

The answer is simple: Because the conditions under which the old paradigm worked well have changed dramatically and, as a result, the paradigm is no longer producing acceptable results. What has changed so dramatically? Let's revisit, briefly, some of the new realities in our business.

- **Unprecedented Business Problems.** Who can say that the management problems they are facing today are not far more difficult and challenging than problems during the Era of Smooth Sailing? Gone is the dependability, predictability, and the relative simplicity that characterized problems during that era. Now we are sailing in uncharted waters, facing new and unique problems. And many of the old solutions are no longer adequate. Managers today need help in solving their new problems.

- **Focus on quality and client satisfaction.** The race clearly is on for client loyalty and referrals that can only be won with consistent high quality, value, and client satisfaction. While good client relations has always been a focus and source of pride within our industry, the expectations have now been raised substantially. We must ensure consistent quality. We must provide value. And this, also, presents managers with unprecedented challenges.

- ☐ **Information technology.** Let's face it: We can not longer afford to be paper driven. We must change our work flows and routines to exploit the cost advantages of technology (while also ensuring consistent quality). This is yet one more challenge for our managers.

Why isn't the old management paradigm solving these problems?

We offer three reasons:

1. In the old paradigm, managers were responsible for solving the problems. Yet, problems like the above can not be solved by management alone. They must be solved *via teamwork* between managers and their Associates. One of the many reasons is that Associates work at the "front lines" every day. They are intimate with clients and underwriters. They bring understanding as well as skill to solving problems.
2. The old paradigm assumed that a focus on quality and client satisfaction could be mandated—just by setting, communicating, and enforcing the standards. Now we know that this is not enough. *It has been proven time and again that quality services start with the attitudes that drive the behaviors of the service providers.* It is consistent behaviors that produce high quality services and highly satisfied clients. So, if managers want an unwavering dedication to quality and client satisfaction they must shape attitudes, they must engage the hearts and minds of their people. And that is impossible to do with the old command and control management paradigm. The hearts and minds of Associates must be won.
3. Our Associates are skilled knowledge workers. They are professionals (you may think of your technical support staff as paraprofessionals). Their value to the organization and to clients is directly linked to the quality and the quantity of the knowledge they bring. And, with the technology of insurance and risk management developing and changing so rapidly, they must now learn continuously. But, continuous learning will not happen via command and control management techniques. Like dedication to quality and client satisfaction, dedication to continuous learning begins with attitudes.

"In the new, information-based organizations that are presently evolving, knowledge and expertise will primarily be distributed at the bottom, held by those who have the most direct contact with the customer."

Peter Drucker in *Harvard Business review*

To summarize, we need a new paradigm for management that will:

- ✓ Engage and align all Associates with the goals of the agency.
- ✓ Include Associates in the management process; and empower them to participate in solving problems that had previously been the exclusive responsibility of management.
- ✓ Enlist Associates' hearts and minds, as well as their energies, in dedication to quality, client satisfaction, and continuous learning.

The New Paradigm: Best Practices Leadership

The good news is that this new paradigm exists and is working.

- The Best Practices leaders we studied are applying it in their agencies, and they are achieving dramatic results.
- Leaders in other industries are also producing results via the new paradigm.
- Books and articles that explain what these leaders are doing abound.

In short, the new paradigm is not a mystery. If you have completed this handbook, you may understand the practices and skills required, and you may know how leaders in our industry are applying them.

> *"Of the best leader, when he is gone, they will say: We did it ourselves."* Chinese Proverb

The Basic Accountability of Best Practices Leaders

Like managers before them, Best Practices leaders are accountable for achieving results through others. Best Practices leaders lead their agency/team in the accomplishment of business objectives such as business development, client satisfaction and retention, cost control and profitability. What separates Best Practices leaders from managers is *how* they achieve the objectives. Managers used command and control techniques. Best Practices leaders use empowerment and inclusion. Managers push workers toward the goals. Best Practices leaders inspire Associates to exceed the goals.

The Four Roles of Best Practices Leaders

When a job has the variation of responsibilities and tasks that agency leadership jobs have, we see advantages in breaking the job into separate roles. To be competent in the job, you must be competent in each of the roles. And, during most work days, you will frequently shift from role to role. In short, you may "play" each role many times, but your overall "performance" will be determined by how well you have "played" each of the roles.

We find that many leaders prefer to think of their job this way. It helps them to focus on the role that is important at the moment, to "play" that role as best they can. It also helps them in assessing their own performance, and their needs to develop skills, since most leaders are stronger in some of their roles than in others.

As we analyzed the accountabilities, responsibilities, and tasks performed by Best Practices leaders, it became apparent that the job contains four reasonably well defined and discrete roles. The most successful Best Practices leaders we have studied perform each of these roles very well.

1. Business Manager Role
2. Performance Facilitator Role
3. Relationship Developer Role
4. Individual Contributor Role

Best Practices Leader: *Business Manager Role*

Principal Accountabilities: Ensure that the mechanistic processes necessary for the agency to accomplish its goals are in place and are working smoothly, e.g.:

- Strategic Goals
- Planning Process
- Systems
- Policies/Procedures
- Work Flow/Process
- Risk Analysis and Avoidance
- Financial & Asset Management
- Employee Selection

1. Ensuring that a sound overall strategic direction and goals for the organization are well defined and communicated.
2. Ensuring that an effective planning process is used, as necessary, to accomplish the goals.
3. Supporting goal accomplishments efforts with such organization, staffing, training, systems, and other resources as may be necessary.
4. Ensures that necessary policies and standards are set and maintained, and that compliance is assured.
5. Ensures that work flow, process, and automated systems are both effective and efficient.
6. Ensures that the likelihood of adverse events impacting the agencies growth, profitability and/or financial stability are minimized.
7. Ensures that the agencies financial and other non-human assets are managed effectively.
8. Maintains effective screening and selection techniques to ensure that new employees hired are highly qualified to join the team.

Notice that in the business manager role, Best Practices leaders *ensure* that these processes, systems and support are in place. This does not mean that they dictate the processes and systems. They may, when they believe it is justified. But more frequently, they will use a *participatory process* to define the processes and systems. Examples of processes and systems used in best practices agencies have been provided in the Handbook, together with how the leaders used participatory techniques to develop them.

Best Practices Leader: *Performance Facilitator Role*

Principal Accountabilities: Ensuring that high levels of performance exist throughout the organization. Best Practices leaders accomplish this by:

- Vision
- Shared Values
- Trust
- Clear Expectations
- Performance Feedback
- Implementation Process
- Coaching and Counseling
- Recognition
- Rewards
- Career Support

1. Aligning all Associates with the agency's vision, values, and objectives.
2. Building and sustaining an atmosphere of trust; ensuring that the worth and dignity of all individuals will be respected at all times; valuing the diversity of experience, opinions, and personal styles throughout the agency.
3. Ensuring that all Associates understand: what is expected of them and of their team; the levels of freedom and control they have in doing their work; the policies and standards with which they must comply.
4. Ensuring that all Associates receive frequent and direct supportive feedback, both positive and corrective.
5. Monitoring activities, plans, and results; facilitating the elimination of bottlenecks and problems.
6. Ensuring that the personal career ambitions and needs of all Associates are understood and supported, to the degree possible.
7. Ensuring that Associates have the information they need to be highly effective in their jobs.

8. Personally coaching and counseling, as necessary.
9. Ensuring that the formal reward and recognition systems are equitable and are administered fairly.
10. Providing frequent informal recognition and rewards.
11. Maintaining a work environment that combines dedication to business tasks and professionalism with appropriate spontaneity, fun, and social collaboration.

Best Practices Leader: *Relationship Developer Role*

We designate this role for emphasis. We believe that the new realities in our business will increasingly place demands on the quality of our relationships with our:

- Associates
- Clients, both external and internal
- Companies/Carriers
- Other suppliers
- Local community

Principal Accountabilities: Ensure that they and their Associates are facile with processes, techniques, and skills for building and sustaining effective business and professional relationships, e.g.:

- Trust
- Communications
- Valuing Diversity
- Feedback
- Relationship Strategies

1. Building foundations of trust and respect in all relationships.
2. Valuing diversity of opinions, beliefs, and personal styles.
3. Using open and direct communications.
4. Reaching understandings and agreements on services to be provided, needs to be met, etc.
5. Establishing standards for service quality.
6. Maintaining processes for soliciting feedback on service quality.
7. Developing and implementing strategies for strengthening key relationships with clients, prospects, carriers.

Best Practices Leader: *Individual Contributor Role*

In our experience with agencies/brokers, rare are leaders who do not carry either personal books of business or close ties to clients, along with their leadership responsibilities. We assume that the accountabilities for this role are understood, and do not need to be defined here.

In Summary: A Best Practices Leader . . .

✓ *Is both* a manager and a leader.

✓ *Manages processes*, the mechanistic systems and procedures required for efficient and effective operations.

✓ *Also manages* the *non-human assets*, e.g., real estate and finance.

✓ *Facilitates* high levels of *human performance* throughout the organization.

✓ *Develops productive relationships* with everyone who can influence the agency's results.

✓ Manages a personal book of business, as required.

Personal Production Plans

Assignment 4

Assignment Objectives

After completing this assignment, you should be able to:

1. Given an insurance agency case, design a personal production plan for a producer.

   In support of the assignment objective listed above, you should be able to do the following:

   a. Explain how the nature of a personal production plan differs depending on a producer's accountabilities for sales.

   b. Illustrate and evaluate goals and objectives in a production plan.

   c. Explain the characteristics of an ideal production plan.

2. Describe how carefully drafted goals and objectives help a producer to meet his or her personal production plans.
3. Establish a personal time management system.
4. Describe various activities that waste producers' sales time.
5. Describe various techniques that will increase goal-related time usage.
6. Explain how the negotiating process can result in a "win-win" situation.
7. Explain how a producer can establish an effective working relationship with an underwriter.
8. Define or describe each of the Key Words and Phrases for this assignment.

Assignment Outline

I. Personal Production Planning
   A. Steps in Personal Production Planning
   B. Personal Planning Summary
   C. An Ideal Production Plan
II. Time Management
   A. The Basics
III. Negotiating
   A. Basic Concepts
IV. Selling the Underwriter
   A. Insurance Company Guidelines
   B. Meeting the Underwriter's Preferences
   C. Providing Information to the Underwriter
   D. Gaining the Underwriter's Trust
V. Summary

Assignment 4

Personal Production Plans

Orient yourself to this assignment by reading the following introduction.

The first three assignments in this text focused primarily on the agency as a business organization; this assignment will be devoted to the producer's individual responsibilities and planning. A thorough understanding of the concepts in the first three assignments is a prerequisite to proper producer planning since, although a producer's success or failure ultimately rests with that individual, producers do not operate independently of their agencies. Agency operations affect the producer's performance, resources, and markets. Agency support can enhance or detract from his or her career.

The last assignment introduced the seven accountabilities of selling insurance—prospecting, fact finding (exposure identification), preparing proposals or quoting, presenting understandable proposals, closing, initial client service, and long-term service. The support the agency gives the producer in these seven accountabilities is determined by the agency's sales management system. Agencies can choose to provide support to producers by taking over many of these accountabilities, thus requiring the producer only to present proposals and close, for example; or agencies may require producers to carry out all of the seven accountabilities itself providing only clerical assistance. Every agency differs.

The producer must understand which of the seven selling accountabilities are his or her responsibility and which are the responsibility of the agency in order to formulate a personal production plan. A **personal production plan** is a plan the individual producer develops. It includes the producer's mission statement and sales goals and objectives as well as the strategies, policies, and procedures used to achieve the stated mission. The personal production plan must be consistent with and supportive of the agency's plans.

Examples of how the seven accountabilities of selling are allocated in various insurance agencies are numerous.

Many insurance agencies do not specialize in any one product or service. Principals in these agencies believe they must offer almost all types of insurance to any insurance buyer. In many small agencies, clerical and support staff are few, and these agencies lack the necessary resources and training to support producers to the extent larger agencies do. Except for the time the principal may be able to spare from full-time production and staff management, no sales manager to guide, train, and supervise the producer is present. For these and other reasons, producers in these agencies must assume responsibility for managing their own activities while handling most if not all of the seven selling accountabilities.

Working in this environment, the producer must develop a personal production plan to encompass a broader range of goals and objectives. A producer in this situation not unusually builds up a book of business gradually, only to find out later that no time is left to solicit new business. The producer becomes so involved in the long-term servicing of accounts that new sales are not possible. If the principals of these agencies want their agencies to grow, they must find new producers to generate new business or begin transferring client service to the support staff. In either case, the job of the agency/owner is difficult. Finding new producers and managing a change in the workings of the support staff are time-intensive and take away from the principal's ability to service his or her own clients. The bottom line for producers in these agencies is that they must plan their sales activities more carefully because they are in charge of more of the ingredients of their success.

Other agencies are more specialized, and the producer may be responsible only for prospecting, fact finding, presenting the proposals, and closing. Support staff handle the other accountabilities. In yet other agencies, the agency provides prospects and leads, leaving the producer to focus on fact finding and selling.

Regardless of how the producer and agency divide the accountabilities, no matter what the size, marketing focus, or management style of the agency, producers encounter different areas of responsibility. The compensation systems for producers (discussed in the previous assignment) should vary based on the producer's account abilities and reflect the duties assumed. More important for this assignment, the producers face entirely different job-related goals and objectives. Every producer must understand his or her role in the agency's sales management system in order to plan effectively and use time wisely.

This assignment addresses the necessity for personal production planning, offers tips for time management, reviews the producer's need for effective negotiating skills, and provides an overview of approaches to selling the underwriter. An ideal production planning system is presented later in this assignment. In addition, the personal production plan assists the producer in time management, an important aspect of producer success.

Read the definition of the *Key Phrase* that follows. Being familiar with this important phrase will help you better understand the first part of this assignment. *Key Words and Phrases* appear in bold in the text when they are defined.

Personal production plan	A plan developed by an individual producer that includes the producer's mission statement, sales goals, strategies, policies, and procedures

Study the first part of this assignment, which includes the following section:

I. Personal Production Planning

Personal Production Planning

General management and sales management begin with the planning function; personal production should begin there, too. George Nordhaus points out, "Yet most agents don't make long-range plans. They seem to be involved with what psychologists call 'the tyranny of the urgent.' The endless details of the moment. . . ."[1] Establishing a personal production plan is the most vital part of self-management.

Steps in Personal Production Planning

A well conceived and drafted personal production plan should be as detailed as an agency's plan (discussed earlier in this segment) and contain the same seven phases:

1. Setting a mission statement
2. Developing strategies
3. Setting goals
4. Setting objectives
5. Developing budgets
6. Setting policies
7. Establishing procedures

To be effective, all phases of the plan must be in writing.

Mission Statement

Because the producer is involved in selling insurance products fitted to the needs of clients, the mission statement should address the needs of those clients. It should not, however, be limited to delivering a particular insurance product to a carefully delineated market segment.

The personal mission statement, like a corporate mission statement, should have these characteristics:

- *It should be broadly stated.* The mission statement generally states the intent of the producer's business career, but refers neither to actual

I. Personal Production Planning
A. Steps in Personal Production Planning
B. Personal Planning Summary

markets the producer will be selling to nor to the specific products to be sold.

- *It should be expressed in terms of meeting the needs of clients or potential clients*. The personal mission statement should state the mission broadly, then narrow it through the strategy statements (discussed below). Since strategies are more flexible and subject to change, narrowing strategies rather than missions is more appropriate.
- *It should be generic (no specific products should be mentioned)*. The producer may want to refer to "insurance needs" rather than "property-liability insurance needs," or, even more broadly, to "risk management needs" rather than "insurance needs."
- *It should be directional*. The final requirement is that the mission statement reveal a career direction for the producer but remain broad enough to allow growth.

The examples used as agency mission statements in a previous assignment in this text can serve as personal mission statements as well:

- "Provide risk management services to my community." A broad statement.
- "To find those people or organizations I can serve within the restrictions of my agency contract." A narrower statement made by an agent of a direct writer.
- "To serve the financial needs of the greater Buffalo community." A statement broad in service and narrow in geographic area.

These examples show that a mission statement, although meeting the four requirements, is still a personal statement that addresses the needs of clients. By its nature, the mission statement does not address the needs of employees, members of the organization, or the person drafting the statement.

Strategies

Personal strategies show a specific approach to accomplishing the individual's mission. The producer's sense of purpose is further revealed by stating strategies that show others within the organization the direction in which the producer wishes to proceed.

Using the Buffalo mission statement as an example, a producer can develop a series of hypothetical personal strategies:

1. To provide total risk management services for small business and not-for-profit organizations
2. To serve the life, health, and employee benefit needs of business and not-for-profit organizations
3. To develop technical competence within our agency in garage insurance, yachts, marinas, and laundries

These three sample strategies show that strategies become more personal, refer to the missions and strategies of the organization, narrow the focus of personal activities, and yet are still broad enough to give a choice of sales activities.

Specific markets should be identified within the strategies for current selling activities, and an educational strategy should be developed if the producer desires to expand the number of markets addressed within the next few planning periods.

Strategies should be shared with others in order to give everyone involved with the plan a specific sense of purpose. Strategies should be written to cover a number of planning periods. They are the foundations of specific short-range planning and should therefore be relatively consistent from planning period to planning period and among all members of the agency.

Goals

Goals are the final target for the planning period. The typical production or sales planning period is one year. The planning period of one year should coincide with the fiscal year of the agency. If an agency operates on a January 1 to December 31 calendar year, for instance, the producer's plan should be the same.

Personal goals should meet seven requisites. They should be (1) specific, (2) measurable, (3) time bounded, (4) end-results oriented, (5) meaningful and challenging, (6) controllable, and (7) written.

Specific

The words and phrases chosen for a goal statement should be clear and unambiguous and should transmit the precise intent of the planner. One reason for this requirement is so the staff supporting the producer's plan knows what is expected of them. Another reason for being specific is to aid in the control process. If exact goals are stated, performance standards and reporting systems will be easier to design.

For instance, assume that a producer sets the following goal:

"I will sell $50,000 of life insurance."

This goal is ambiguous. The producer's sales manager reading this goal has no idea whether the $50,000 refers to annualized premiums, annualized commission, or face amount of protection. In other words, selling a $50,000 mortgage redemption policy may meet this goal, but if the producer meant commissions, the same sale would be only a small step toward the goal. Further, in designing the reporting system, is the crucial figure commissions, premiums, or face amount? The statement is too ambiguous.

Measurable

Measurability can be viewed in two different ways. A goal is measurable if some sort of a yardstick can be used to determine results. Assume that the producer modified the previous life insurance statement to read, "I will sell $50,000 of face amount of permanent life insurance." This example has yardstick measurability. At the end of the planning period, a yardstick of $50,000 is measured against the actual result.

The second type of measurability is a "yes" or "no" measure. Suppose a producer's goal is, "I will add an insurance license in 2004." There are at least two problems with this goal. First, the type of license desired is not specified. Second, because it is not specific, it cannot be measured. The statement also lacks a "standard of performance" as the life insurance sales goal earlier.

The rephrased goal "I will become licensed to sell variable annuities in 2004" is specific and now also meets the "yes" or "no" measurability standard. At the end of that year, if the producer has the license, the goal is met; if not, the goal is not met.

The specificity requisite assists in establishing the reporting system, and the measurability requisite assists in establishing the performance standards.

Time Bounded

Each goal must include a specific time for completion. Goals that say "this year" or "in this period" do not tell the reader when "this year" or "this period" ends. The specific date must be mentioned.

For example, "I will sell five automobile dealers accounts this year" should read, "I will sell five automobile dealers accounts by June 30, 2004." A reader in the second case will clearly know that the "five automobile dealers" yardstick must come out to measure results on June 30, 2004. A personal production goal should be written to allow anyone to read and understand the goal statements. Without a specific date, no goal statement meets that criterion.

End-Results Oriented

A goal statement should clearly express goals as the end results of the activities undertaken to accomplish those results.

A new producer may set this goal: "To make progress on my company's personal lines sales program." "Making progress" is not an end result, nor is it specific, measurable, or time bounded. Problems in the area of end results usually occur when some activity cannot be completed by the end of the planning period. In those cases, the producer should establish an end result acceptable to the producer for the end of the planning period even though it will not be the end result of the activity involved. In this case, the producer could have said, "I will complete seven of the eighteen assignments in Crowley Fire and Marine's personal lines course by December 31, 2004." The completion of seven assignments is not completion of the course, but completion of the seven assignments is a valid end result if the entire course cannot be completed in the planning period.

Meaningful and Challenging

Meaningful and challenging personal goals can be the source of many problems in the goal-setting process. So far, most people not associated with the producer could look at a goal statement and determine whether it meets the requisites. However, the individual producer determines whether a goal is meaningful and challenging. What may be challenging for one producer may not be for another.

Meaningful suggests that the goal is necessary or helpful to the producer in order to meet the producer's strategies and mission. It also means that the goal is in line with other goals of the producer and of the firm. *Challenging* means that the goal is not set either unrealistically high or low. If a producer annually generates $25,000 in commissions from referrals alone, a goal that states, "I will sell $20,000 in commissions from referrals between December 1, 2003 and December 1, 2004," is clearly not challenging. At the other end is a new producer who sets as a goal, "To sell insurance to three-fourths of the people I call on during 2004," thereby establishing a standard of performance that is probably not attainable. One of the reasons for setting goals that meet these requisites is to help establish standards of performance. Setting goals that are too low or unrealistically high is psychologically unsound. However, research indicates that high achievers set high, but realistically achievable, goals.

Controllable

Accomplishing each goal should be within the control of the producer. If the success of the plan depends on activities that are outside his or her control, the producer is establishing performance standards and goals for some other person. A producer should never be held responsible for or blame his or her failure on other people's activity or inactivity. A goal that states, "I will telephone five prospects each week with X-dates from my files during 2004," is within the control of the producer. The producer's activities will require that a file of X-dates be available and that the producer has clearly made a personal commitment to telephone five of them a week. A goal that states, "I will telephone ten prospects a week my company sends to me," is not within the control of the producer. If the insurer does not send any prospects, the producer cannot reach the goal; such a goal is meaningless.

Goals that are important yet not personally controllable need to be restated in terms that make them controllable. Using the previous example, the producer could say, "Each week I will telephone ten prospects from prospect lists, if any, my company sends to me during 2004." Here the producer has made the commitment to call ten people a week from a specific list, but only if the insurance company sends the list. If no prospect lists are sent, no calls need be made, and the goal is still valid. The number of these restated goals must be kept minimal, however, or the producer risks having many valid goals with no income.

Written

The final requisite for a goal is that it be written. Writing goals makes them available to others. Goals expressed in writing are easier for the producer and the sales manager to examine to be sure that they meet the other requisites and are consistent with other goals the producer and the firm develop. Written goals allow the sales manager to review those that are not being met to determine how the staff or the producer can meet them. A written goal establishes a real target for the producer's actions;

one simply kept in mind can be easily forgotten or neglected, or may change with circumstances.

A written goal keeps the producer from too easily revising the goal to meet the actual results, thus creating a false sense of success when in fact the producer is failing. For example, at the beginning of the year the producer declares, "I'll place forty new life policies." By November, the producer has written only three policies and states, "Well, that's pretty good since I only wrote two last year."

Marketing Tip

Commit your goals to writing to test how meaningful they are. If you are reluctant to write a goal down, ask yourself if the reason is that you just don't believe you can do it. If that's the case, the goal is bad, and you need to revise it until you believe it is realistic and attainable.

Writing down goals also has one other advantage. Everyone, including your agency's support staff, wants to back a winner. If you put your goals in writing and share them with others on your team, they have the chance to help you succeed by looking for opportunities that meet your goals. Without knowing what your goals are, how can they help you? If they are unaware of your goals, they may unknowingly distract you from them or even act contrary to them. By writing down your goals and sharing them, you will more likely succeed.

Goal Examples

Usually, a producer will generate a number of goals, and goals should be established in every area of accountabilities and developmental activities. In addition to production goals, education, training, income, supervision, or any other area in which the producer wishes to make significant progress should be addressed in goal format. By clearly establishing goals and showing the relative priorities among the goals, the list serves to help budget the producer's time, a producer's most precious commodity.

An Education Goal. "I will study CPCU this year."

The intent of the goal is a good one, but its form fails in five of the seven requisites. The goal is not specific. CPCU is an eight-part program; which of the eight parts will be studied? During which exam window will the producer sit for the CPCU exam? Does the producer intend to take the national examination at all?

The goal is not measurable. How is "study" measured? There is no yardstick to measure accomplishing the goal and the statement does not even measure on a yes or no basis. If the goal were stated "I will take a CPCU examination," at least the yes/no measurement could be used.

The goal is not time bounded. "This year" does not give the reader any information. Is it the American Institute's academic year, or the calendar year, or the agency's planning (fiscal) year?

The goal is not end-results oriented. Studying in and of itself is not the end result. Taking or passing an examination, or taking a CPCU classroom course, would be end results of studying.

Finally, the goal is potentially not meaningful and challenging. Perhaps studying does come hard for this producer, but the act of reading a chapter in a book can be considered studying. And reading a chapter in a book "this year," although meeting the goal, might not be considered challenging. Also, reading one chapter may or may not be meaningful.

If this producer has as a strategy "To become a professional, a CPCU," the goal is meaningful in that studying CPCU leads to obtaining the designation. But because the goal lacks specificity, measurability, time bounding, and an end result orientation, it cannot yet be considered meaningful.

The goal is, however, both controllable and written.

To make this a goal statement, the deficiencies must be corrected. Any of the following reformulations would meet the requisites of a goal:

1. "I will pass CPCU 510 in the May–June examination window."
2. "I will take the CPCU 510 and CPCU 555 examinations in December–January and May–June, respectively."
3. "I will take the CPCU 510 course offered by the Atlanta Chapter of CPCU during the spring and take the examination in June."

Each of these goal statements is specific, measurable, time-bounded, end-results oriented, meaningful and challenging, controllable, and written.

A Supervision Goal. "During 2004 I will cross-train the people in my unit."

This goal is not specific or measurable. Cross-training means that one person learns the duties and responsibilities of another person within the unit. But which duties and activities will be part of the cross-training? Is the intent to make everyone in the unit able to handle everyone else's job if necessary or just a portion of the total job? Those same questions then make difficult measuring the accomplishment of the goal. Unless the cross-training is specified, it cannot be measured.

The goal is time bounded, end-results oriented, meaningful and challenging, within the producer's control, and written.

A Production Goal. "During calendar year 2004 I will sell $100,000 of new personal lines premium other than life insurance."

The goal is specific. Each personal lines product will be included except for personal life insurance sales. Homeowners, auto, personal umbrella, recreational vehicles, and mobile homeowners all qualify. Premium

I. Personal Production Planning
A. Steps in Personal Production Planning
B. Personal Planning Summary

volume can be measured. Using a commission or policy count would be appropriate, but this producer chose, presumably for valid reasons, to use premiums.

The time bounding is during the year 2004. A number of activities must generate $100,000 of new personal lines business, so the goal is end-results oriented. This goal appears both meaningful and challenging to the producer. It certainly is within his or her control *if* other goals will not take too much of the producer's time and energy to accomplish. Finally, the goal is written.

Any producer reading this goal may want to change the statement that makes it personally understandable. That is one of the advantages of goal setting. No one producer's goals will exactly suit another producer. One may want a commission measure; another may want the premium (or commissions) stated per line within personal lines. A third may want to eliminate any personal lines goals and concentrate on commercial lines. Criticizing a goal statement should emphasize the *format,* since a goal is a personal responsibility.

Objectives

Objectives are milestones toward goals. In football, if the goal is to score a touchdown—to cross the goal line—the objective may be to advance the ball at least ten yards every three plays. The objective is essential to accomplishing the goal and will usually be accomplished before the goal.

Requisites for an Objective

The requisites for a statement of objectives are the same as those for goals: specific, measurable, time bounded, end-results oriented, meaningful and challenging, controllable, and written. However, applying each requisite to objectives is slightly different.

Goals state the strategy the producer adopts toward a personal mission. The strategy is relatively "loose," and the mission statement is broad and geared toward the producer's clients. Objectives should be directed at accomplishing the goals they support.

Objectives should be as clear as the goals. When writing goals and objectives, the producer should list the goal beginning on the far left-hand side of a page and indent the objectives that support the goal. The hierarchy of the plan becomes clear and shows how the specific objectives relate to one goal. Exhibit 4-1 exemplifies this plan.

The cross-training goal discussed earlier, now revised to meet the requisites of a goal, reads: "By the end of 2004, each of the three support people in my unit will be able to handle the duties of the others." The intent is to operate the unit efficiently in the absence of any one member, and the producer has until the end of the year to accomplish the cross-training. Logically, what steps must be taken between now and the end of the year to accomplish the goal? That question should lead to a list of activities necessary to reach the goal:

1. Meet with the unit to explain what must be done.
2. Ask each member of the unit to describe his or her major job functions to the others.
3. Be sure each member spends some time each day with the others observing and doing their jobs. How much time?
4. Surprise the unit periodically and switch positions.
5. Ask each unit member to prepare a short oral test for the others to see whether they understand each other's duties.
6. Reward the unit for their efforts.

This list is not intended to be the objectives, but rather a list of some of the activities that could take place to reach the goal. In this example the producer first decides to get the unit's support before proceeding—a good idea. In answering the questions, the producer could rephrase the activities and convert them to objectives for the cross-training that will be done.

Exhibit 4-1
Education Goals and Objectives for Joan Producer

I will sit for CPCU 520 and 560 examinations during 2005.

- I will take the CPCU 520 class offered by the local chapter in the fall of 2004.
- I will take the CPCU 560 class offered by the local chapter in the spring of 2005.
- I will read each assignment and complete the course guide for each assignment as they are assigned.
- I will reserve 8:00 A.M. to 8:30 A.M. and 4:30 P.M. to 5:15 P.M. each workday to study my CPCU assignment.

I will complete a property insurance educational course by June 2004.

- I will find a property insurance course to take by January 31, 2004.
- I will register for the course by March 31, 2004.
- I will buy a new tennis racket if I complete the course as planned.

I will teach INS 21 for my office during 2004–05.

- I will hold classes once a week for 15 weeks (two review sessions).
- I will actively solicit attendance within the office three weeks prior to the beginning of classes.
- I will start the class no later than October 1, 2004.
- I will spend two hours each Sunday preparing for the class.
- I will take each student who attends 13 of 15 classes to lunch.

Objective #1

"Meet with the unit as a group before May 1, 2004, to discuss cross-training and how to accomplish it." When the producer calls the meeting, before the first of May, the members of the unit will have a clear idea why they are meeting and what ideas they should bring with them.

I. **Personal Production Planning**
   A. Steps in Personal Production Planning
   B. **Personal Planning Summary**
   C. An Ideal Production Plan

Some of the ideas the other members of the unit suggest may be better than the ones the producer's list of questions originally suggested. A general planning rule is to be flexible. Changing plans should not worry the planner. If a better and more effective way can be found to accomplish a goal, that new way should be adopted. If a goal and its objectives turn out to be unattainable, the plan should be changed.

Objective #2

"During the initial meeting, members of the unit will be asked to contribute their ideas for cross-training." The time bounding is during the meeting that, according to objective #1, is to be held before May 1. The objective states that each member will be *asked* rather than each member will *contribute*. It may seem subtle, but "asking" is controllable, whereas "each member *will* contribute" is not controllable.

Objective #3

"Each unit member will spend one hour per day with each other member during the first month of cross-training to learn other job duties." As the unit's supervisor, the producer has the right to ask the unit members to do certain job-related tasks. In this case, the producer can state the time period for training. But assume that during the meeting the unit members suggest that because of their close association, they already have a good idea about each other's job duties. One month is too long a time, and if they take two hours from their current jobs to study other jobs and have to spend another two hours cross-training for their own jobs, they will get little work done. Therefore, the unit suggests that the three members meet to decide on a cross-training schedule that will meet the goal and objectives but still allow the normal workload. The producer agrees, and the objective can now be revised to reflect the unit members' real world: "The unit members will devise a cross-training schedule to last a maximum of two weeks, by May 15, 2004."

The producer knows that if the members of the group are allowed to participate in a decision, a better decision will be made. The unit members know their job tasks better than the producer and can work out the details more effectively than the producer. And if the objective is a suggestion of the unit, the unit will more likely be committed to it and work harder to accomplish it.

Establishing the objectives for this particular goal continues until the producer and the unit are satisfied that everything can be accomplished within the constraints and by the appointed time. The producer must now establish a reward objective for the unit. A two-hour lunch, a day off, or more frequent casual days may show the unit that the supervisor appreciates their efforts.

Budgets

Because a budget is designed to allocate scarce resources, producers, for their personal planning, should think about how to budget time as well as how to budget money.

Time budgeting is the allocation of available business-related time toward the accomplishment of the producer's goals. Budgets for time should be drafted *after* goals and objectives, since they set many constraints on the producer's time. Time management will be discussed later in this assignment.

Policies

Remember, policies are generalized guidelines to carry out activities; they also limit those activities. The producer could have as a policy, "All agency billed accounts that are fifteen days past due on premium payment will be sent notice of cancellation. Any exceptions must be approved by management." This policy, if communicated to the support staff who process and mail the necessary paperwork, limits the staff to a course of action unless management chooses to make an exception.

Policies should always be written. Since most of the activities that are affected by policies are delegated, a written reference would help the persons responsible. A manual is not necessary unless the delegated activity is complex, but the more that is committed to writing, the more likely it is that the policies will be followed.

Procedures

Procedures state the way to do things. For instance, in developing a personal sales plan, the producer decides to use, as a portion of the plan, an introductory mailing program. Since most processing related to the mailing program is routine, it should be delegated. The support staff creates and mails the letters in a controllable fashion. If the producer has a list of 100 automobile dealers in the area, mailing letters to all of them at once would not make sense. Some auto dealers would eventually be contacted so long after being mailed the letter that the letter would not accomplish the objective. Therefore, a procedure is established such as, "On Monday morning, mail form letter 37 (auto dealers) to five names on the auto dealer's prospect list." The producer can then be reasonably sure that only five dealers will have to be contacted within a short time.

As with policies, procedures should be written out.

Personal Planning Summary

The production planning of all producers may result in formalizing the organization's sales plans into a manual. Certain aspects of goals and objectives may be reduced to policies and procedures. Exhibits 4-2 and 4-3 are examples of pages from such manuals. The first portion of Exhibit 4-2 relates the organization's goals to an X-date inventory and solicitation goals for commercial and personal lines. In the next portion, a producer has selected goals from the array of agency goals. The third portion projects the solicitation goals into revenue goals.

I. **Personal Production Planning**
   A. Steps in Personal Production Planning
   B. **Personal Planning Summary**
   C. An Ideal Production Plan

Exhibit 4-2
Broad Individual Solicitation Goals

Annual "Inventory" Goals
- a. 600 X-dates for personal lines prospects
- b. 150 X-dates (all lines) commercial account prospects

Key Solicitation Goals
- I. Personal Lines
  - A. 400 Homeowners X-dates
  - B. 200 Automobile X-dates
- II. Commercial Lines X-dates
  - A. 5—Volunteer fire departments
  - B. 15—"Main street" type small business accounts
  - C. 5—Fire prospects
  - D. 20—Small, medium building trades contractors
  - E. 5—Attorneys
  - F. 5—Office tenants
  - G. 5—Funeral homes
  - H. 5—Printers
  - I. 10—Medical professionals
  - J. 5—Churches
  - K. 5—Veterinarians and/or animal hospitals
  - L. 5—Auto parts wholesalers
  - M. 5—Air conditioning and refrigerator wholesalers
  - N. 10—Fast food businesses or restaurants
  - O. 5—Fraternal clubs
  - P. 10—Hardware dealers
  - Q. 5—Drug stores or pharmacies
  - R. 5—Scrap and secondary material dealers (recycling)
  - S. 5—Motels
  - T. 5—Apartment projects
  - U. 5—Banks, savings and loans
  - V. 5—Private schools

Specific Solicitation Goals
- I. Weekly X-dates
  - A. 12—Personal lines prospects
  - B. 3—Commercial account prospects
- II. Telemarketing Program

Annual "Inventory" Goals
- A. 800 X-dates for personal lines prospects
- B. 50 X-dates (all lines) commercial account prospects

Key Solicitation Goals
- I. Personal Lines
  - A. 600 Homeowners X-dates
  - B. 200 Automobile X-dates
- II. Commercial Lines X-dates
  - A. 5—Volunteer departments
  - B. 15—"Main street" type small business accounts
  - C. 5—Fire prospects

D. 5—Office tenants
E. 5—Churches
F. 5—Veterinarians and/or animal hospitals
G. 5—Fraternal clubs
H. 5—Private schools

Specific Solicitation Goals

I. Weekly X-dates
    A. 16—Personal lines prospects
    B. 1—Commercial account prospect
II. Telemarketing Program
    A. Every Monday, 5:30 P.M. to 8:30 P.M.
        1. Phone prospecting using
            a. Tot finder referrals
            b. Utility direct mail leads
            c. New homes/resale home leads

Key Market Objectives:

1. 16—Homeowners: Average premium = $200
2. 8—Automobiles: Average premium = $800
3. 4—Commercial: Average premium = $5,000

Specific Market Objectives:

A. 10 HO-3s
    1. 6—with replacement cost endorsement
    2. 4—with inland marine endorsement
B. 6 HO-2s
    1. 2—with $300,00 Section II
    2. 2—with replacement cost endorsement
C. 8 Automobile
    1. 2—with limits = $300,000
       —with limits = $5,000 medical

Reprinted with permission from George Nordhaus, IMMS of California, 1992.

To assist all personnel in the firm, top management established policies and procedures for the routine aspects of reaching the goals. The first part of Exhibit 4-3 is a written guide for policies and procedures. According to that guide, (1) some homeowners policies are to be upgraded from HO-2s to HO-3s; (2) liability limits are to be upgraded to $300,000; (3) the limits on medical payments are to be upgraded to a minimum of $2,000; (4) deductibles are to be upgraded according to the value of the home; and (5) additional Section I perils are to be added.

The rest of Exhibit 4-3 contains specific renewal objectives for personal lines and commercial lines.

In an organization using a planning system, producers have a clear idea of what management expects and can select those organizational goals that reflect personal interests and goals. Such a system makes personal planning easier and helps assure both the producer's success and the organization's success.

Exhibit 4-3
Policy and Procedure Guide

Subject: Key Personal Lines Renewal Objectives

A. Homeowners
   1. Upgrade HO-2s to HO-3s
   2. Upgrade Section II limits to $300,000
   3. Upgrade medical limits to $2,000 minimum
   4. Upgrade deductibles to $250 minimum on homes valued under $100,000; to $500 minimum for homes valued over $100,000
   5. Offer:
      a. Earthquake coverage
      b. Backup of sewers, drains, etc. coverage

B. Automobile
   1. Increase liability limits to $300,000
   2. Increase medical limits to $5,000
   3. Increase deductible collision coverages to $500 on all medium- to high-priced luxury cars
   4. Increase comprehensive deductibles to $250
   5. Offer:
      a. Towing and labor
      b. Accidental death and dismemberment
      c. Rental reimbursement

Subject: Specific Personal Lines Renewal Objectives

A. Homeowners
   1. Upgrade _____ HO-2s to HO-3s
   2. Upgrade _____ Section II limits to $300,000 and _____ to $500,000
   3. Upgrade ____ policies deductible to $500 and _____ to $250
   4. Increase ____ policies medical limits to $2,000
   5. Sell _____ earthquake coverage endorsements and ____ water/sewer backup endorsements
   6. Sell ____ inland marine endorsements

B. Automobile
   1. Sell ____ towing and labor endorsements
   2. Sell _____ rental reimbursements
   3. Increase _____ policy limits to $300,000
   4. Increase ____ policies medical payment limits to $5,000
   5. Increase ____ policies deductible limits to $250 and ____ policies deductibles to $500
   6. Increase comprehensive deductibles in ____ policies to $250
   7. Sell ____ car rental endorsements
   8. Sell ____ accidental death/dismemberment endorsements

Subject: Commercial Lines Renewal Objectives

I. Internal Broad Commercial Lines Renewal Objectives
   A. Complete customer information cards
   B. Update 3-5 year loss history records

C. Obtain current financial information for surety purposes (where bonds in effect)
D. Review file 90 days prior to renewal with sales representative
E. Give written record of recommendations for discussion with client to sales representative
F. Complete risk management surveys for each account
G. Check all accounts for experience ratings; take necessary steps to experience rate those eligible
H. Review accounts for implementation of:
    1. Self-insurance capabilities
    2. Higher voluntary deductibles—all eligible areas

II. Internal Key Commercial Lines Renewal Objectives
A. Increase liability limits to $1,000,000 for accounts with net worth $100,000 or more
B. Increase liability limits to $500,000 for accounts with net worth less than $100,000
C. Add on special pak or similar package coverages
D. Assist accounts in completion of OSHA and ERISA requirements imposed by law (refer to account sales representative)
E. Obtain applications for commercial umbrella
F. Place all eligible accounts on dividend workers compensation program

III. Internal Specific Commercial Lines Renewal Objectives
A. Increase ____ policies liability limits to $1,000,000
B. Increase ____ policies liability limits to $500,000
C. Sell ____ commercial umbrellas
D. Sell _____ license and permit bonds
E. Sell ____ special pak coverages (or similar packaged deals)
F. Sell ____ contract pak coverages (or similar packaged deals)
G. Obtain ____ commercial referrals each month
H. Complete _____ risk management surveys in coordination with sales representative
I. Complete _____ account information review sheets
J. Increase ____ policies deductibles on collision coverages—fleet auto to $500
K. Increase property damage deductibles to $500 on _____ policies

Reprinted with permission from George Nordhaus, IMMS of California, 1992.

An Ideal Production Plan

The ideal production plan for a producer should possess the following characteristics. It should (1) be negotiated with the sales manager, (2) give the producer self-guiding activities, (3) give the sales manager a tool with which to evaluate the producer, (4) allow the agency to reduce both the time and money invested in the producer, and (5) be consistent with the agency's overall plan. Producers should consider the following:

- The producer's production plan should be negotiated with the sales manager or principal for several reasons. First, of course, the producer should direct his or her efforts towards the kind of business the agency wants to sell. Also, the producer's plan may involve assistance from members of the agency staff. For example, the support staff may have to produce letters, and account representatives or service representatives may have to learn new coverages.

- A well-written personal production plan gives the producer a set of self-guiding sales activities. A saying is attributed to life insurance agent Ben Feldman: "The sale of insurance is a procedure and not a problem. It only becomes a problem when it ceases to be a procedure." A property-liability producer can adopt the same philosophy by establishing goals and objectives that are sales procedures.
- A negotiated personal production plan, with stated goals and objectives, gives the sales manager or agency principal an ideal evaluation tool. If a producer is not meeting a particular sales goal, the sales manager and producer can talk about the objectives. They may discover, for example, that florists are generally not willing to make appointments with producers over the phone and that a new objective based on some other initial contact is necessary. It may become obvious that the goal itself is unrealistic and that sales efforts would be better directed towards another target market. In other cases meeting the goal was easy because the objectives were extremely effective. The agency could encourage other producers to use the same system to develop agency expertise in this type of sale.

  It is important to the sales manager that the producer clearly agree to the goals and objectives. If the producer does not meet the goals because he or she did not use the procedures established by the objectives, then the sales manager may decide to terminate the producer. If there is no sales manager, the producer must be honest enough to see when activities are not accomplishing the expected results and when he or she is consistently missing objectives. The producer should then revise the goals and objectives. If the failure is consistent and apparently irreversible, the producer should acknowledge the situation and resign before the relationships with the principal and other agency staff deteriorate to bitterness and blame.
- When a manager must make a firing decision, using a negotiated production plan and checking on the producer's progress enables the sales manager or principal to recognize a mismatch between the individual and the job much earlier than otherwise, saving the agency both time and money. On the positive side, since most producers want to succeed, negotiating a plan and helping the producer meet goals and objectives will help the producer generate new business more rapidly; the producer will contribute to the agency's profits more quickly—again reducing the time and dollar investment in the producer.
- The producer must formulate an individual plan that fits into the agency's plan. Staff support depends on trained personnel. Insurance company representation will determine the size and types of business that the agency can produce. If the agency emphasizes commercial versus personal, property and casualty versus life and health, and

large versus small account size, the producer's goals must agree. If the producer has one set of goals, and the agency has another, neither will have much success in meeting their goals.

Personal production plans are vital. They must contain the same components as the agency's plan and be consistent with that plan. Managing time, negotiating, and building relationships with underwriters are also important issues for producers. These topics will be discussed in the second part of this assignment.

Check your understanding of the *Phrase* found in the first part of this assignment.

Personal production plan (p. 1)

Review the concepts presented in the first part of this assignment by answering the following questions. **Note: Acceptable answers to all questions appear at the end of this segment.**

1. What are the seven selling accountabilities? (p. 1)

2. How does the number of accountabilities affect a producer's production plan? (pp. 1-2)

3. What are the steps in personal production planning? (p. 3) 7 STEPS

   Mission — Budgets
   Strategy — Policies
   Goals — Procedures
   Objectives

4. What are the four requirements for a personal mission statement? (pp. 3-4)

   - meets needs of clients
   - generic
   - directional
   -

5. Write a personal mission statement for yourself.

6. Write three strategies you believe will help you accomplish your mission.

7. What are the seven requisites of a goal or objective? (p. 5)

8. Evaluate the following statements and determine whether they meet the requisites for a goal:
   (a) "I will improve my sales by 25 percent this year."

   (b) "I will become better organized."

   (c) "I will take the AAI 83 exam soon."

9. Explain the relationship between goals and objectives. (pp. 10-11)

10. What are the five characteristics of an ideal production plan? (pp. 17-18)

- negotiated w/ sales manager
- self-guiding activities
- measurable goals for evaluation by sales mgr.
- time/money should reduce over time agent can produce
- be consistent with agency's overall plan.

Apply the concepts presented in the first part of this assignment by answering the following questions.

1. Bill James has developed a production plan stating that 200 new personal lines clients will be sold by the end of the current year. Halfway through the year only 75 new clients have been added to the books. Bill is concerned, and he is considering scrapping the entire plan, feeling that there is no way to accomplish the goal. Bill has asked for your advice. What issues would you discuss with Bill?

2. An ideal production plan for a producer requires negotiation with the sales manager.
   (a) Why is this negotiation important?

   (b) What adverse consequences might arise without such negotiation?

Read the definitions of the *Key Words and Phrases* that follow. Being familiar with these important words will help you better understand the second part of this assignment.

Negotiating	Discussion ending in mutual agreement
"Win-win" scenario	Agreement where both parties believe they have won

Study the second part of this assignment, which includes the following sections:

II. Time Management
III. Negotiating
IV. Selling the Underwriter

Time Management

After the producer has developed a personal production plan, he or she must find the time to get out and sell. If a producer spends a great deal of time identifying markets and approaches to those markets, it would be a shame to have the plan fail because he or she is not selling to those markets. Yet producers commonly spend most of their time on nonsales activities—one estimate is less than one hour of selling for every four hours of nonselling time. Three reasons are often cited for this low percentage of time spent selling:

1. Producers spend most of their time servicing existing clients and managing.
2. Producers have attained personally acceptable levels of income, and the potential gain in income does not motivate them to keep working as hard at finding new clients.
3. Producers prefer to service rather than to sell insurance.

The popular definition of management is to "get work done through the efforts of others"; good management skills may help to overcome the first reason. As discussed in previous assignments, effective delegation and understanding are crucial when turning management and service duties over to others is more profitable.

Also as discussed in previous assignments, income is not the only motivator. Management and the producer can build meaningful rewards into the production plan to overcome the second reason.

Finally, one major aversion to selling is the effect of rejection on the ego. Assuming the producer could be an effective salesperson, the production plan and its control procedure, in conjunction with training in effective selling techniques, can help the producer to increase the number of "yes" responses and hence decrease the fear of selling.

The purpose of time management is to overcome the reasons that producers don't sell and to increase the time available for selling. In other words, time must be focused on those activities that lead the producer to attain the goals and meet the objectives of the personal production plan.

The Basics

Many time management texts discuss tips and techniques, as if the problems would be solved if one just becomes clever enough at using these techniques. For example, here are some problematic tips:

- *Save your time*. Saving time is a misnomer. Time is going by in a constant stream. One cannot acquire more time. One has exactly the same amount in a given day as everyone else, no more or less.
- *Get more done in less time*. A fallacy many fall prey to is "high efficiency" time management. Rather than finding the most valuable use of time, they focus on getting more done in a given length of time. This can lead at worst to burnout, at best to a triumph of motion over meaning. One feels busy but seems to be accomplishing nothing. As management writer Peter Drucker says, "There is nothing quite so useless as doing with great efficiency that which should not be done at all."
- *Make a to-do list*. Not a bad idea, but too often list making then becomes a simple game of "How many items did I cross off today?" without regard as to whether the items should have been done at all.

Some people get so enamored of this idea they will actually spend considerable time on activities not on their list, then add them later just to cross them off. At the end of the day, looking back on a long list of crossed-off "accomplishments," they consider the day well spent when in fact they did nothing of consequence.

- *Delegate everything possible*. Another good concept, as discussed in this text. But if the activity wastes time, delegating it simply makes another person waste time. First decide what is important to do, *then* delegate what others can do more effectively.

There are many other tips, but all may have the unfortunate result of giving a sense of effectively managing time when the wastefulness already costing you one of your most precious resources is merely rearranged. One may as well rearrange all the papers on the desk without actually working on any of them. One feels a sense of accomplishment, but nothing really happened.

The important question in time management is the same as in money management—If this is all you have, where is the best place to "spend" it? Once it is gone, will you be able to look back at your "purchases" and know you chose wisely? Was it properly allocated or did you just "use it up"? And the key to getting limited time allocated to its best uses is to eliminate time wasters and start setting priorities.

Eliminating Timewasters

Eliminate those activities that waste time without providing any meaningful benefit. Dr. R. Alec Mackenzie, an expert in time management, cites sixteen major timewasters.[2]

- Responding to crises instead of to what is important
- Inadequate planning/objectives
- Telephone interruptions
- Visitors
- Paperwork/red tape
- Ineffective delegation
- Attempting too much
- Personal disorganization
- Procrastination and indecision
- Meetings
- Inadequate staff
- Socializing
- Lacking self-discipline
- Inability to say "no"
- Incomplete information
- Leaving tasks unfinished

These sixteen timewasters are in the order of importance producers indicated in Dr. Mackenzie's study. In almost every case, if a producer establishes a sales system with a production plan and works that system, he or she will mitigate the timewasters. In some cases, such as telephone

I. Personal Production Planning
II. Time Management
A. The Basics
III. Negotiating

interruptions and visitors, the producer should seek the cooperation of others on the staff.

Eliminating these timewasters is not as easy as it may seem, but doing so is crucial. Everyone likes to have a positive attitude, as well as to be seen by coworkers as helpful and cooperative. And many people have difficulty saying "no." Yet saying "yes" to too many activities leaves no time to do those things that are meaningful to production plans.

Producers must learn to recognize these timewasters and eliminate or at least minimize them.

Setting Priorities

Setting and sticking to priorities are the heart of an effective time management system. Everyone has priorities, whether writing them down and designating them as such or not. But just as with goals and objectives, the failure to actually establish written priorities makes it far too easy to ignore them or let other activities get in their way. If they deserve attention, take the time to think them through and then write them down.

A myriad of time management systems discuss setting priorities. All begin with making a to-do list of every task that needs to get done in a given amount of time. A letter (or number) is then assigned to each task, establishing its relative importance. Some systems use three levels of priorities, others four or five. Which system a producer chooses is not as important as the process itself.

For our purposes, four priority levels will suffice. These can be labeled as priorities A through D.

1. Important and urgent (As)
2. Important but not urgent (Bs)
3. Urgent but not important (Cs)
4. Not important and not urgent (Ds)

(All of Dr. MacKenzie's sixteen timewasters listed above could be labeled as either Cs or Ds.)

Once the to-do list is labeled, nearly all time management texts claim that worries are over. Simply focus on finishing As, then move on to Bs, then Cs and, if time allows, do a few Ds. Why, then, do so many people fail to accomplish their goals? The potential trap lies in how the terms "important" and "urgent" are defined.

Many producers never define those terms. They let others define "important" and "urgent" for them. For example, you walk into your office early in the morning and find several phone messages already on your desk (or in your voice mail); the receptionist has just called to warn that your client who has been giving grief to every CSR in the agency is in the lobby and the support staff want you to handle him this time; and there are fresh doughnuts (your favorite) in the coffee room in honor of the bookkeeper's birthday. No matter what you decide to do at this point, who really determined what was important and urgent for you this morning? The client is important, but the support staff referred him to you. You didn't bring in the doughnuts, but they certainly got your attention. And those phone messages are crying out to be returned. You will probably be busy this entire day without getting to any task *you* would have chosen as important or urgent. Unfortunately, the priority list in this scenario is beyond your control; that client will have to come first.

A first step in gaining control of time allocation is to learn that the term *urgent* does not necessarily mean *automatic priority*. Your focus must be on the term *important*. Important is any task that leads to accomplishing the goals you have set for yourself. *Priorities* are those tasks you choose that lead toward those goals; the tasks that do not are not priorities. Once you determine which tasks are *important*, then you can separate those tasks into *urgent* (those items that may need immediate, short-term attention) or *not urgent*. If a task is not *important*, then any sense of *urgency* attached to that task is probably incorrect or at least a misplaced priority.

Once you have properly classified your tasks, *then* you can begin to focus on maximizing important items—As and Bs—and minimizing Cs. Remember, the only proper approach to Ds is to eliminate them.

Focusing on Important Activities (A and B Priorities)

Since important activities are those that lead toward goals, every possible minute of production time must be allocated to these areas. If in doubt, ask yourself how this activity brings you closer to your goals. If you are not sure, it is probably not an A or B priority. Examples of important activities include prospecting, fact finding, preparing proposals, and closing interviews.

Producers should not think that the best use of their time is always an A item, and they only move on to Bs when all As are completed. Both A and B items are important; the difference is the sense of urgency and immediacy of an A item. Constantly working only on items that seem urgent leads to what has been called the "tyranny of the urgent," treating priorities as if all plans, goals, and objectives were only laid out for one day. Since plans actually cover months and years, a short-term focus on A items will lead to stress, burnout, and eventual failure.

Management author Stephen Covey, in *The Seven Habits of Highly Effective People*, calls the need to back off from handling only the current emergency and spend time preparing for future needs "sharpening the saw." The analogy is clear—if you spend all your time cutting, you may get work done, but at some point the saw (you) is going to get worn down and useless. At least some time must be spent in rest and preparation if the "saw" is to remain sharp and ready. In fact, Covey is so convinced of the wisdom of this, he suggests spending the most time doing B items.

For the producer, B items include investing time in training and education, which are preparation for opportunities farther along in planning periods. Choose training that will enable you to be of more help to your clients and prospects. Another B item is prospecting and X-dating. The prospects should be those who will become next year's clients, not just the one who will buy today. For B items, always think in terms of an investment now for a long-term payoff.

Management Tip

Taking the long-term view of priorities can be tough, particularly for a new producer who sees every sale as food on the table. The new producer may overpromise or give up too much just to get the sale. The agency and the producer will later pay the price for this desperate act by losing money on the account or a possible E&O claim, but that is all in the future, and the producer is often focused entirely on the immediate need to succeed.

A number of sound psychological ways can increase the amount and effectiveness of time spent on A and B items. The producer should, for instance, pick the peak emotional time of the day to concentrate on selling activities. During that peak time, the producer feels the freshest and most alert. For some it will be the morning, but others will find the afternoon or evening best.

Producers can manage their time with clients in several ways. On calls to prospects and clients with appointments, be prompt. No one likes to wait when an appointment has been made. The producer is trying to make a good impression, and tardiness is not helpful in creating that impression.

In appointments of every sort, be clear and concise. The simpler the language, the easier it is to make a point. Some clients may want detailed explanations of recommendations or ideas; others will accept the wisdom of an expert without further explanation. Give clients and prospects the opportunity to accept suggestions without a lengthy dissertation on the importance of the suggestion.

Have a specific goal in mind before any appointment. If the call is to obtain an X-date, every effort should be made to obtain the date and end the appointment. Without a goal, an appointment can drag on long past its useful period.

In any sales call, know the essential points to make. A short outline of why a producer wants the expiration date can help to organize the call. If the appointment is to present technical suggestions about coverage changes or risk management procedures designed to minimize premium dollars, arrange the suggestions and arguments logically beforehand. This procedure also helps to avoid a rambling sales presentation.

Marketing Tip

A good way to prepare for a crucial presentation is to try it out on a member of the agency staff, preferably a nontechnical person. In this way, the producer not only gets practice to help get the nerves settled, but also the presentation is held up to the "jargon quotient." If the producer tends to use too many insurance terms

(CGL, BAP, UM, Comp, and so forth), a technical person listening in wouldn't notice since the terms are all familiar. A nontechnical person can point out when the terms used are vague or confusing, helping the producer translate insurance talk into the prospect's language.

Set time limits in advance and make them known. If a producer sets an appointment, it is just as important to know when the appointment will be over as to know when it starts. For instance, "Jim, I need to pick up your insurance policies to review your program. I will be in your neighborhood Friday at 2:30 and I am sure we can be done by 2:45." Time is a producer's (and a client's) most valuable resource and should be invested wisely.

Use normal meal times for appointments or meetings. A common practice in many areas is to begin the day with a breakfast appointment. The producer has to eat anyway, so why not turn the mealtime into a sales opportunity? Lunch for many is essentially C time. It can become an A or B with a sales-related appointment.

Plan the next day or week at the end of the current day or week. Elaborate allocations of time are not necessary, but a review of what needs to be done tomorrow or next week will help the producer allocate time.

Finally, make the time allocated appropriate to the task. For instance, three hours to pick up a personal auto policy X-date is excessive. Those same three hours may be inadequate, however, to complete a commercial insurance exposure analysis.

Minimizing C Priorities

It seems difficult to imagine how something could be urgent but unimportant. Yet the concept is important to understand because once the obvious timewasters have been eliminated, the producer can find real time management improvements in these C items.

Controlling the Phone A common example of a C task is phone calls. The phone rings and we feel compelled to answer it. How many times have you been in the middle of a serious and productive face-to-face conversation with another person, only to have the phone ring and the other person say, "Just a moment while I get this"? Why would any intelligent person consider the unknown caller to be a priority over the person actually present? Although many people dislike the use of voice mail and answering machines in screening calls, both of these tools can help a producer manage the priority of phone calls.

There are two helpful hints when composing the outgoing message with voice mail. First, make the outgoing greeting personal. Record a greeting in your natural voice, with the current date and a promise of when the caller can expect a return call. If you normally answer the phone jovially but your voice mail message sounds robotic, you reinforce the idea that the caller is talking to a machine and not a human. Even though recorded, your natural voice will be welcoming.

Second, tell your callers in your message how they can use *your* voice mail to help *them*. Often callers are simply instructed to "leave your name and number." But if the caller does not leave a more detailed message, then the producer has no idea what the call is about. Assuming the producer reaches the person on the return call and not his or her voice mail, the producer may be forced to take notes on the problem and call back after doing the necessary research to answer the question. Now the producer must make a *third* phone call, risking getting voice mail again. Some people hate voice mail since all they do is endlessly trade phone numbers. A better method is to ask in the greeting for the caller to record the reason for the call. Then, when you call back, you will be prepared with the necessary information to solve the problem. If you get voice mail, you can leave a complete answer to his or her question—which is exactly what the caller wanted.

Also mention in your greeting that if the caller would like information faxed or e-mailed, he or she should record the information requested and a fax number or e-mail address. Then no return call is needed, and you (or better yet a member of your support staff) can obtain the information and deliver it to the client.

Cellular Phones and Pagers As producers become more mobile and spend more time out of the office, they would seem to have less worry about phone interruptions. Naturally, someone else or their voice mail will need to take the calls, and the clients will have to understand.

But many producers have avoided this potential solution and have continued the problem by purchasing a cellular phone. If the client is given the cellular number (and many producers put the number on their business cards), in effect the producer has given the client the right to interrupt whatever the producer may be doing twenty-four hours a day. *Now* who is setting the priorities? Turning the phone off is no answer, since again, calls go unanswered, which is the problem the cellular phone was to solve.

A better solution for the mobile producer may be a pager. These devices keep the producer in touch, but beyond the beep or the vibration (depending on the type of pager and options chosen) the producer is free to choose to continue the task at hand, returning the call at the most appropriate time. Many pagers simply display a phone number, which is the least costly option, but this feature also creates the potential for phone tag. More complex pagers and services are available that allow messages to be delivered directly to the pager or stored in voice mail. No matter what the choice, that choice belongs to the producer, who must remember his or her priorities.

One suggestion for cellular users is also to get a pager and give out the pager number and not the cellular number. When calls come in, the producer can review the pager message and return the calls according to *priorities*—either immediately with the cellular phone or later upon returning to the office. Thus, the producer has the convenience of the cellular while retaining the control.

The cellular phone does give the producer the option of making or returning calls while away from the office. Many producers spend hours driving daily; this time could be productive if the producer uses the cellular phone to answer client questions that otherwise would be answered from the office phone. This approach leaves more office time available for priorities that require that type of time.

Management Tip

The "tyranny" of the telephone is well documented but often difficult to control precisely because our cultural bias suggests that it's rude not to be immediately accessible when someone wants to speak with you. This is compounded by the often ingrained fear that any call unanswered is an opportunity lost. This fear has probably sold the majority of the millions of cellular phones now carried by business people. Yet the phone call is a classic example of having priorities set by others—namely, the caller. If you are to set your priorities, then the phone must be managed like any other activity. Find a way, even if it is rude.

Other Suggestions Being in the office creates opportunities for interruption of the producer's time. A producer can do two things to the physical arrangement of the office to decrease casual conversations that interrupt the producer.

First, turn the office around. Instead of the front of the desk facing the door, where passersby can catch the producer's eye, arrange the desk so that the producer's back is to the door. The sight of the back of a person bent over a desk is more discouraging to idle conversation than the ability to make eye contact. Closing the office door may have a similar effect. The second suggestion is to place only one other chair, in addition to the producer's chair, in the office. People tend to feel more uncomfortable sitting when there is no other unoccupied chair. Alternatively, if the producer stands, the uninvited visitor feels uncomfortable sitting.

Finally, this question is often heard: "Got a minute?" One way to control loss of time in those cases is to say, "No." If the issue is important, arrange a time to see the person, but "no" will discourage idle conversation.

Personal Time

Although the discussion has focused on business activities, no one can spend every hour of every day in business activities. Activities outside the office that are rewarding to producers personally, such as time with the family, sports, and the like, must be considered essential in planning time use. The producer should attempt to estimate how much personal time can be allowed in a business day. An alternative is to decide first how much time will be spent in business activities and allocate the balance of the twenty-four hours to personal time.

Negotiating

Few skills will serve the producer as well as the art of negotiation. Unfortunately, the term is often misunderstood to mean getting the best possible deal from the other party. Speaking of negotiating a deal often has negative connotations to many people, including producers.

The term **negotiating** actually means "to arrange or settle by discussion and mutual agreement." The key word is "mutual." As Roger Dawson states in *Roger Dawson's Secrets of Power Negotiating*, true negotiating is "a creative way that both you and the other person can walk away from the negotiating table feeling that you've won."[3] Negotiating, when done correctly, results in what is known as the **"win-win" scenario**. This "win-win" situation, where both parties believe they have won, is important for the long-term, relationship-building interaction that is required in an employment or client service arrangement.

But the reason so many people handle negotiations so badly is they assume that one side will win and that the other must lose. Their entire goal in negotiating becomes not to be the loser.

To these people, negotiating is like a singles tennis match, in which the two opponents take their positions on opposite sides of the net and then hit the ball back and forth until one misses. After enough misses, one player is declared the winner and the other the loser. Even if they shake hands before walking off the court, both know exactly where they finished in the match and the loser is *never* happy with the result.

In many insurance selling situations, the producer goes in intent on making the sale, and the client goes in just as intent to get the lowest possible price or wear the producer down in the attempt. Invariably, one or both end up disappointed and disillusioned after the meeting. Have you ever had a client agree to buy but say, "because I have to. If they ever repeal that work comp law, you can kiss this account goodbye"? It often seems insurance has found a way to turn negotiating into a "lose-lose" scenario.

Learning how to negotiate effectively focuses on creating only the "win-win." Professional negotiators consider anything other than a "win-win" to be a loss.

True negotiators would consider the tennis match analogy as a doubles match in which both parties are on the same side of the net. Both want to avoid losing the benefits of the deal, and both want to gain the advantages. How is this possible? Both sides must try to get what they want. Producers should approach negotiations in this way with their clients and their underwriters. If both sides win, everyone gets what they want, and everyone is happy. The result is usually a long-term relationship that continues to benefit the various parties.

Basic Concepts

Detailing negotiating techniques is beyond the scope of this text. Many excellent reference texts or audio cassette programs are available on the subject. Some steps are very important to producers, however, so they will be discussed here. These steps include knowing the opponent, avoiding "single issue" negotiation, not milking the win, and always delivering more than promised.

Know Your Opponent

Knowing your opponent is not that different from the fact-finding and prospecting every good producer must do. You are looking for two basic things: (1) what is the opponent's style of doing business, so you can tailor your approach to be meaningful; and (2) what is it he or she wants from the negotiation.

Personal Style

Some people are difficult to deal with; others are nonconfrontational. Some like to have fun in their work; others are more serious. Some appreciate a good relationship; others want to get straight to the bottom line. Knowing the prospect's style of doing business can dictate the style you use in negotiating. For example, if the person is highly competitive and loves to win at everything, be prepared to fight to get what you need while still allowing the other to claim "victory."

What Does the Prospect Want?

The second step may not be as obvious as it seems. For example, many producers, when asked the one thing every client is seeking from his or her agent, gave near unanimous response: "a low price!" When one producer was confronted with a survey of clients where price actually came in eighth on the list, he simply responded, "So they lied to the survey."

The point is not that price is not a significant issue, but that the producer may be mistaken to assume it is *the* issue. For example, the prospect may have taken the lowest price product last year and found when a claim arose how bad the coverage was. He is now prepared to acknowledge he made a mistake but still wants reassurance he is getting a good deal. A producer with knowledge of the facts will approach the prospect emphasizing a sound coverage package, but not pointing out, "We're a bit expensive, but as you have learned, you get what you pay for." A "win-win" statement is "We offer an exceptional value considering the breadth of the coverage." The producer can meet both of this client's needs and still make the sale.

Avoid "Single Issue" Negotiation

Another common mistake is to think that if all the problems have been resolved except for a single issue, things are going well. If the negotiation ever turns on a single issue, then a "win-lose" scenario results. Whose position on the single issue will prevail? For example, many producers try to avoid the price issue, but by holding it until last, they risk falling into the "single-issue" trap. Once the producer and client have agreed on everything but price, the haggling begins. The producer spends an hour convincing the prospect what a great policy he is getting, but then spends

II. Time Management
III. **Negotiating**
A. **Basic Concepts**
IV. **Selling the Underwriter**
A. **Insurance Company Guidelines**
B. **Meeting the Underwriter's Preferences**
C. Providing Information to the Underwriter

days going back and forth to the underwriter trying to lower the price to what the buyer wants. Every new price the producer secures the client either refuses or threatens to go to another agent who is offering a better deal.

One way to avoid this "single issue" trap is to have more issues on the table, price being only one. For example, lay out all the major benefits the prospect wants along with the price you want. Then negotiate the items in groups. For example, the price can be lowered, but only if the prospect gives something back in another area. Perhaps a convenient payment plan will offset a slightly higher annual premium.

Don't Milk the Win

When you clearly have the advantage over the prospect, do not push the advantage too far. For example, you know the prospect needs a certain coverage, and you are the only agent in the area who can secure it for him. The mistake is to reinforce the helplessness of the prospect by hinting, "You're lucky to get this at any price." One day the market may turn, and he will remember how you treated him. No matter how much the situation results in your favor, find a way to give the prospect a little extra to help him feel that you treated him fairly. Perhaps attention to his need for certificates of insurance, or an unexpected package discount on his standard coverages will pay dividends when business later becomes more competitive.

Always Deliver More Than You Promised

In quality management, this concept is expressed as "always seek to exceed customer expectations." In negotiating, it means that after the negotiations are over, give something more than you promised. An unexpected bonus often will be remembered far more than the details that seemed so important during the negotiation.

This bonus does not have to be extravagant or costly, just unexpected and pleasurable. For example, cut out and send a new client an article in the paper about her son's making the Little League All-Star Team. Offer to help cook at the insured's company picnic. If the client is a retailer, be sure to patronize his or her store and recommend it to others. If the client works in real estate, refer him or her to some people who want to buy or sell a house. If the client owns a restaurant, hold an agency party there.

Selling the Underwriter

Another assignment in this course more completely discusses selling to an underwriter, but it will be highlighted here since it is an important activity for many producers. Basically, it means satisfying the following criteria of the underwriter:

- Submitting business within the underwriter's authority as established by the insurance company's guidelines

- Submitting acceptable classes of business that meet the underwriter's personal preferences
- Providing the underwriter with accurate and complete information with which to make a decision
- Gaining the underwriter's trust through an open, honest exchange

Insurance Company Guidelines

Over years of operations, an insurer, branch office, or regional office develops experience in certain lines. Even an all-lines insurer may prefer certain types of business. For example, some companies prefer home-owners policies. Knowing these preferences, the producer can decide which insurance company to approach.

Any information a producer can obtain about the carrier's underwriting guidelines will be helpful because a producer's submissions go to the underwriter, and the underwriter will have to respond within the corporate underwriting guidelines. For instance, assume an insurer says it will accept any good property insurance business. An application is submitted for $1 million on a frame construction building in fire protection class 10. The company has a clear guideline in its underwriting manual that says it will not accept frame buildings in class 10. The producer has wasted both his and the underwriter's time and efforts by submitting business the underwriter is going to refuse.

Meeting the Underwriter's Preferences

Most underwriters develop preferences and expertise in certain lines of business. This expertise makes the underwriter more knowledgeable about these classes of business and how to underwrite them.

From the producer's standpoint, dealing with experienced underwriters may be easier or more difficult than dealing with less experienced underwriters. Underwriters who are expert in workers compensation, for example, may be able to recommend innovative rating, retention, and loss control programs acceptable to the insurer, producer, and insured. Additionally, these experienced senior underwriters may have been given responsibility for this particular product line in their territory; thus, they are concerned about premium volume as well as loss ratio.

On the other hand, an experienced underwriter may have had negative experience. That is, the underwriter's expertise in a particular line of business may make him or her wary of submissions in that class based on poor experience. An underwriter expert in products liability, for example, knows what to look for, what to look out for, and what classes to avoid altogether.

In any event, producers should seek out underwriters and insurers with the greatest expertise in the class of business being underwritten. In the long run, these experienced underwriters will provide the producer with the necessary technical support and creative insurance programs that will help to establish the producer's reputation in that class of business. If underwriters with expertise reject certain submissions in a class, the producer should probably not handle these accounts.

Marketing Tip

When an experienced underwriter refuses an account, always ask why. Simply asking is a great way for a producer new to a certain line of business to learn the good and bad things to watch out for when surveying the prospects. Besides, the producer can save time and effort by not soliciting business for which no insurer is interested.

Underwriters who receive a regular flow of submissions from a producer are more likely to accept as many as possible if the producer understands and accepts their occasional declinations.

Providing Information to the Underwriter

Producers must provide underwriters with as much relevant information as the underwriter believes is necessary to make a decision on a submission. Such information includes, first, submissions that are within the underwriting guidelines or rules of the insurer; second, all information contained on the ACORD or company application; and third, because of the personal preferences of the underwriter, information the underwriter believes necessary. Finally, the information should be legible and easily understandable.

Marketing Tip

The topic of providing information to the underwriter is discussed in detail in the other two courses in the Accredited Adviser in Insurance program. AAI 81, *Foundations of Insurance Production*, and AAI 82, *Multiple-Lines Insurance Production*, include a section titled *What the Underwriter Needs to Know* following every discussion of an insurance policy. This section advises producers on the types of information that underwriters want to accompany an application for coverage or quotation. By providing complete and accurate information in the initial submission, the producer saves time for everyone involved in the transaction and often receives a better quality (and priced) insurance program for the insured.

Gaining the Underwriter's Trust

Underwriters will be more cooperative with a producer they know and trust. The producer and the underwriter should freely exchange information. Sadly, some producers still do not provide underwriters with the most basic information source—a completed application.

Building trust and free, open communications can also help the producer. In a difficult submission, a thoughtful underwriter may offer advice on how a borderline submission may be made acceptable. This good relationship among producers and underwriters is worth building. For instance, during a new underwriter's training period, an experienced one may say, "Watch everything from Harry; he always tries to get away with something." On the other hand, "Shawn gives us complete information and clean business. It is a pleasure to work on one of her accounts." The new underwriter will likely look kindly on accounts from Shawn and watch Harry's work suspiciously.

Human relations and a genuine concern for the underwriter's feelings will go a long way. Producers should place themselves in the underwriter's position. What they would want to know about a submission if it were being submitted to them. They may get a hint as to what information to give the underwriter.

Underwriters will have to be sold on some submissions. The more complete the information the producer gathers and presents to the underwriter and the more the underwriter is taken into the confidence of the producer, the better the producer's results will be in the future.

Check your understanding of the *Key Words and Phrases* found in the second part of this assignment.

Negotiating (p. 30) – to arrange or settle by discussion & mutual agreement.

"Win-win" scenario (p. 30) – Both sides get what they want.

Review the concepts presented in the second part of this assignment by answering the following questions.

11. Illustrate five of your timewasters. (p. 23)

12. Describe a technique to eliminate each of the timewasters identified in Question 11. (pp. 24-30)

13. What is meant by a "win-win" situation in negotiating? (p. 30)

14. Why should a producer always deliver more than promised to a client? (pp. 32-33)

15. Why are insurance company underwriting guidelines important to a producer? (p. 33)

16. Explain what is meant by "meeting the underwriter's preferences." (pp. 33-34)

17. Explain how a producer can gain an underwriter's trust. (p. 35)

- Anticipate what they need to make decisions, give them info before they ask for it.
- honest & complete info.

Apply the concepts presented in the second part of this assignment by answering the following questions.

3. Many agents believe that selling underwriters has always been underrated in the importance of education of producers.
   (a) Do you agree with this statement?

   (b) How could you build trust with underwriters?

(c) How would you approach the selling of underwriters in a hard market? In a soft market?

4. A priority system can help a producer minimize time spent on nonselling activities. Three of these nonselling activities are listed below. How can a producer minimize time spent

 (a) on the telephone?

 (b) in meetings with office employees?

 (c) in conversations in the office?

Summary

Each agency provides different levels of support to its producers. In order to develop the producer's production plan, the producer must know which of the seven selling accountabilities are a personal responsibility and which are the responsibility of the agency. A personal production plan includes the same ingredients as an agency plan: a mission statement, strategies, goals, objectives, budgets, policies, and procedures. The heart of a personal production plan is the goals and objectives. Goals and objectives should be specific, measurable, time bounded, end-results oriented, meaningful and challenging, controllable, and written. The ideal plan is negotiated with the agency's sales manager or principal, provides a self-guiding system for the producer to follow, is an evaluation tool, allows a reduced time and money investment in the producer by the agency, and is consistent with the agency's plan.

Time management should be both efficient and effective for a producer. Timewasters must be identified and reduced or eliminated. In a time management system a producer allocates business time by assigning priorities to business activities.

For a producer, effective knowledge of negotiating skills can make the difference between a struggle to survive or an enjoyable process of dealing with clients. By learning the basics of the process, the "win-win" scenario is not only possible but probable.

A producer must not only sell a prospect, but also sell an underwriter on a submission. Selling the underwriter means presenting proposals that are within the insurer's underwriting guidelines, that meet the underwriter's personal preferences, and that contain complete and accurate information; thus the producer will gain the underwriter's trust and confidence.

Notes

1. George Nordhaus, telephone interview, 1992.
2. Alec Mackenzie & Associates, Inc., "Timewaster Matrix," *Making Time Productive*, pp. 27-28.
3. Roger Dawson, *Roger Dawson's Secrets of Power Negotiating* (Hawthorne, NJ: Career Press, 1995), p. x.

Answers to Review and Application Questions

Assignment 1

Answers to Review Questions

1. An agency is a fiduciary relationship in which one entity (the principal) authorizes another (the agent) to act on its behalf in business dealings with third parties.
2. • Duty of loyalty—An agent must not undertake any business venture that competes with or interferes in any manner with the business of the principal.
   • Duty of obedience—An agent owes a duty to obey the lawful instructions of the principal.
   • Duty of reasonable care—An agent is required to exercise the degree of care and skill that a reasonably prudent person would exercise under similar circumstances.
   • Duty of accounting—An agent owes a duty to account to the principal for all property and money of the principal that comes into the agent's possession.
   • Duty to give information—An agent owes a duty to keep the principal informed of all facts relating to the agency relationship.
3. • Bring an action for breach of the agency contract
   • Sue in tort for the harm done
   • Sue for the value of the benefit received by the agent
   • Sue to require the agent to transfer to the principal the property improperly held
4. • Period of employment—The principal retains the power, if not the contractual right, to terminate the relationship.
   • Opportunity to work—The principal must make reasonable efforts to enable the agent to continue performing as required by the terms of the contract of employment.
   • Duty of compensation—The principal must pay the agent the agreed compensation for the services performed by the agent.
   • Duty of reimbursement—The principal must reimburse or repay the agent for any disbursements and expenses incurred for the proper discharge of agency duties.
   • Duty of indemnity—The principal must indemnify the agent for any losses or damages from the agency relationship but suffered without the agent's fault.
5. The broker may be the agent of the insured in securing a policy and, as is generally required by specific statute, may also be the agent of the insurer in receiving premiums.
6. An insurance agent can become a dual agent when the broker is an agent for one principal for part of a transaction (the insurer) and an agent for another principal (a client) for the remainder of the transaction.
7. A producer might prefer a commission because the commission is a part of the premium and not visible to the insurance buyer (as fees are). When the insured knows the fees charged, that insured can evaluate the cost of producer services separately from the cost of insurance protection. The fee visibility allows the client to negotiate it separately.
8. • Express authority—Anything legal that is agreed to by the agent and the principal
   • Implied authority—Acts deemed necessary to carry out the agent's express authority
   • Apparent authority—Reasonable belief, from appearances created by the principal, that the agent has authority

9. When facing a loss with an undisclosed principal, the agent is not absolved of responsibility, as the agent normally would be if the principal had been disclosed. The third party has the choice of suing the agent or the principal for performance on the contract should the principal attempt to back out of the contract. The third party is in a superior position after discovering the principal as compared to the position if that third party had dealt with an agent of a disclosed principal.

10.
    - Term of agreement/termination
    - Rehabilitation
    - Ownership of expirations
    - Payment procedures
    - Indemnification
    - Amendments to contract
    - Arbitration
    - Sale of the agency

11. The arbitration clause of an agency contract provides a formal method for the agency and insurer to resolve disagreements arising under the contract.

12.
    - Profitability of business written by the agency based on the trade-loss ratio
    - Meeting minimum volume commitments
    - Meeting growth incentive levels based on a percentage growth in premiums
    - The average profitability of the book of business over a period of years

13.
    - Sole proprietorship—A business owned by a single individual
    - Partnership—A voluntary association of two or more persons as co-owners of a business operating for a profit
    - Corporation—A legal entity with a life beyond that of the owners (shareholders) and unaffected by the death or disability of an owner

14.
    - Advantages:
        1. Limited liability of the owners and unlimited life of the corporation
        2. More favorable tax treatment than other forms of business organization
    - Disadvantages:
        1. Additional work and costs to document the activities of the corporation
        2. Additional work and costs to file a corporate tax return

15.
    - Advantages:
        1. Cluster members can combine premium volume to receive special treatment from their companies.
        2. Cluster members have greater clout for negotiating agency-company contracts. Some cluster members report a 2 to 3 percent increase in average commissions.
        3. Agency clusters can provide funds to upgrade to a more productive system.
        4. Insurance companies can deal with one entity, instead of several, and realize economies and efficiencies in communication and work flow.
        5. Agency clusters bring specialists together to form a new entity that provides expertise for better serving clients.
        6. Agency clusters provide an alternative to merging or selling the agency.
        7. Agents may enjoy delegating personnel administration and other management tasks to an operations manager and returning to selling.

8. Agency clusters can provide economies in physical space, staffing, and insurer relations.
9. Agency clusters pool advertising expenditures effectively.
10. Agency clusters provide the "engagement" period before the "marriage" for agents who have reservations about whether a merger is appropriate for them.

- Disadvantages:
  1. Independent businessowners may have difficulty agreeing on agency management issues. Individuals who have successfully built agencies may not share their decisions.
  2. Cluster members share financial information with other members. Loss of privacy in financial matters may make many businessowners uncomfortable.
  3. Cluster members lose direct, personal control of agency cash flow.
  4. Agency clusters require an operations manager, and some agents have difficulty letting go of the administration of the agency.

16. When considering an affiliation with a support group, the producer should:
    - Develop a questionnaire profiling potential cluster members.
    - Inventory insurance companies that potential members represent and the products offered.
    - Decide whether participating members should occupy the same building or whether the cluster should be established as a separate entity apart from member offices.
    - Appoint start-up committees addressing resources, finance, management, automation, and personnel.
    - Structure the board of directors.

Assignment 1
Answers to Application Questions

1. There are several ways that the agent might "stay in the picture." First, if any problems occur concerning the coverage or service provided by the agent or the company, the insured might sue either or both, which obviously brings the agent into the picture. Second, if a third party sues the principal and is successful, the principal might sue the agent for causing the problem. Third, the principal might initiate a suit against the agent for violating some of the duties owed to the insurer under their contract. Additionally, the agent has an obligation to provide service to the client and represent the principal.

2. (a) A written contract contains the express authority granted by the insurance company to the agent. The agent also has the implied authority to carry out the express authority. Implied authority might come about through the actions of the insurer; apparent authority is based on the perception of the insured and has nothing to do with the agency contract.

   (b) Customary business procedures are the essence of implied authority, because they are necessary to fulfill the agent's obligations. Express authority would not apply, but apparent authority would. Because most agents have binding authority, it would appear to a client that issuing a binder is a normal business procedure and that the binder was in force.

   (c) An insurance company plaque on the agency's wall would give the appearance of an agency relationship with the insurer (apparent authority). Neither express nor implied authority would apply here.

   (d) Most agency contracts do not give express authority to bind an umbrella. In fact, many contracts state that the umbrella cannot be bound without prior insurer approval, so there is no implied authority either. But, from the insured's standpoint, it would appear that an agent could bind any coverage or policy. Thus, apparent authority applies. The fact that the binder is oral doesn't matter because an insurance binder does not have to be written to be valid.

3. (a) 1. Loyalty—The agent should provide undivided loyalty to the principal. An agent may not secretly represent his or her own interest or a third party's interest to the detriment of the principal.
   2. Obedience—The agent should obey all lawful instructions of the principal.
   3. Reasonable care—The agent should exercise the degree of care and skill that a reasonably prudent person would exercise under the same or similar circumstances.
   4. Accounting—The agent should account for all property and money of the principal in the possession of the agent.
   5. Information—The agent should relay account information to the principal. Knowledge of the agent is legally considered to be knowledge of the principal. The principal is entitled to all information that materially affects its interest.

   (b) 1. Employment—The principal should employ the agent during the period of the contract.
   2. Opportunity to work—The principal should give the agent the opportunity to work as described in the contract.
   3. Compensation—The principal should pay the agent the agreed compensation for services performed.
   4. Reimbursement—The principal should reimburse or repay the agent for any disbursement and expense necessarily incurred for the proper discharge of agency duties.
   5. Indemnity—The principal should indemnify the agent for any losses or damages arising because of the agency and without the agent's fault.

   (c) If an agent fails to fulfill his or her duties to the principal, the principal can sue the agent. The specific remedies are suits for:
   - Breach of contract
   - Tort for harm done
   - Value of any benefit received by the agent
   - Transfer to the principal of any property inappropriately held

4. The typical agency contract contains eight major provisions. Each provision should be clearly understood by both parties and negotiated to the extent that both parties agree to and are comfortable with the terms.

   Term of agreement/termination deals with the length of the contract and what activities can cause contract termination. This provision also addresses the agency/principal relationship after the contract has terminated.

   Rehabilitation provides an opportunity for an agency to avoid termination.

   Ownership of expirations delineates the right to control the relationship with the client. This provision will be different for independent agencies than for exclusive or direct writing agencies.

   Payment procedures describes how premiums will be collected and paid to the principal/insurer.

   Indemnification spells out when the insurer will indemnify, defend, or hold harmless the agency if a claim arises solely or partially through the insurer's error.

   Amendments to the contract must be made occasionally. This provision details how and when those changes can be made.

   Arbitration provides a formal method for the agency and insurer to resolve disagreements.

   Agency sale describes the future of the agency/insurer relationship if the agency is sold or how the relationship would be terminated if it is not going to continue.

5. • Advantages:
   1. The producer experiences a reduction of bad debts.
   2. The producer saves time and money by not having to prepare bills, follow up on late payments, and process the checks
   - Disadvantages:
   1. Paperwork has not disappeared. The insurer sends frequent computer billings, reminders, and cancellation notices to the agency as well as to the client.
   2. The insurers now hold funds that were at one time held by the agency or allowed to earn interest. This has been detrimental to cash flow and is apparent when interest rates are high.
   3. Some producers believe they have lost control over the account. Producers no longer prepare and maintain the direct billed policy. Producers also miss the contact with the insured at renewal.
   4. Direct bill systems are not perfect, and mistakes are made. When mistakes are made, the client frequently notifies the agent even though the agent was not responsible for the error.

6. The two important economic factors that occurred simultaneously in the early 1980s and indicated weaknesses in using the trade-loss ratio as a basis for contingent commissions are:
   - The highly competitive "soft" market drove rates to rock-bottom levels. Although the premium base decreased, a similar decrease in losses did not occur. This automatically shrank the agencies' commissions and hurt their loss ratios. Therefore, in a "soft" market, loss ratios tend to increase and contingent commissions tend to decrease.
   - High interest rates made "cash-flow" underwriting a popular concept. The underwriter accepted business at a premium that was expected to generate a loss. The insurer, however, expected to more than offset this underwriting loss with interest earnings. This practice destroyed loss ratios even though insurers recorded earnings from investment income. Because the investment income was not reflected in the contingent commission formula, agents did not benefit from the cash-flow practices.

7. For many years, principals of agencies have been getting together informally to discuss important matters such as insurance companies, sales techniques, automation, and personnel problems. Although informal, these affiliations have often led to the resolution of problems or to mutually beneficial activities among agencies. A second type of affiliation has been a formal management affiliation in which one group operates the agency and seeks producers who will affiliate with them. A third type of affiliation is an insurer-sponsored group. Several insurers have selected exclusive agents in certain areas to market a special product. The fourth type of affiliation is the franchiser. This system operates much like the real estate industry; the franchiser works nationally and, for a fee, will provide management assistance, marketing tips, advertising, risk management, financial management, and national image.

Assignment 2
Answers to Review Questions

1. • Planning—Determining the desired results and formulating ways to achieve them
   - Organizing—Managing activities and resources logically
   - Leading—Influencing employees to work together to achieve the organization's goals
   - Controlling—Monitoring activities and making revisions necessary to achieve the desired results

2. • It enables organizations to move toward specific goals by improving their chances to succeed
   - It facilitates decisions on what to do and how, when, and where to do it.

- It identifies the goal, the resources needed, and the choices for using resources, and it relates the organization to its environment.
- It reduces costs and increases profits, in an ideal scenario.

3. - Simple
   - Practical
   - Severable
   - Flexible

4. - Organizational plans—Address survival, independence, and public image
   - Functional plans—Address profit, growth, product line, and personnel

5. - Strategic plan—Long-range plan with ideas of what the organization hopes to achieve; a general plan that is three to five years long
   - Action plan—Detailed plan with concrete steps applied to the immediate future of the organization

6. (1) Set a mission statement.
   (2) Develop strategies
   (3) Set goals (long-term).
   (4) Set objectives (short-term).
   (5) Develop budgets.
   (6) Set policies.
   (7) Establish procedures.

7. A mission statement should:
   - Be broadly stated.
   - Be phrased in terms of meeting client needs.
   - Be generic (no mention of specific products).
   - Be directional.

8. Objectives are milestones or intermediate steps toward goals, whereas goals are the final targets for the planning period.

9. Both goals and objectives:
   - Have time bounds.
   - State desired results.
   - Are easily understood and measurable.
   - Do not specify how to accomplish.

10. - Sales budget—Forecasts sales and used for monitoring and control
    - Expense budget—Projects when the expense is incurred and when it is paid
    - Cash budget—Combines the short-term sales and expense budgets

11. - The sales and expense budgets in summarized form
    - The capital budget— A plan for expenditures on assets whose returns will extend beyond one year (computer hardware) and the long-term investment of excess cash

12. (1) Line—Authority flows vertically, in a direct line, from top to bottom. Responsibility flows in the opposite direction, from bottom to top.

(2) Functional—The owner retains line authority but can staff each function with an expert in the respective area. Experts each have some employees reporting to them, lengthening the line.

(3) Line and staff—Merging the line and functional organizational structures. The functional or staff specialists advise the line when expertise is needed. The staff organization exists to serve the line functions, which are paramount. The specialist serves in an advisory capacity with no line supervisory authority.

13. (1) Position in the organization—Title of the position, the reporting relationship, and the department in which the position is located

(2) Summary of responsibilities—General activities of the person holding the position

(3) Primary accountabilities—Responsibilities of the job and the basis on which their relative success or failure on the job is measured

(4) Nature and scope—How the position fits within the department associated with that position

14. • In-house—Employees in the organization itself might be better suited to handle another type of job or might be in line for a promotion.

- Other organizations—Good employees in one business are often good in another.
- Recent graduates—Recent high school or college graduates require more training but may not have to be paid as much as a person with some work experience. Recent graduates are generally enthusiastic and receptive to learning new things.

15. Screening a potential employee involves:
    - Initial contact
    - An application
    - A short interview
    - An in-depth interview
    - Testing
    - Reference checks

16. An open probe expects a variety of responses and accepts all answers. Open-ended questions encourage explanations that will provide insight into the person's attitudes and desires.

17. • Physiological needs—Oxygen, food, water, constant body temperature

- Safety needs—Organization, security
- Love, affection, and belongingness needs—Sense of belonging
- Esteem needs—Stability, self-respect
- Self-actualization needs—Striving to fulfill one's "calling"

18. • Benefits—Health insurance, life insurance, disability insurance, and a pension or retirement plan

- Ownership—Shares of the agency earned as performance recognition, employee stock ownership plans (ESOPs), or the sale of shares in the agency to important employees as a means of perpetuating the agency
- Fringe benefits—Auto allowances (company car), expense accounts, and club memberships
- Time off—Vacations, holidays, and flexible work hours (flex time)

19. (1) Establishing reporting systems

(2) Developing standards to measure performance

(3) Measuring results against standards

(4) Correcting undesirable deviations from standards

(5) Rewarding desirable results

20. • Total Quality Management (TQM)—Focuses on (a) developing a system of tools and procedures that, if used systematically, would enhance the quality of the process and the products and (b) meeting and exceeding customers' wants and expectations.
    • Return on Quality (ROQ)—Focuses on what the company can expect to gain from a given investment in quality concepts (the greatest gains given the amount of time and resources invested)
    • Continuous Quality Improvement (CQI)—Focuses on analyzing and improving the quality and efficiency of business operations (continuous process improvement)

Assignment 2
Answers to Application Questions

1. (a) In a line-only organization, the top management is directly responsible for all employees of the firm in a straight, vertical manner. Several layers of management might exist, such as an office manager or a supervisor, but they are directly responsible to the top management, usually the principal. In a line and staff structure, functions are created that are served by staff specialists in order to accomplish specific organizational objectives. Staff persons serve as advisers only, while line managers have the authority and responsibility to carry out policy.

   (b) The advantage of the line-only structure is its simplicity. Everyone knows who is responsible for what and who reports to whom. Quick decisions are made possible by this form of organization. Many disadvantages are also apparent. First, the structure usually becomes unworkable as the agency grows. Second, specialists do not develop, and therefore all members of the organization may not be competent in all areas. Finally, the principal is often unwilling to delegate authority, which causes most of the other employees to feel that they cannot grow and gain responsibility.

   A properly designed line and staff structure has the advantage of fixed responsibility and authority as staff persons serve only in an advisory role. Coordination among members is usually improved, and efficiency is enhanced through the specialization that results. Delegating authority is also easier because the structure is designed for more decentralized responsibility and authority. The major disadvantage is the potential conflict between line and staff personnel. Staff people often become frustrated if their advice is not heeded. Hiring for staff is sometimes difficult because the staff person might need to be highly skilled but will not be making decisions or seeing all recommendations followed.

   (c) The best structure depends on the circumstances. Smaller agencies often find the line-only setup desirable, while larger agencies invariably use some type of line and staff structure. The key factor to examine is which structure will achieve the agency's objectives.

2. (a) The steps in the planning process are as follows:

   (1) Setting a mission statement.

   (2) Developing strategies.

   (3) Setting goals.

   (4) Setting objectives.

   (5) Developing budgets.

   (6) Setting policies.

   (7) Establishing procedures.

   (b) Strategic plans (including the mission statement, strategies for the next three to five years, strategic goals, and strategic objectives) should be done first. These set the direction for the agency and show all personnel what the agency should be like in the future. From the generalized, long-run plan, individual departments and employees set action plans, which help accomplish both agency and personnel goals.

(c) Because action plans follow strategic plans and because more people within an agency are involved in action plans, the strategic plan should be simple so that everyone can understand it. It should also be practical so that employees can address their action plans to the portion of the strategic plan that affects them. Finally, it should be flexible so that if conditions change, people are not asked to accomplish the impossible. These same statements can be repeated with action plans because accomplishing action plan goals involves many people within the agency.

3. This question will generate a variety of answers. Refer to the text exhibits on pages 2-21, 2-22, and 2-24 for examples of organizational charts. Compare these exhibits with the chart drawn of your own agency.

4. A job description is a written summary of a particular job in an organization. The job description:
   - States where the job fits in the hierarchy of the organization.
   - Provides a summary of job responsibilities.
   - States the nature and scope of the position.
   - Shows the individual where he or she fits within the organization and what he or she would do in that position.

   Job qualifications include the accountabilities of the position and the tasks, knowledge, skills, and personality traits necessary to do the specified job.

5. *Money* is the first human need and perhaps the most basic. Money serves to motivate employee productivity and to inhibit productivity if the employee believes that he or she is not being paid adequately or equitably. The importance of the *work* and the job responsibilities are important motivators. If employees feel that their jobs are not important or are not contributing to the firm, productivity will fall.

   Job security is another important need. People need to feel secure in order to perform at their best level.

   Another human need is the ability to *grow on the job*. Few people feel satisfied staying in exactly the same position.

   People also need *a personal place* or territory. Most people feel unsettled and are unproductive if they do not have some privacy and a place of their own.

   Recognition is another factor most people need. Employees want to know they are appreciated for the work they perform.

   Finally, *incentives or rewards* for good work are important. The most obvious incentive is the first need, money. But other incentives such as ownership, a package of benefits, time off, or unique fringe benefits (such as the use of a condominium at the beach or of a yacht or sailboat) also encourage an employee to work harder and more efficiently while improving his or her standard of living.

6. (a) Your answer should include examples of explicit transfer of authority and responsibility for a task or a lack of explicit transfer.

   (b) Your answer should include communications related to motivational items and incentives to motivate employees.

   (c) Your answer should include an office operations manual and agency policies and procedures.

7. Automation will change what is done and how it is done in an agency. Implementing automation in an agency requires reviewing job descriptions and the various qualifications needed in those jobs. If the current staff does not have the necessary qualifications to work with the new automation systems, hiring additional or replacement personnel might be required.

8. An agency cannot discriminate against a prospective employee because of that person's disability. When hiring employees, the agency may need to make reasonable accommodations for the disabled employee. As long as the modifications do not place an undue hardship on the agency, these accommodations may include modifications to:

- The building or office.
- The job itself.
- The manner in which the job is performed.

Assignment 3
Answers to Review Questions

1. The sales manager manages all agency activities that put producers in touch with the right customers and prospects at the right time, in the right place, and with the right product or service. The sales manager assigns producers these accountabilities:
   - Prospecting
   - Fact finding
   - Preparing proposals
   - Presenting proposals to clients/prospects
   - Closing
   - Initial service
   - Long-term service
2. - Selling insurance policies—Policies that are not sold cannot be serviced.
   - Servicing insureds— Policies that are not serviced will become some other firm's sale.
3. An agency should hire a nonproducing sales manager to take care of the sales management functions and free the best producers for selling.
4. - Top-down systems—Management sets the long-range and year-to-year sales goals for the organization and determines how they will be achieved.
   - Bottom-up systems—Each producer outlines what he or she expects to achieve during the year in new sales, retention, and personal and technical development. Managers then compile these plans into the overall agency plan.
5. - Property and liability commissions
   - Life and health insurance commissions
   - Fees for services rendered pertaining to insurance operations
6. - Compensation to producers
   - Commissions to others
   - Bad debts
   - Entertainment
7. To a traditional income statement, the agency can add an additional column showing the last twelve months of activities. This revised income statement will indicate general areas for concentrating the sales manager's efforts.
8. Management should establish a structure for sales management that includes:
   - A sales mission statement—To provide a broad statement of purpose.
   - Sales strategies—To describe methods for meeting goals for volume, business mix, and specialization.
   - Sales goals and objectives—To define the size of accounts for the agency to pursue.
   - Agency sales-related budgets—To allocate money, people, and time to serve the agency's goals.

- Policy statements—To explain what to do in certain situations and define the general rules of work.
- Procedures—To facilitate training and help maintain quality control in the field.

9.
- Judgment and experience standards—Based on the judgment and experience of management
- Historical standards—Internal or external standards based on past performance
- Engineered standards—Based on an objective, quantitative analysis of a specific work situation and designed to measure the potential output of individuals
- Internal financial standards—Based on the company's past performance and budgets

10. The best method is to compare actual financial results to the budget or to goals. This comparison alerts the financial manager to cost and income trends while highlighting specific areas that need attention.

11.
- Bases for the evaluation
  - Quantitative—Premium, commission, new prospects, and accounts sold
  - Qualitative—Self-organization, knowledge, customer relations, appearance, and attitude
- Standards against which to judge the performance
- A comparison of performance against standards
- A discussion of the evaluation with the individual and method to establish a plan for the coming review period

12. Sales meetings can provide:
- Feedback for identifying problems and taking corrective action.
- Communication and information sharing among peers.
- Continuous education, coverage review, new product introduction, motivation, and training.

13.
- Set an objective.
- Have an agenda.
- Stay on schedule.
- Keep meetings short.

Assignment 3
Answers to Application Questions

1. (a) The first producer is working with a top-down sales management system in which individual goals are set by top management and then given to the producers. The second producer works with a bottom-up system in which producers set their own goals. Top management combines these goals to form the agency's goals.

   (b) In the top-down system, management first establishes the budget. Total income is then used to establish production goals for each producer. In the bottom-up system, producers first establish their individual goals. Management, after agreeing to the goals, then uses the goals for all producers to establish the agency's income in the budget.

2. (a) A producer might not want this promotion because:
   - Producers generally have a sales orientation that desires independence and sales activities. The producer might not like the idea of managing people.
   - Producers often earn less in a management position than in sales. The producer may have no financial incentive to accept the promotion.

   (b) A producer-sales manager should determine how much money he or she generates from selling. When the lost sales revenue from time spent in management exceeds the cost of hiring a full-time sales manager, the agency would be better off hiring a full-time sales manager and returning the producer-sales manager to full-time sales.
   (c) The agency would lose the value of the top producer's sales, and the skills needed to be an effective manager are different from the skills needed by an effective producer. Few people have both sets of skills. The agency should choose someone with good management skills for the position.

3. An agency could show two sources of income—controllable and noncontrollable—on its income statement. With this change, the agency would identify how sales affect income and design its management system to increase sales.

4. (a) All insurance product commissions and any fees for service are controllable revenue sources.
   (b) The major source of noncontrollable revenue is contingency income (profit sharing). It is noncontrollable because it is based on the agency's loss ratio, and the agency cannot prevent losses from occurring. Agents should not depend on contingency income when preparing budgets, since it is beyond the control of the agent.

5. (a) An agency can develop sales performance standards by using information that is internal or external to the agency.
   - Internal standards use the judgment and experience of the agency's management, information about the agency's past performance, and standards engineered or developed by the agency to measure quantitative work output.
   - External standards, based on facts or designed by organizations outside the agency, are used to compare the agency's performance to a level that agency management believes is desirable.

   (b) An agency owner should measure performance with:
   - Judgment and experience standards—Based on the judgment and experience of management
   - Historical standards—Based on past performance (internal standards or external standards)
   - Engineered standards—Based on objective quantitative analysis of a specific work situation and designed to measure the potential output of individuals

   (c) An agency should measure its results against the selected standards.
   - An agency that does not meet the standards should either take corrective action or revise the standard to a more appropriate level.
   - An agency that meets or exceeds the standards should revise those standards to set higher standards for future performance.

6. (a) A poorly run sales meeting can be a waste of time. It occupies time that could be used more productively. On the other hand, a sales meeting that helps rejuvenate producers, provides for good communication among the producers and the principals, and is well organized can be highly beneficial.
   (b) The boss is probably not using an agenda for the meeting and is certainly not following an agenda, if there is one. If the meeting is important enough to hold, the boss should follow a fixed agenda of items to discuss.
   (c) The meetings obviously do not have a scheduled ending time. Sales meetings should have a set beginning and ending time that is not violated so that the staff can schedule appointments.

Assignment 4
Answers to Review Questions

1. (1) Prospecting
   (2) Fact finding (exposure identification)
   (3) Preparing proposals or quoting
   (4) Presenting understandable proposals
   (5) Closing
   (6) Initial client service
   (7) Long-term client service
2. To formulate a personal production plan, the producer must understand which accountabilities are his or her responsibility and which are the responsibility of the agency. The producer's personal production plan must be consistent with and supportive of the agency's plans. The producer must understand his or her role in the agency's sales management system to plan effectively and use time wisely.
3. (1) Setting a mission statement
   (2) Developing strategies
   (3) Setting goals
   (4) Setting objectives
   (5) Developing budgets
   (6) Setting policies
   (7) Establishing procedures
4. - It should be broadly stated.
   - It should be expressed in terms of meeting the needs of clients or potential clients.
   - It should be generic (no specific products should be mentioned).
   - It should be directional, revealing a specific career direction, but remain broad enough to allow growth.
5. This question will generate a variety of answers.
6. This question will generate a variety of answers. The answers should relate to your own personal mission statement written for Question 5.
7. A goal or an objective should be:
   (1) Specific
   (2) Measurable
   (3) Time bounded
   (4) End-results oriented
   (5) Meaningful and challenging
   (6) Controllable
   (7) Written
8. (a) This statement meets the seven requisites for a goal if it is in writing.
   (b) This statement does not meet the seven requisites for a goal because it:
      - Does not have a specific yardstick for measuring the results.

- Does not have a specific time for completion.
- May not be written.

(c) This statement does not meet the seven requisites for a goal because it:

- Does not have a specific time for completion.
- May not be written.

9. Goals are final performance targets, whereas objectives are milestones—steps along the way—toward accomplishing the goals.
10. An ideal production plan should:
    (1) Be negotiated with the sales manager.
    (2) Give the producer self-guiding activities.
    (3) Give the sales manager a tool for evaluating the producer.
    (4) Allow the agency to reduce its time and money invested in the producer.
    (5) Be consistent with the agency's overall plan.
11. This question will generate a variety of answers.
12. This question will generate a variety of answers. The answers should relate to your time wasters listed for Question 11.
13. A "win-win" situation in negotiating is a mutual agreement in which both parties walk away from the negotiating table believing they've won.
14. The producer who delivers more than promised will exceed the client's expectations, thereby solidifying the relationship.
15. The producer's submissions go to the underwriter, and the underwriter responds with the corporate underwriting guidelines. Knowledge of the insurer's underwriting guidelines will prevent the producer from submitting business the underwriter is going to refuse.
16.
    - Submitting business within the underwriter's authority
    - Submitting classes of business that meet the underwriter's personal preferences
    - Providing the underwriter with accurate and complete information
    - Gaining the underwriter's trust through open, honest information exchange
17. A producer gains an underwriter's trust by gathering complete information, providing this information to the underwriter, and taking the underwriter into the producer's confidence.

Assignment 4
Answers to Application Questions

1.
   - Bill should set shorter term objectives, such as the number of new clients per month. Setting shorter-term objectives can focus sales efforts, and Bill may not have a plan to accomplish this goal.
   - Bill should determine how many contacts he needs to make a sale. A common formula for this purpose is 10 prospect contacts = 5 expiration dates = 3 proposals = 1 sale.
   - Bill should review his past sales to see where he was successful. This could help Bill with future sales.
2. (a) Negotiation is important when developing a production plan because it will focus the producer's efforts on the proper classes of business, will draw on assistance from the staff, and will ensure the feasibility of the plan.

(b) The producer would surely fail to reach the goals of the plan without staff support and without the producer's plan being consistent with the overall agency plan.

3. (a) Yes. Producers are usually trained in technical insurance topics and selling skills in dealing with prospects. But if the producer does not make a good sales presentation to the underwriter, the producer will not have anything to sell to the prospect.

(b) Building clout with underwriters includes providing complete information, dealing fairly and honestly, meeting the underwriter's business preferences, and producing a volume of business.

(c) In a hard market, presenting the preferred class of business is very important because insurers often restrict new production to the most profitable classes. Another important characteristic is the loss ratio of the prospect, which also helps the insurer's profitability. In a soft market, a large premium would be attractive to the underwriter. In both market cycles, honesty is crucial to gain the underwriter's trust and build clout.

4. (a)
- Telephone calls should be carefully screened so that the producer does not waste time on a call that should be handled by others, such as the claims department or bookkeeping department.
- The producer should choose times in the office to take calls that are not critical calls. This time might be one hour a day or any calls after 3:00 P.M. This action will give producers more time to concentrate on particular projects.

(b)
- Meetings with office employees should have a predetermined time limit.
- Topics not relevant to the producer should be discussed without the producer being present.

(c)
- Rearranging the producer's office can reduce conversation. Fewer people will engage in casual conversation if the desk faces away from the door.
- Close the office door. (This action may be the best step.)

Index

A

B

C

D

E

R

S

T

U

W